Stop Global Street Harassment

Stop Global Street Harassment

GROWING ACTIVISM AROUND THE WORLD

Holly Kearl

 PRAEGER™

An Imprint of ABC-CLIO, LLC
Santa Barbara, California • Denver, Colorado

Library of Congress Cataloging-in-Publication Data

Kearl, Holly.
  Stop global street harassment : growing activism around the world / Holly Kearl.
    pages cm
  ISBN 978-1-4408-4020-3 (hardback) — ISBN 978-1-4408-4021-0 (ebook)
1. Sexual harassment of women—Prevention.   2. Women—Violence against—
Prevention.   3. Public safety.   4. Public spaces—Social aspects.   I. Title.
  HV6556.K427 2015
  364.4—dc23   2015015914

ISBN: 978-1-4408-4020-3
EISBN: 978-1-4408-4021-0

19 18 17 16 15   1 2 3 4 5

This book is also available on the World Wide Web as an eBook.
Visit www.abc-clio.com for details.

Praeger
An Imprint of ABC-CLIO, LLC

ABC-CLIO, LLC
130 Cremona Drive, P.O. Box 1911
Santa Barbara, California 93116-1911

This book is printed on acid-free paper ∞

Manufactured in the United States of America

To individuals, groups, organizations, and government
agencies who are challenging the status quo and are
working to make public spaces safer for everyone.
Also, as always, this is dedicated to
my life partner, Mark Hutchens;
my parents, Beckie Weinheimer and Alan Kearl;
and my sisters, Heidi and Mary Kearl.
I love you all.

Contents

Acknowledgments

In late October and early November 2014, street harassment was a prominent news story after Rob Bliss Creative released a viral video showing a New York City woman's street harassment experiences across 10 hours. Out of the media interest came the possibility of this book. Thank you so much to my editor, Jessica Gribble at ABC-CLIO, for contacting me, advocating for this book, and being so supportive and kind throughout the process.

Thank you to my friends and activist allies Nuala Cabral, Soraya Chemaly, Dr. Laura S. Logan, Patrick McNeil, Chai Shenoy, and Joanne N. Smith for providing valuable feedback on the book outline and content. Thank you to professors Dr. Gina Daddario, Dr. Linda Garber, Dr. Melanie Klein, Dr. Jennifer Martin, Dr. Amy Sarch, Dr. Shira Tarrant, and Dr. Karol Weaver for advocating for this book and, in many cases, for providing feedback on the book proposal.

Thank you to the activists who took time to answer questions for the book and gave permission to use excerpts of their writing and photographs, including: Angie Abdelmonem, Christy Abraham, Manuel Abril, Noorjahan Akbar, Lisa Arntzen, Tara Ashford, Samer Aziz, Laura Bates, Bryony Beynow, Nuala Cabral, Laura Capobianco, Rebecca Chaio, Sarah Chang, Simona Chirciu, Tilly Grove, Andrea Gunraj, Elsa S. Henry, Kasumi Hirokawa, Mark Hutchens, Aikanysh Jeenbaeva, Ileana Jiménez, Pallavi Kamat, Marty Langelan, Caroline Laurin, L'Heureux Dumi Lewis-McCoy, Fran Luck, Damon Mackin, Lauren McEwen, Patrick McNeil, Lindsey Middlecamp, Dr. Mari Morales-Williams, Linnet N. Mwangi,

Jasmeen Patheja, Adriana Pérez-Rodríguez, Carolina Pineheiro, Shawna Potter, Seanna Pratt, Raquel Reichard, Nihal Saad, Nathalie Sanchez, Nancy Schwartzman, Radhika Takru, Kathryn Travers, Kristi Weir, Jake Winn, Zoneziwoh M. Wondieh, and Rachael Wyant. Thanks also to STOP Harcèlement de rue in France, ProChange in Germany, Paremos el Acoso Callejero in Peru, and Touche Pas à Ma Pote in Belgium.

I am extremely grateful to Ana Flores, Mark Hutchens, Alan Kearl, Zosia Sztykowski, and Beckie Weinheimer for providing feedback on the book manuscript. Extra thanks to Mark, Beckie, and Alan for regularly being a sounding board and source of support throughout the writing process. I am also grateful for the kind words and understanding offered by my colleagues at the OpEd Project, Aspen Institute, and U.N. Women during my marathon writing months.

Each day, I'm inspired by individuals worldwide who decide to do something about street harassment. I have tracked their resistance and bravery on the Stop Street Harassment blog and, to the extent that I had space, featured and honored them in this book. I am so grateful for everything that these ordinary yet incredible people are doing to make the world a safer place. All of our lives are better because of them.

Introduction

In December 2009, I finished writing my first book, *Stop Street Harassment: Making Public Places Safe and Welcoming for Women*, also published by Praeger, and it was released in 2010. It is an introduction to the issue of street harassment: what it is, how it is a global problem, the impact it has on harassed persons, why it matters, why it happens, and what we can do about it. I wrote it after experiencing street harassment hundreds of times myself, writing a master's thesis on the subject in 2007 at The George Washington University, and launching the Stop Street Harassment website in 2008. This book looks at the issue five years later. What has happened? What has changed? What comes next? Before focusing on the period from early 2010 to early 2015, the introduction looks further back and answers the two most common questions I am asked: is street harassment a new problem? And if not, is the activism in response to it new?

The short answer to both questions is no. Harassment in public spaces has always been a problem; it is the manifestation of inequality based on gender, sexual orientation, race, class, and disability. However, an important difference is that today there are more opportunities for harassment to occur. Since 2008, most of the world's population has lived in cities, where people encounter more other people in their daily lives than in previous eras,[1] and anonymity can embolden harassers. While there have always been efforts to challenge street harassment, the Internet has allowed that resistance to be more visible and has fostered collaborations and idea sharing at faster and larger rates among individuals, groups, and government agencies across regions and countries.

The longer answer starts with a brief overview of the historic problem of street harassment. Men harassing women is the most common form, and it connects to the reality that in many societies, public spaces have traditionally been male domains where unaccompanied women have been unwelcome. "Equating domestic space with women and public space with men is not new as there are many cultures that have segregated domestic space based on gender, dating back to ancient Greek houses," wrote Susan J. Drucker and Gary Grumpert in their article "Voices in the Street: Explorations in Gender, Media, and Public Space." "For example ancient Greek houses had separate courtyards for men and women. Islamic homes have for centuries created secluded places within the home for women. The Turkish yurt has a defined particular place within the home for women, paralleling the outside world."[2] They continue: "The 'public woman' was associated with the nonrespectable, the prostitute, who was segregated from the respectable woman . . . This was typified by the mores of the Victorian age, which held it indecent for a lady to so much as walk on the street unaccompanied by a husband, father, brother, or male servant."[3]

In her 1991 book *The Sphinx in the City*, Elizabeth Wilson wrote about how both western and non-western societies have regulated women's movement in cities. "With few exceptions, males dominate public space, and if women are given access it is not equal access. Examples of women being restricted to the home, chaperoned, or veiled in public, or denied access to certain public areas abound in cultures around the world. Some of these restrictions apply only to women of certain social classes—upper class women are restricted while lower class women are not."[4]

Indeed, women who were servants or slaves or part of poor households always had to work, and that often involved moving through public spaces alone. In the late 1800s, for instance, many working-class women lived in cities and traveled to and from jobs in factories and wealthy people's homes. We know little about their experiences in public spaces, but given that exploitative sexual violence was not uncommon against them in the households and establishments where they worked, it is logical to assume they faced unwanted sexual encounters in public spaces, too.

Beginning in the mid- to late-19th century, more middle- and upper-class women left their homes alone to go shopping—especially with the introduction of department stores like Bon Marche in Paris in 1852 and Macy's in New York City in 1857.[5] They began attending college and working as teachers, sales clerks, secretaries, and nurses. And as they left their homes unaccompanied, they encountered harassment from men who were used to public spaces being their domain. U.S. newspaper articles show that phrases used by street harassers more than a century ago sound the same as today: "Hey, baby," "Hey, honey," "How much for you?"[6]

Dr. Estelle Freedman wrote about U.S. street harassers in a chapter of her 2013 book *Redefining Rape: Sexual Violence in the Era of Suffrage and Segregation.* She found documentation of women expressing concerns about "sexual dangers" in public spaces from as early as the 1700s, as well as evidence of their desire to have the "liberty to travel freely."[7] By the late 1800s, street harassers were so common they were described with terms like "mashers" and "sidewalk sheiks." Kerry Segrave's 2014 book *Beware the Masher: Sexual Harassment in American Public Places, 1880–1930* looks at street harassment during this time period, particularly the laws and ordinances passed to address the growing "menace."

In Hispanic cultures, the genderized public space (a common description of machismo to this day is "man on the street, women in the house"[8]) was compounded by the tradition of *piropos.* Originally, *piropos* was the term for compliments that aristocratic Spanish men gave to women about their beauty, charm, or grace, but with time, *piropos* became more vulgar and were uttered by men in every social class. They became a normal part of everyday life and made women feel less comfortable in public spaces. "*Piropos* [permit] men to intrude and sexually harass women in their personal space in public areas," wrote Joan Fayer in her article "Changes in Gender Use of Public Spaces in Puerto Rico." "This hostile environment serves to restrict the access women have to public spaces."[9]

To cope with or avoid harassers, women were often given advice to dress more modestly, be polite and demure, and try to avoid going places alone. For example, in 19th-century Paris, Madame de Saverny issued this advice to women readers of her magazine: "a simple style of dress would insure that the wearer could stroll unmolested, even in the most public of streets . . . the actions of the honest stroller were marked by a steady reserve and refusal of contact with other walkers."[10] A religious leader in the United States in 1912 urged women to wear skirts that nearly touched the ground to ensure their ankles did not incite harassment.[11] In Hispanic cultures, women were advised to avoid areas where men making *piropos* were common, thus limiting where women could go.[12]

CHALLENGING AND ADDRESSING STREET HARASSMENT

People have been challenging and addressing street harassment for as long as it has happened, but there have been pockets of time when it was more prominent. "While street harassment was probably going on consistently through the centuries, the condemnation of harassment strongly correlates with the height of the suffrage movement in the early

1900s—and in more recent decades, with the feminist movement—and other claims to space and rights,"[13] Freedman told me in an interview for the Stop Street Harassment blog.

Looking at the United States from 1880 to the 1920s, for instance, both Freedman and Segrave wrote about news articles detailing women who reported harassers, hit them with parasols, and poked them with hatpins. There were news stories about self-defense classes for women and how the first policewomen in urban areas like Chicago were specifically tasked with looking out for street harassers. In Washington, D.C., in the early 1920s, there was even an "anti-flirt club" that focused on actions we describe today as street harassment.[14]

Notably, the newspaper stories were primarily about white men who harassed either white or black women. When black men harassed black women, the women rarely said anything about it publicly, and almost no black men would dare harass a white woman for fear of severe punishment and even lynching. White men preying on black women was a huge problem, especially in the segregated South. From the 1940s to the 1960s, a large number of black women collectively challenged the centuries-old practice of white men harassing and raping black women with impunity.

In 1944, for example, white men attacked and gang-raped 24-year-old black sharecropper, wife, and mother Recy Taylor as she walked home from church with female friends. Her story caught the attention of a Montgomery, Alabama, NAACP member, Rosa Parks, an established anti-rape crusader. Parks led a national campaign for justice for Taylor that resulted in the assailants admitting they committed the crime—despite white male police trying to cover for them—and the case went to trial. Sadly, the all-white, all-male jury did not indict any of Taylor's assailants.[15] Despite not gaining justice for Taylor, Parks's campaign laid the foundation for other campaigns. In Danielle McGuire's 2011 book *At the Dark End of the Street: Black Women, Rape, and Resistance*, she chronicles Taylor's story and how the civil rights movement began not only out of outrage over the lynching of black men, segregation, and general discrimination, but also because of people's indignation over white men's assaults of black women in public spaces.[16]

During the 1970s and early 1980s, street harassment was occasionally addressed within Women's Liberation actions, the rape crisis center movement, and Take Back the Night rallies. Women hung up and distributed flyers, patrolled places with high rates of reported rape, and even held demonstrations. An example of a demonstration occurred in New York City in June 1970. At that time, newspapers routinely printed the commuting schedules and physical measurements of pretty women who worked on Wall Street, and some men lined up outside their work-places to harass them. In response, Karla Jay and Alix Kates Shulman organized an "ogle-in" during which they yelled sexualized "compliments" at men on the street. "We're trying to point out what it feels like to be whistled at, pointed at constantly every time we walk down the street . . . they think that we're just sexual objects. And we don't want to be sexual objects anymore,"[17] one of the women participants said in an interview.

The term "street harassment" was first used in Michaela di Leonardo's 1981 article "The Political Economy of Street Harassment." More on-the-ground actions focused specifically on street harassment took place in the 1980s. Notably, in Washington, D.C., Marty Langelan, the director of the D.C. Rape Crisis Center, Nkenge Toure, the center's director of community education, and other women led the first large, comprehensive city-wide campaign to stop street harassment from 1985 to 1987. They collaborated with groups like the D.C. African Women's Committee for Community Education, unions, and religious organizations and organized hundreds of street actions, public speak-outs, demonstrations, leafleting, harassment intervention training sessions, and sustained neighborhood action to take back specific public spaces.[18] They tested different ways of responding to harassers, and Langelan later published their suggestions in her 1993 book *Back Off: How to Confront and Stop Sexual Harassment and Harassers*.

Starting in 1989, a popular way of documenting street harassment and women's feelings of insecurity in public spaces was through a Safety Audit. That year, after the media reported on numerous cases of men attacking women in a popular city park in Toronto, Canada, the most dominant response from community leaders and the media was to tell women not to go out at night, not to go places alone, and to avoid the park. At first, frightened women in Toronto stayed home. But then, several women came together and decided instead to examine what made that particular park conducive to acts of violence. Without yet having a name for it, they conducted a Safety Audit and took their findings to the local municipality. That process was formalized by the Toronto-based nonprofit organization Metropolitan Action Committee on Violence against Women & Children (METRAC).[19] The United Nations (U.N.) took on the audit model in the 1990s, particularly in its work in African countries. Safety Audits conducted by women in Dar es Salaam and Nairobi, for instance, contributed to local governments pedestrianizing more city streets, reorganizing transit routes, and installing more street lights.[20] Today the audit is a component of every international Safe Cities initiative (see Chapter 5).

During the 1990s, violence against women gained recognition as a problem both internationally and in the United Sates. In 1993, the U.N. adopted the Declaration on the Elimination of Violence Against Women in 1993. It was first time an international human rights doctrine included violence against women. In the United States, the Violence Against Women Act of 1994 was signed into law by President Bill Clinton. The 1995 Fourth World Conference on Women recognized the elimination of gender-based violence as central to gender equality and the empowerment of women. Much of the focus in the years that followed was on violence against women in private or intimate settings: domestic violence, incest, and rape between non-strangers.[21]

The 2000s saw the start of many campaigns and efforts focused specifically on street harassment. During this time, the first website where people could share their stories, StreetHarassmentProject.org, went on-line. Groups like Young Women's Action Team and Girls for Gender Equity, with young women of color as leaders, organized actions like the RESPECT campaign in Chicago and the Youth Summit on Street Harassment in Brooklyn. The anti-harassment groups Blank Noise and the Gulabi Gang began in India in 2003 and 2006, respectively. The Egyptian Centre for Women's Rights started an anti-harassment campaign in 2005. In New York, RightRides for Women's Safety was formed in 2004, and Hollaback! launched as a website in 2005. The Stop Street Harassment website and blog launched in 2008.

Since 2010, efforts to stop street harassment have accelerated. On a daily basis, social media—from Twitter and Tumblr to Facebook and YouTube—is flooded with stories, images, songs, and campaign ideas about the topic. There is a groundswell of individuals who are holding rallies and marches, conducting surveys, putting up flyers, meeting with government officials, and leading youth workshops. Where we once had almost no data on street harassment, we now have scores of studies. Influential entities like the U.N. have Safe Cities initiatives and work with grassroots groups and governments to address sexual harassment and assault in public spaces. Many major media outlets regularly cover the topic. Countries like Belgium, Egypt, and Peru have new laws that touch on street harassment, and there has been an explosion of new transit campaigns in countries worldwide. These efforts, of course, build on the work of our foremothers and their male allies.

During 2014 specifically, there was a sharp increase in attention to and action around this issue, even compared to 2013 as Google Trends attests.[22] Some of the contributing factors were influential Twitter hashtags and widely viewed videos, including one by Rob Bliss Creative that has been seen 39 million times to date. Stop Street Harassment released the most comprehensive study on street harassment in the United States and oversaw the largest International Anti-Street Harassment Week with hundreds of actions by participating groups in 25 countries.

After the biggest year for street harassment news, activism, and action to date, it is worth taking time to look at the past five years to reflect on what has transpired and to consider where we go from here. I am grateful that Praeger is providing the space for this discussion. Here is what this book entails: Chapter 1 is an overview of what street harassment is and why it is a serious social problem. Chapter 2 lists new street harassment studies and excerpts of stories that show the global and complex nature of the problem. Chapter 3 features examples of the amazing offline community action that individuals have led in dozens of countries. Chapter 4 focuses on the utilization of technology to challenge street harassment. Chapter 5 summarizes the launch or expansion of seven global initiatives to address street harassment. Chapter 6 examines what several governments have done to address street harassment. Chapter 7 looks in depth at both Egypt and India and how global headline-making news about attacks on women in public spaces spurred community and government responses. Chapter 8 concludes with suggestions for what comes next.

Of course, this book is just a snapshot of a very complex and globally diverse issue. Deciding what to include and exclude was challenging. Many of the initiatives I write about are so new that there has been no evaluation of their effectiveness. Thus, a significant portion of the book is simply a narrative of what has transpired without an analysis of outcomes.

It is my hope that this book can show the global scope of the problem—and the solutions people are trying. I hope it can help move the issue and the movement forward in important ways. I also hope this book inspires readers to know that any and every action taken helps. We are where we are today thanks to individuals who decided to do something. You can join us, do something, too, and propel the movement forward.

Chapter 1

A Human Rights Violation

Sidewalk chalk message in Washington, D.C., 2013. (Mark Hutchens)

Since 2010, public awareness of street harassment has increased. Yet there are numerous people who still do not understand why the issue matters, trivialize it as a joke, call it a minor annoyance or a compliment, or blame the harassed person for causing it. These attitudes are reflected in movies, TV shows, and music videos, and also by companies like Fiat, Lego, and Snickers in their marketing materials. In reality, street harassment is a serious problem that should not be trivialized. It is a human rights violation that prevents equality, it falls along the spectrum of gender violence, and it connects with other social justice issues. Before discussing these different points, it is important to first define street harassment.

There is no standardized definition for street harassment yet. My working definition is: Gender-based street harassment is unwanted comments, gestures, and actions forced on a stranger in a public place without his or her consent that are directed at the person because of his or her actual or perceived sex, gender, gender expression, or sexual orientation. Harassment includes unwanted whistling; leering; sexist, homophobic or transphobic slurs; persistent requests for someone's name, number or destination after the person has said no; sexual names, comments or demands; following; flashing; public masturbation; groping; sexual assault; and rape. Not all people use the term "street harassment" to describe these behaviors. Some call it "sexual harassment in public spaces," "Eve teasing," or "men's intrusions."

Of course, people are also harassed because of factors like their race, nationality, religion, disability, or class. Some people are harassed for multiple reasons within a single harassment incident. Harassment is about power and control, and it is often a manifestation of societal discrimination like sexism, homophobia, Islamophobia, classism, ableism, and racism. No form of harassment is ever OK; everyone should be treated with respect, dignity, and empathy.

When it comes to men harassing women, it is important to recognize that these intrusions often begin for women at a young age. A 2010 study by the Bangladesh National Women Lawyers Association, for instance, found that almost 90 percent of girls aged 10–18 years had faced street harassment, particularly by street vendors, rickshaw pullers, bus drivers, and bus passengers.[1] Some Bangladeshi girls have committed suicide as a result, like 13-year-old Nashfia Akhand Pinky who was routinely harassed by young men as she walked to and from school. Her harassment included "ribald comments, smutty jokes, coarse laughter, sly whistles, and even indecent exposure," and the men escalated their attention to stalking and physical harassment. No bystanders present ever intervened. Pinky became traumatized and suffered such "serious mental torment" that she hanged herself from a ceiling fan with a sari.[2] That year, Bangladesh Education Minister Nurul Islam Nahid said in a BBC interview: "In some places, schools have been shut down and exams delayed because of the problems caused by Eve teasing [street harassing] stalkers. Those who are teased do not like to go to school, and sometimes guardians do not allow them to go to school for their safety and honour. So the dropout rate of female students in many schools is increasing."[3]

A 2014 national survey on street harassment in the United States conducted by the survey firm GfK and commissioned by Stop Street Harassment (SSH) reported that 65 percent of women and 25 percent of men had been harassed, and half of all harassed persons said their first experience happened by the time they were 17 years old.[4] Based on stories, however, we know that street harassment often begins around puberty. A woman wrote on the SSH blog: "Since I was in middle school, I've been honked at, stared at, and had vulgar things of a sexual nature yelled at me. In high school, my friends and I would count how many times we got honked at during the seven-minute walk from our campus to a restaurant nearby. If I remember correctly, our record was 17."[5] For some, harassment begins even earlier, as it did for this woman, who also shared her story on the SSH blog: "The first time I was sexually harassed by men . . . I was 7 years old. I was crossing in front of my house when a carload of men drove by and hooted and whistled at me and yelled that I was sexy. Although young, I knew the implication of their catcalls, and I ran as fast as I could into my house, my head ducked down and my cheeks hot with shame."[6]

In poor inner-city communities, the level of harassment girls face is often higher than in other communities. In 2011, researchers Susan Popkin and Robin Smith found that sexual comments, groping, pressure for sex, and dating violence were extremely normalized and "so visible that the people we interviewed no longer find it shocking."[7] Popkin and Smith discovered that "living with daily harassment, coercion, and dating violence takes a toll on girls growing up in these communities and may contribute to the high rates of depression and other health problems there."[8] In an Urban Institute article about their research, Popkin and Smith called for the sexual coercion and harassment of girls to be taken as seriously as gun violence and drug trafficking.[9]

Harassment can have negative implications on all girls' self-esteem, sense of safety, and ability to live full lives. In 2011, counselor Dr. Kathryn Stamoulis wrote for *Psychology Today* about meeting with a 14-year-old girl whose parents felt she wasn't exhibiting enough independence for her age. Eventually the teenager confided to Stamoulis that men harassed her when she went places alone, so she tried to avoid it by not running errands for her parents or traveling to and from school alone, and she also turned down a paid job walking her neighbor's dog.[10]

IT PREVENTS EQUALITY

Often starting at an early age, street harassment can restrict people's mobility in public spaces, as it did for the girl Stamoulis counseled and the girls in Bangladesh. The fear of and actual acts of street harassment can dictate where, when, and with whom people go and how they dress. It can inform their hobbies and habits, their routes and routines. It even causes some people to move or quit jobs because of harassers in the vicinity. Street harassment limits resources and opportunities that should otherwise be available, including an education, employment, recreation, political participation, and positions of leadership. Stories shared on the SSH blog often illustrate this. There was the woman in Kansas who nearly dropped out of her PhD program because she was routinely harassed by men near her campus;[11] a woman in Mississippi who quit her job at a retail store because male customers began following her to her car after her shift;[12] and a woman in California who was harassed so many times while she waited for a bus to campus that she finally went home and missed the class.[13]

Harassment can be used as a tool to intimidate people, to make them leave and give up. As women strive to gain equal rights worldwide, some men harass them to try to keep them from advancing, to prevent their equality, and to try to force them to retreat to their homes. In countries like Kenya, South Africa, and Zimbabwe, for instance, groups of men have harassed and stripped young women wearing clothes that the men deemed inappropriate. "Public strippings represent the front lines of a cultural war against women's advancements in traditionally conservative but rapidly urbanizing societies. They aren't really about what women are wearing. They are much more about where women are going," wrote Sisonke Msimang, a South African columnist, in a January 2015 op-ed for *The New York Times*. After describing the advances African women have made in education, employment, and political leadership in a short amount of time, she said, "Street harassment is often a sign of deep-seated resentment of women's changing status in society. For men who were raised to believe that they are entitled to be breadwinners and receive sexual gratification and domestic subservience from women, the shift hasn't been easy."[14]

Girls who attend school sometimes face backlash for doing so. A famous example is when the Taliban shot 15-year-old Pakistani schoolgirl Malala

Yousafzai on her way to school in 2012 because she was an outspoken advocate for girls' education. She survived the attack and continued her advocacy, particularly for girls' education in Pakistan, which has the world's second-highest number of children out of school. In 2012, 8.3 million children there were not attending school, and among those who were, boys outnumbered girls by 19 percent.[15] In 2014 Yousafzai became the youngest person to receive the Nobel Peace Prize in recognition of her advocacy.[16]

Women may also face backlash if they participate in politics. In Bolivia, for instance, 35 percent of ministers in 2012 were female, but typically only 9 percent of women ran for office a second time. But no wonder. Bolivian councilor Juana Quispe was strangled and dumped in a river after she helped female colleagues file complaints of sexual harassment. Councilor Daguimar Rivera Oritz was shot for exposing local corruption. Councilor Petronila Aliaga said in a BBC interview that she was experiencing intimidation and death threats. "They came to my house three times to get me to resign. My family were terrified." From 2004 to 2012, there were more than 4,000 official complaints of violence and harassment filed by Bolivia's female politicians.[17]

While the street harassment of people who are male or identify as transgender is less understood or documented, there is no doubt that they also experience harassment that is meant to slow the progress of their discriminated identity groups toward more rights. Transgender individuals in particular face high rates of harassment, assault, and murder, and each year those who have been murdered are remembered during the November 20 Transgender Day of Remembrance.

Victim Blaming and Risk Reduction

Too often people's response to street harassment and assault is to blame victims and to tell them to change how they dress or act and where they go. These "risk reduction" tactics limit a harassed person's mobility and equality and can make the harassed person feel as though the harassment was deserved if every directive was not followed. The focus on the actions of harassed people instead of harassers is not only harmful and disempowering, but it also means the root causes of harassment are never addressed.

It is not just family members and friends who may blame harassed people and tell them to change. In region after region, people—mostly men—in leadership positions, including governors, mayors, police officers, and transit authority directors, do too. "Women complaining about sexual harassment on the streets of the eastern province of Muş should deal with the problem by simply staying at home," said the Turkish province's mayor Necmittin Dede in 2011. "Do not walk around; sit in your homes," he declared to Muş representatives of the Women's Center, or KAMER, when they told authorities that men were sitting in teahouses verbally harassing women passing by.[18]

That same year, Fauzi Wibowo, the governor of Jakarta, Indonesia, told women: "Wear sensible clothes; don't wear 'inviting' clothes. You can imagine, if [a woman] wears a short skirt and sits next to the driver, it could be 'inviting.'" His statement was in response to reports that recently a bus driver raped a female passenger late at night, and in a separate incident, another bus driver and unidentified perpetrators gang raped and killed a university student.[19] After more than 50 people in Jakarta protested in the Muslim-majority country by wearing mini-skirts and holding signs that read, "Don't tell us how to dress; tell them not to rape" and "My mini-skirt is my right," he apologized for his comment.[20]

In January 2011, a representative of the Toronto Police Service infamously advised college students that "women should avoid dressing like sluts in order not to be victimized."[21] This led to a "Slutwalk" protest march in Toronto that then inspired around 200 other Slutwalks worldwide in which people of all ages, genders, and races marched in clothes ranging from bikinis to burkas to protest rape culture and victim blaming. But Toronto Police Service officers did not all learn from this incident. A few months later, after school officials reported that a man was harassing girls on their way to school by trying to look up the skirts of their school uniform, Toronto police advised that female students should only change into their school uniforms once they arrived at school.[22]

Police in Swaziland in 2012 banned women from wearing mini-skirts, any shirts revealing the midriff, and low-cut jeans. "The act of the rapist is made easy, because it would be easy to remove the half-cloth worn by the women,"[23] police spokeswoman Wendy Hleta said. That same year, after a rise in reports of indecent exposure, lewd acts, and upskirt photos, China's Shanghai No. 2 Subway company posted an image to the company's official social media account of a woman standing on a subway platform in a semi-transparent dress with the caption, "If that's what you wear on a subway, then no wonder you will be sexually harassed! There are too many perverts riding the subway every day, and we can't catch them all. Girl, you've got to respect yourself!" Two young women protested the victim-blaming message at a Shanghai subway station by wearing black veil over their faces and holding up signs that read, "I want my coolness under the sun but not the pervert in the subway," and "I can reveal myself, and you cannot bother me."[24]

Also in 2012, a drunk Arizona male police officer named Robb Evans "walked into a bar, walked over to a woman, and reached up her skirt and assaulted her." A jury convicted him of sexual abuse, and he was fired from the police force. But Arizona trial Judge Jacqueline Hatch decided that Evans's actions did not warrant jail time. She simply sentenced him to probation and 100 hours of community service and then surprisingly had harsh words for the woman he assaulted. She chastised her saying, "bad things can happen in bars," and "if you wouldn't have been there that night, none of this would have happened to you."[25]

For people who are gender non-conforming or in the LGBTQ community, it is not uncommon for others to tell them, regardless of their true gender expression, to avoid harassment by dressing within the stereotypical gender boundaries expected of them and by not holding hands or showing affection for same-sex love interests and partners. In some places it is even illegal to be openly gay—including in 38 out of 54 African countries—which forces people to hide their authentic selves, particularly in public places. In Nigeria, for example, a 2014 anti-gay bill created a mandate of up to 14 years in jail not only for sex acts between people of the same sex, but also for public affection between people of the same sex.[26]

Instead of stopping harassment, the "advice," mandates, and laws simply prevent harassed persons from having equal access to public spaces and the resources available there.

In 2013, the United Nations recognized the reality that street harassment prevents equality during the annual Commission on the Status of Women meeting, a convening of the highest global normative body on women's rights. For the first time ever, the commission included several clauses about the safety of women and girls in public spaces in its Agreed Conclusions document. The conclusions expressed "deep concern about violence against women and girls in public spaces, including sexual harassment, especially when it is being used to intimidate women and girls who are exercising any of their human rights and fundamental freedoms." The U.N. called on its member states "to increase measures to protect women and girls from violence and harassment, including sexual harassment and bullying, in both public and private spaces, to address security and safety, through awareness-raising, involvement of local communities, crime prevention laws, policies, and programs."[27] It was an important moment.

IT FALLS ALONG A SPECTRUM OF VIOLENCE

Street harassment is also a harmful and serious social ill because it falls along a spectrum of violence. It can start as verbal harassment and escalate to sexual assault and rape—and even murder. In the U.S. national street harassment survey conducted by GfK and commissioned by SSH, for instance, 23 percent of women and 8 percent of men said they had been sexually touched by a stranger in a public space, and 9 percent of women and 2 percent of men had been forced by a stranger to do something sexual. Overall, more than two-thirds of harassed women (68 percent) and 48 percent of harassed men said they were concerned their experiences of harassment would escalate.[28]

This fear of escalation also encompasses a not uncommon concern that a harasser may pull out a knife or gun and then might use it, in large part because this occasionally does happen. Here are just a few of the tragic stories from 2014: A man in New York slashed the throat of a woman who refused to go on a date with him.[29] A man in Seattle pulled out a gun after a woman ignored his repeated invitations to "hang out."[30] A harasser in England put a woman in a hospital after punching her when she told him to stop touching her.[31] Men harassed and violently attacked two transwomen in Atlanta in a subway car, and this prompted them to move from the city.[32] A woman in Detroit was shot dead by a harasser after refusing to give him her phone number.[33] In India, two teenagers committed suicide because young men in the area kept following them.[34] In Brazil, between January and August 2014, 12 young women aged 13–29 were shot and killed by a motorcyclist as they stood in public spaces, simply for being female.[35]

Sometimes bystanders also experience violence and murder, as several did in 2014. A San Francisco man sustained life-threatening injuries after asking a harasser to leave his girlfriend alone.[36] A Philadelphia man was hospitalized after he told a harasser to watch what he was saying to women nearby and the harasser got out of his vehicle and attacked him.[37] A harasser killed a Chicago man in front of the man's 15-year-old daughter after he confronted the harasser for making "inappropriate gestures" at her.[38] An Egyptian teenager was stabbed to death while stopping to help young women experiencing harassment.[39] In Germany, Tugce Albayrak, a 23-year-old student, died at the hands of a street harasser when she spoke out to protect two teenage girls.[40]

These attacks and deaths never should have happened. But they did. And the fact that they did causes people to live with a certain degree of fear each time they are harassed. In a 1991 article, scholar Elizabeth Arveda Kissling called street harassment a form of sexual terrorism because one never knows when it may happen—or how far it may escalate.[41]

It Can Be Traumatic

Street harassment also relates to violence because it can cause retriggering and be especially upsetting for rape survivors. A woman in Kentucky eloquently wrote on the SSH blog:

Every time I am harassed by men on the street, I am re-victimized. From leering, catcalls, and comments about my body to stalking and groping—they all reduce me to an object. Not a person, but a thing. Something to have power over. All of these forms of harassment are triggers for me. They all induce the same sense of powerlessness, the feeling of invasion—they all take me back to when I was raped. I know I am not the only one. There are so many other survivors, like me, who every day are forced to relive the experiences of their rapes by men on the street. Street harassment IS a big deal. It perpetuates the society that allows men to treat women as objects, to have power over them, to assault them, to rape them.[42]

A study released in late 2014 conducted by researchers at the University of Mary Washington supports this. They found that sexual harassment is traumatizing for women, especially for those who have experienced sexual abuse. "Women who experienced frequent sexual harassment displayed signs of trauma and post-traumatic stress disorder (PTSD). Those who had a history with sexual abuse endured a greater degree of trauma, regardless of how often they were harassed."[43]

In early 2015 researchers at the University of Missouri-Kansas City released a study showing that the treatment of women as sexual objects, including through street harassment, contributes to increased feelings of anxiety about their physical safety, causing them to fear both physical and sexual harm. African American women felt more afraid and had more psychological stress than white women, likely because they are more likely to be sexually objectified in the first place.[44] A 2008 study of college women by Dr. Kimberly Fairchild and Dr. Laurie Rudman found that street harassment was significantly related to self-objectification (which predicts negative outcomes like depression and eating disorders), marginally related to fear of rape, and reliably related to perceived risk of rape.[45]

The frequency and acceptance of street harassment contribute to people seeing larger issues of gender-based violence as "normal." According to a study conducted in 2014 by Dr. Heather R. Hlavka at Marquette University, most teenage girls interviewed assumed that all people experience being harassed, assaulted, or abused simply because they experienced it everywhere: at parties, in school, on buses, in cars, and on the streets. They saw it as acceptable and "natural" for boys to act this way. "They're boys; that's what they do," said one 13-year-old, after she shared that boys had groped and grabbed her.[46] A 2013–14 U.N. Women research project about mobile phones and sexual harassment (see Chapter 4) that I worked on included focus groups and interviews with women in Brazil, India, and Morocco. It had similar findings: most women thought that sexual harassment and assault in public spaces was normal and almost never spoke out against it or reported it.

On the flip side, of course, is the reality that if perpetrators of street harassment never face consequences and in fact receive support and acceptance for their acts, it creates a culture more accepting of serious forms of abuse. This is not OK.

IT CONNECTS WITH OTHER ISSUES

Street harassment and activism to stop it are not occurring in isolation. They have happened amidst influential movements like the Arab Spring political revolutions that took place in several countries in the Middle East and North Africa, the Occupy Wall Street protests that happened in financial capitals around the world to challenge the influence of the richest 1 percent, and the SlutWalk marches during which people challenged rape culture and victim blaming in more than 200 cities worldwide. They also happen amidst natural disasters and conflict, making life that much harder for women and girls, as these four examples illustrate.

In 2010, after an earthquake in Haiti killed an estimated 200,000 people and displaced even more, women and girls living in sprawling tents and under tarps faced high rates of harassment and assault. For instance, a 21-year-old woman told The Grio news site how she was gang-raped by three men when she left her tent to use the public toilet one night. After the earthquake, few women reported rapes for fear of being retaliated against and because so many police blamed them for assaults based on how they dressed. KOFAVIV, a group of Haitian women who survived political rapes in 2004, worked to help and support rape survivors.[47]

Women and girls who fled famine in Somalia in 2011 by traveling to refugee camps located in countries like Ethiopia and Kenya faced street harassment and rape during their long journeys. Once at the refugee camps, they often continued to face harassment and assault, both in the camps and when they left to gather firewood.[48] A 17-year-old girl, for example, told Capital News reporters about the man who raped her while she collected firewood near a refugee camp in Ethiopia.[49] In response to the attacks in and near refugee camps, U.N. workers tried to move women located on the outskirts of camps into more populated areas and supply them with firewood.[50]

Libya was one of the countries that saw political revolution during the Arab Spring movement. But for women, the revolution brought more harassment. Various women interviewed for a 2013 *Voice of America* article said that harassment "was bad under former Libyan strongman Moammar Gadhafi with men jostling, groping, and pestering women in shops, universities, and offices and demanding sex, but since his ouster two years ago, harassment has worsened . . . with lawlessness making the country more dangerous."[51] Women shared how they now try to work from home, avoid shopping alone, and drive by car to places as close as a block away. Few women ever report incidents to police because there is a good chance the police will harass them, too. In 2013, activists launched a Don't Harass Me website to record incidents with the goal of pressuring Libyan leaders to act.[52]

Since 1964, there has been armed internal conflict in Colombia, with the fighting between government forces, paramilitaries, and guerrillas rooted in poverty and inequality. Since Juan Manuel Santos became president in 2010, he has facilitated many peace talks and as of January 2015, the largest rebel group and the government were continuing to work toward peace. Through the 50 years of conflict, more than 220,000 people have been killed and countless people harassed and raped.[53] A survey spanning 2000 to 2009 found that an estimated 12,809 women were victims of conflict rape, with higher rates among Afro-Colombian and indigenous women.[54] Colombian Adriana Pérez-Rodríguez wrote for the SSH blog that for women and girls in conflict areas, "sexual slavery, rape, and harassment become a continuum in their lives from as early as 12 years old."[55] Police often blame women who are harassed or raped, so few women turn to them. Since 1996, Alianza Ruta Pacífica de Las Mujeres has been peacefully protesting gender violence, documenting sexual violence and assisting survivors, and advocating for change.[56]

In the United States, gender-based street harassment and efforts to address it connect to many social justice issues that are being addressed, like racial profiling and police brutality, bullying and sexual harassment in schools, rape on campus and in the military, online harassment, and rights for LGBTQ individuals. The rest of this section looks at racial profiling and police harassment as an example.

Racial Profiling and Police Harassment

Racial profiling and police harassment have been problems for decades in the United States. The American Civil Liberties Union states on its website, "More than 240 years of slavery and 90 years of legalized racial segregation have led to systemic profiling of Blacks in traffic and pedestrian stops. Since September 11, 2001, members of Muslim, Arab, and South Asian communities have been profiled by airline personnel, federal law enforcement, and local police. The federal government's encouragement of raids of immigrant communities and workplaces by local law enforcement in cooperation with federal agencies has targeted Latino communities."[57]

A report published in the journal *Crime & Delinquency* in January 2014 found that by age 23, half of black men have been arrested at least once.[58] In 2013, the report of the Sentencing Project to the United Nations Human Rights Committee found that black men are six times more likely to be incarcerated than white men.[59] A study of the New York Police Department's records between 2002 and 2014 showed that black and Latino communities were disproportionately targeted for the controversial "stop and frisk" practice in which nearly 9 out of 10 stopped-and-frisked New Yorkers were innocent.[60] In 2013, a federal court judge found the practice unconstitutional because it facilitated racism, and in 2014, Mayor Bill de Blasio reached a deal with civil liberties groups to end it.[61]

Three years before "stop and frisk" ended, Dr. L'Heureux Dumi Lewis-McCoy, associate professor of sociology and black studies at the City College of New York, wrote about the parallels of street harassment and police harassment for the SSH blog:

In hearing the testimonies of women enduring street harassment, I couldn't help but hear the testimonies of young men of color regarding police harassment. While street harassment and police harassment have key difference, in many important ways they're similar. Here are three important parallels:

First, it's everywhere: I live in New York City, the mecca of diversity. However, when you look at the stop-and-frisk numbers for the city, you find that Black and Latino (predominantly male) residents are singled out. . . . The harassment that men of color often undergo via the police is a constant pressure. When walking through Harlem, I routinely see Black boys approached by undercover officers and forced to submit to "random searches."

Second, it's targeted: These searches are anything but random and serve to make young boys and men feel unsafe in their own communities. In the same way that young men of color are subject to an "invisible force" that disrupts their life without consent, young women of color feel the same. Somehow we live in communities where both men and women of color feel unsafe, displaced, and harmed by harassment. Neither form of harassment leads to safer communities or healthy relationships.

Third, it's illegal: When we look at the stop-and-frisk data from NYC, we see the number one reason someone is stopped and frisked is "furtive movement." Do you know what that is? Me neither. In fact, you're not supposed to! The goal is to find any reason possible to stop and deter you from going where you're going or living your life peacefully. Sound familiar? . . .

It's going to take those that are the most and the least affected by street harassment and police harassment to come together to fight them. One-sided action is not enough.[62]

It's not just cis-gender men ("cis-gender" means those whose gender identity matches the sex they were assigned at birth) who are profiled.

Transgender individuals and cis-gender women are, too. A 2012 report by the National Coalition of Anti-Violence Programs found that "transgender people across the United States experience three times as much police violence as non-transgender individuals. Those numbers are even higher for transgender people of color."[63]

Young cis-gender women of color and transgender women of all ages are disproportionately stopped by police under the charge of "loitering for prostitution" even when they are not.[64] In April 2014, for instance, Monica Jones, a transgender woman of color, social work student, and activist was found guilty for "manifesting prostitution." Under a controversial Arizona law, police officers can arrest a woman if they even suspect she is a sex worker, including if a woman waves at cars, talks to passersby, or inquires if someone is a police officer. Jones's crime was accepting a ride to a bar from two undercover cops. Many saw her case as an example of "walking while trans," a saying that "refer[s] to the excessive harassment and targeting that trans people experience on a daily basis."[65]

When it comes to killings by police officers, the data shows it is overwhelmingly white male police officers killing black men.[66] Analysis of data by ProPublica further shows that young black men are 21 times more likely to be killed by cops than young white men.[67] The Centers for Disease Control and Prevention compiled data that shows that people of color are most likely to be killed by cops.[68]

In recent years, the alarming reality of racial profiling ending in death has become more visible to the larger (namely, white) population. In 2012 George Zimmerman, the coordinator of his neighborhood watch program administered by the local police department, killed unarmed black teenager Trayvon Martin because Zimmerman thought Martin looked "suspicious" wearing his hoodie and carrying a bag of skittles in his pocket. Zimmerman's 2013 trial for second-degree murder and manslaughter ended in acquittal. Marches and rallies took place across the country after both Martin's death and Zimmerman's acquittal.

In August 2014, white police officer Darren Wilson shot and killed unarmed teenager Michael Brown in Ferguson, Missouri. Wilson was not indicted by a grand jury in December, and neither was Daniel Pantaleo, the police officer in Brooklyn, New York, who choked to death unarmed black man Eric Garner while on camera. #JusticeforTrayvon, #IAmMikeBrown, #ICantBreathe, #HandsUpDontShoot and #BlackLivesMatter were some of the many rallying messages on social media and on signs at marches and die-ins. There were also calls for all police officers to wear body cameras and go through sensitivity training.

Women of color have made women's stories known, too. In Brooklyn, Girls for Gender Equity participated in a National Walk Out on Dec. 1,

2014, and "convened in front of the Barclay's Center in Brooklyn, highlighting the names of cis and trans women, men, and genderqueer people who have been killed—and largely overlooked—in recent years."[69] When *Ebony* editor Jamilah Lemieux started the hashtag #Alivewhileblack in early December after the grand jury voted not to indict the officer who killed Garner, women and men alike tweeted personal stories about police harassing them, questioning them, and needlessly arresting them for things that should have been non-issues and likely would have been if they had been white.[70]

Because men of color may be both street harassers of women and/or LGBTQ people *and* victims of harassment by police, many anti-street harassment advocates have taken a more nuanced approach to talking about street harassment in these communities than in those of their white peers. In 2014, Nuala Cabal and Mari Morales-Williams, Philadelphia-based activists and co-founders of FAAN Mail, wrote about this for the Black Youth Project:

To engage male allies of color around this issue without acknowledging the harassment that they face from police is a missed opportunity for mutual understanding. As women of color who are actively concerned about the criminalization of black and brown bodies in this country, we are interested in lifting up the voices of everyday victims, encouraging bystander intervention, and reclaiming public space as a safe space—without police intervention.

For the past five years, we have organized young women of color and our allies to hit the streets and raise awareness on International Anti-Street Harassment Day. Our outreach—from workshops and film screenings to street theater and rallies—has required creativity, reflection, and tough conversations about freedom, justice, and safety. Engaging youth, male allies, and LGBT folks (a group that disproportionately experiences street harassment) has been critical in our efforts to end street harassment. . . . Our goal is to raise awareness of street harassment and eradicate it through a transformative justice approach: community accountability and community healing. We do this work as a part of FAAN and Black Youth Project 100, two collectives committed to ending race-, sexual, and gender-based violence.[71]

While there is a long way to go before we will see racial profiling and gender-based harassment eradicated, it is encouraging to see both gain more visibility and recognition since 2010. As 2014 SSH blog correspondent Sarah Colomé wrote in an article about Ferguson, when it comes to issues like racial justice and gender-based harassment, "our oppressions are intertwined."[72] We cannot hope to solve one issue without acknowledging and working to solve the other, either directly or indirectly as an ally.

Each day, people change their lives to try to avoid harassment. They face victim-blaming accusations when they are harassed. They may find themselves traumatized by harassment or feel their mobility is restricted because of it. Sometimes harassment escalates into rape or murder. It is always a human rights violation and happens in all kinds of contexts and to various marginalized groups. With street harassment impacting so many people's lives in very real ways, it is imperative that individuals, groups, and government entities work together to stop it. And a growing number are, as the rest of the book attests.

Chapter 2

Research and Personal Stories

A sign at the Akihabara subway station in Tokyo, Japan, that says: "Many upskirt photo-taking incidents reported here. Women in miniskirts, please be alert and don't get yours taken!" (Kasumi Hirokawa)

Two of the most important components for shifting attitudes and creating new policies around a societal issue like street harassment are data and personal stories. In news articles, speeches, and policy briefings, these two components together can create a compelling argument for change. Since 2010, the numbers of studies and personal stories about street harassment have increased enormously, improving our understanding of the issue and creating more advocacy tools. Indeed, the acts of sharing, reading, and listening to street harassment stories—online or in person— combined with data are gaining the attention of people for whom the problem was invisible before. They are debunking the myth that only one demographic of people is harassed as is often portrayed in the media (attractive, young, white, straight women in big cities who wear high heels and short skirts), and they are showing that it is a global problem. And they are inspiring individuals, community groups, international entities, and governments to care more about the problem, take action, and design initiatives to address it.

RESEARCH PROVES STREET HARASSMENT IS A PROBLEM

Documenting a problem is an important first step for addressing it. Data about street harassment not only provide evidence that it exists, but they also demonstrate the scope, frequency, specific behaviors, and impact street harassment has on people's lives and on communities. Since 2010, there has been an increase in research conducted on street harassment. But there were a few data collection efforts before then, too.

In the United States, for example, there were a handful of studies. Carol Brooks Gardner, associate professor of sociology and women's studies at Indiana University, Indianapolis, conducted one of the first. She interviewed 293 women in Indianapolis, Indiana, over several years in the late 1980s and early 1990s. Gardner found that every single woman could cite several examples of being harassed by unknown men in public, and all but nine of the women classified those experiences as "troublesome."[1] In a country-wide study, Penn, Schoen and Berland Associates conducted a nationally representative telephone survey of 612 American women ages 18–64 in June 2000 and found that 87 percent had been harassed by a male stranger. Over half had experienced "extreme" harassment including being touched, grabbed, rubbed, brushed, or followed.[2]

Through the efforts of local research groups and guidance from international entities like U.N. Women, more countries and communities have been conducting street harassment studies since 2010. Several groups have also conducted informal surveys, including Hollaback! sites in countries like Canada, Croatia, and Poland, and individuals in Bulgaria, India,

Nicaragua, and Serbia who have worked with Stop Street Harassment as Safe Public Spaces (SPS) mentees or blog correspondents. For example, the SPS team in Serbia surveyed more than 600 college students at six institutions during the second half of 2014. They found that most women had experienced street harassment. As a result of their findings, the school's psychologists plan to hold educational workshops on street harassment, and the board commission for gender equality of the city of Nis, Serbia, will conduct another survey to find out where people feel the least safe so the board can create a targeted strategy to address it.[3]

What follows is a sampling of the formal studies conducted or completed since 2010; studies specific to harassment on public transportation are found in Chapter 6.

Global: The annual World Economic Forum releases a Global Gender Gap Report each October. Year after year, it shows that no country has achieved gender equality though Scandinavian countries come the closest every year.[4] Gallup data from surveys in 143 countries in 2011 showed that in every country, men are considerably more likely than women to say they feel safe walking alone at night in their communities.[5] When Patrick Ryne McNeil surveyed 331 gay and bisexual men around the world about their experience with street harassment for his George Washington University master's thesis in 2012, about 90 percent said they are sometimes, often, or always harassed or made to feel unwelcome in public spaces because of their perceived sexual orientation.[6]

Europe: A 2013 study of 93,000 LGBTQ individuals in the European Union and Croatia found that half of them avoided public spaces sometimes because of street harassment and most reported high levels of fear of harassment and assault in locations like restaurants, public transportation, streets, parking lots, and parks.[7]

Australia: Research conducted by the Australia Institute in 2015 found that 87 percent of women were verbally or physically attacked while walking down the street. Forty percent of women feel unsafe in their own neighborhoods at night. In addition to verbal harassment, 65 percent of women experienced physically threatening harassment.[8]

Bangladesh: The Bangladesh Bureau of Statistics and United Nations Population Fund surveyed 12,600 women across the country in 2014, and most said they regularly face sexual harassment in their daily lives. About 43 percent said public spaces were the spots where they experienced it the most.[9]

Chile: The Organization Against Street Harassment found in its first opt-in study in 2014 that almost 40 percent of Chilean women are harassed on a daily basis, and 90 percent of women reported having been harassed at least once in their lives.[10]

Ecuador: A scoping study conducted by U.N. Women in 2011 found that 68 percent of women had experienced some form of sexual harassment and sexual violence in public spaces during the previous year.[11]

France: Researchers from the National Institute of Statistics and Economic Studies found in 2013 that one-fourth of women ages 18–29 were fearful when walking down the street. Twenty percent had experienced verbal harassment, and one in ten had been kissed or sexually touched against her will.[12]

India: We the People Foundation's 2012 study found that 80 percent of women in Mumbai had been street harassed, primarily in crowded areas like trains and railway platforms.[13]

Israel: A 2011 study by the Tel Aviv-Jaffa Municipality's committee for advancing the status of women found that 83 percent of women in Tel Aviv had faced street harassment. This included suggestive remarks (40 percent), touching (21 percent), stalking (18 percent) and sexual abuse (6 percent).[14]

Papua New Guinea: In Port Moresby, a 2011 scoping study conducted by U.N. Women in six markets (Gerehu, Gordons, Tokarara, Malauro, Waigani, and Hohola) found that 55 percent of women had experienced sexual violence in the market spaces the previous year.[15]

Peru: The Paremos el Acoso Callejero group and Pontifical Catholic University of Peru surveyed 800 women in 2013 and found that nearly 60 percent of women had experienced street harassment, including more than 80 percent of those ages 18–29.[16]

Rwanda: A baseline study conducted by U.N. Women in Kigali in 2012 revealed that women's fear of sexual harassment and other forms of sexual violence limited their participation in activities outside the home during the day and at night. Forty-two percent of women said they were concerned about going to educational institutions during the day and 55 percent after dark. Over half of women said they were concerned about participating in leisure activities during the day and after dark.[17]

Saudi Arabia: Nearly 80 percent of women ages 18 to 48 said they had experienced sexual harassment—including street harassment—in a study reported in Al-Monitor in 2014.[18]

United Kingdom: In a 2012 YouGov poll commissioned by the Ending Violence Against Women Coalition, 43 percent of young women ages 18–34 in London had experienced street harassment just during the past year alone.[19]

United States: According to a 2011 report by the Center for American Progress, LGBT individuals report high rates of discrimination in public spaces.[20]

The results of Gallup's annual crime survey, conducted in 2014, showed that 37 percent, of U.S. adults said they would not feel safe walking alone near their homes at night. By gender, 45 percent, of women said they do not feel safe walking alone at night, compared with 27 percent of men.[21]

In a 2,000-person national survey on street harassment in the United States conducted in 2014 by the surveying firm GfK and commissioned by SSH, 65 percent of women and 25 percent of men said they had experienced street harassment. The majority of both women and men said men were the harassers. While verbal harassment was most common, nearly 1 in 4 women had been groped or sexually touched, 1 in 5 had been followed, and nearly 1 in 10 had been forced to do something sexual. Most harassed persons said it happened more than once. Half of all harassed persons said their first experience happened by the time they were 17 years old.[22]

Street harassment is complex, and factors like gender, sexual orientation, race, ability/disability, age, income level, educational attainment, weight, and region all impact people's experiences. As more people share stories, it is clear that some of the most marginalized and vulnerable groups experiencing street harassment are teenagers, homeless women, transgender individuals, disabled women, and sex workers. Due to the sample size, the SSH study could not delve into all of these complexities, but it did show that persons of color were more likely than white people to experience street harassment. It showed that homophobia is common, particularly for men. The most frequently cited form of harassment for men of all sexual orientations was homophobic speech (for women it was the least frequently cited, even less than sexual assault). Women of all sexual orientations were about as likely to experience street harassment, while among men, those who identified as gay, bisexual, transgender, or queer experienced much higher rates of street harassment than did straight men. The full report and findings, including findings from 10 focus groups, are found at www.stopstreetharassment.org.

STORIES ILLUSTRATE COMMONALITIES AND COMPLEXITIES

For a long time, street harassment has been normalized, and this has kept many harassed persons silent, which in turn has made harassment largely invisible to those who do not experience or perpetrate it. While people have always told their harassment stories—usually in hushed tones in safe spaces, between close family members and friends—now more and more people share them online, creating a ripple effect. As more people share stories, more people read them, realize they are not alone or to blame for the harassment they experience, and then share their own.

Thousands of people have shared their experiences on the approximately 100 international and regional anti-harassment blogs and websites such as Collective Action for Safe Spaces, Everyday Sexism Project, Harass-Map, Hollaback!, and SSH. More people are using op-ed writing to connect their personal stories to the larger issue, and today individuals can seamlessly share their harassment stories alongside other thoughts and experiences on their personal web pages and social media accounts. Sometimes these stories go viral, and news outlets and larger blogs cross-post them, garnering hundreds of thousands of views. Facebook and Twitter are other platforms where people regularly write about their experiences, raising the awareness of friends and family and other members of their online network.

Their stories help us understand the many manifestations of street harassment in different countries and communities and the unique ways issues like racism and homophobia can intersect with gender-based harassment. They help us understand why street harassment is a human rights violation, how it negatively impacts our societies, and why it is urgent that we act to end it.

Excerpts of several essays and stories follow to illustrate the global nature of the problem and, using the U.S. as an example, to illuminate how race, sexual orientation, and disability intersect with gender-based harassment.

Afghanistan: A Letter to My Harasser

Hello sir,

I do not know your name, but you passed by me a week after Eid-ul-Fetr in the Bazaar in Kabul. You might remember me. I was the young woman wearing a white scarf and a long red embroidered tunic with dark pants. I was standing by a vegetable stand and bargaining the price of fresh mint when you passed me and nonchalantly pinched my bottom. I turned red. The old man who was selling vegetables noticed but didn't say anything. He probably sees this every day. This had happened to me more than once, but this time I felt more embarrassed because the old man noticed.

I ran after you and grasped your wrist. Scared and sweating I started yelling, "Why did you do that? How dare you? Do you do this at home to your family members, too?," and you started yelling back louder, "You crazy woman! I haven't done anything. You are not worth doing anything to."

I was still ashamed to tell people what you had done. You probably remember how everyone was watching us. Other women advised me to keep calm, that this would only ruin my reputation, but I wasn't going to give up now. I started yelling. Soon the police arrived and took us both to the station.

A tall man in uniform asked me what had happened. I told him. You opened your mouth, and the police officer yelled, "You, shut up!" Next thing I knew he was beating you. You were on the floor, and he was kicking you with his gigantic shoes. Sweat was dripping off his thick eyebrows. He must have been as angry as I was.

I didn't see you again, but the friend who was walking with you followed me all the way home. He told me, "What is the big deal?! It is not like he f***ked you." But I was too tired for a second fight that day.

You and your friend probably both claim to be Muslims. You probably even pray at the mosque every Friday or more often. You probably tell your wives that they should not get out of the house because the world out there is filled with horrible men who will disgrace them. You probably even believe that you had a right to touching my bottom because you think a "good" woman would never be out on the streets without a man. Your sisters are "good." They stay at home when you pressure them to. If I were a "good woman," I would do the same. These streets belong to men.

I am writing this letter to tell you that I never intended for you to get beaten and humiliated, but I am not sorry for speaking out. I am writing to tell you that I know what you are up to. You want to threaten me, scare me, and keep me shut at home where I will learn to tend to many children and cook food for your kind and be submissive to a man that might someday marry me. You want me to be terrified of the world outside and not find my way and my place in it. You want me to believe that the only safe and "decent" place for me is in the kitchen and the bedroom. But I am writing you to tell you that I am not buying that ever again. Not you, not the Taliban, not this government, not my brother or mother, nor anybody else can convince me that I am less than a man, that I cannot protect myself, that I cannot be what I want to, and that the best life for me is in a "safe" kitchen where a man or a mother-in-law has control over my every move. I am not buying that. Not ever again.

I will come out of the home every day and walk bravely down the streets of my city, not because I need to, but because I can and neither your harassment or sexual assault nor an oppressive government will ever be able to take that ability from me again.

With Defiance,

A Woman You Harassed[23]

Australia: Challenging Islamophobia

On December 15, 2014, Islamist extremist Iranian-born Man Haron Monis held 18 people hostage for 17 hours in a café in the middle of Sydney. During the siege he forced several of the hostages to hold up a black flag with the shahādah on it in white lettering. Knowing and seeing that Muslims, especially women who wear the hijab or other religious garb, would likely experience an increase in street harassment as backlash, Tessa Kum created the Twitter hashtag #IllRideWithYou to express solidarity and offer what assistance she could to people feeling vulnerable. It trended globally on Twitter, and all of my friends were talking about it.

When the hashtag took off, opinions varied as to just what effect the hashtag was having. I know many of the first articles I saw referring to it had glowing praise for this "lesson in how to respond to terrorism." However, there has also been no shortage of criticism as attention to this hashtag grew. These have come from two opposing directions. First, there have been a few conservative politicians and commentators who contend that the street harassment of Muslim women is not something that happens, or at least not with any frequency, and as such #IllRideWithYou is unnecessary and offensive. But, this point is not debatable. We know that street harassment is a major problem. We know that Muslim women, in particular, are subject to street harassment. And we know that Australia is no magical safe haven from racist and sexist abuse.

More worthy of our attention is criticism from members of the Muslim community. They seek to remind us that there are huge, insidious, systemic issues at play here, and we haven't even come close to addressing the prejudices and hate that lead to street harassment . . . we need to be reminded that a hashtag is not enough. We need to join in with the conversation that demands more. I disagree with those who would call #IllRideWithYou hollow, but there is truth in the sentiment that this is not a solution. I think that's okay, though. Few people using the hashtag set out to solve street harassment and discrimination, and so long as we remember that there is still a big problem that needs solving, we can also take joy in having made a positive contribution to our community.

It is clear to me that #IllRideWithYou has had a positive impact on many people—making them feeling safer when the tide of misogyny and islamophobia would have them forced out of public spaces with a million micro- and not so micro-aggressions . . . Of course, this was not a huge organised campaign against street harassment and bigotry. In the scheme of things, a hashtag is just a small gesture. But small can still be valuable. If we have learnt one thing from street harassment, it's that one interaction can flavour an entire day.

It is my belief that #IllRideWithYou won't continue as a massive movement for change; it won't be a singular triumph in the history of Australian race relations or gender equality. But for at least a few days, people around Australia had days that tasted of solidarity and support.[24]

India: Festivals and Street Harassment

India is a diverse country; people of all faiths, religions, castes, and creeds openly practice their way of life. In Mumbai, the city where I live, it is not unusual to find several places of worship almost adjacent to one another—be it a temple, a mosque, a church, or a gurudwara (a Sikh place of worship). Celebrating various festivals is important.

Some of the most important festivals in the city are Holi (the festival of colors), Dahi Handi (which comprises a human pyramid constructed to break an earthen pot strung above), Ganpati (where the elephant headed-God is worshiped over a period of 10 days), Dassera (the celebration of the victory of Ram over Ravan), Diwali (the festival of lights), and Christmas (the birth of Jesus Christ). Unfortunately, they are not free from street harassment.

Festivals like Holi can take an ugly turn as people look at it as an opportunity to indulge in all sorts of harassment, including pelting women with water balloons as they walk down the street and rubbing colour on women's bodies, including women the men do not know. There have been several incidents where women who were pelted with these balloons on the train lost a part of their eyesight. Due to such risks, a lot of women, including me, fear stepping out of the house as the festival comes near. Specially, on the day of the festival, I do not leave the comforts of my home till evening after all the revelers would have gone home.

The scene is no different during Dahi Handi. Truckloads of men move from one part of the city to another in their eagerness to form higher and higher pyramids to break the pot and win the prize money. Sometimes these men harass women passersby en route; they pass lewd comments and do not hesitate to indulge in absolutely disgraceful behavior. As a result, women who would usually have been a part of these festivities hesitate to stick around to see who wins the prize.

Ganpati is my most favourite festival of all—it is when Lord Ganesha comes into our humble abode and stays with us for 10 days. It is also celebrated in a big way on a common platform—localities have a common idol complete with a theme and decorations. Going from one mandal (locality) to another, or mandal-hopping, is a common thing for families in Mumbai, and it continues late into the night. However, this can be marred by the increasing incidences of Eve teasing (street harassment) and molestation against women. There are hardly any women outside on the last day of the festival. This year the Mumbai commissioner of police finally had to ask all of the Ganpati mandals to ensure there were no cases of sexual harassment.

During festivals, perpetrators take advantage of the crowds knowing well that it is next to impossible for them to be caught by the authorities.

Also, if a woman does raise her voice, say against inappropriate touching, the perpetrators can always plead innocence under the guise of there being little space as hundreds of thousands of people have descended onto the streets.

Women have as much of a right as the men to enjoy each and every part of the festivals that are so intrinsic to our culture. Women should not fear stepping out of their own homes worrying about harassment or molestation. If such acts continue, we would soon have celebrations that would feature only men. Men need to make these festivals and their celebrations safer for women. If each one of them took a pledge to ensure a harassment-free experience for women at each of these events, it would make a world of difference, and not just to the women![25]

Japan: Camera Phone Shutters and Women-Only Subway Cars

Recently, I ran into a friend from Penn State who was on a month-long graduation trip to various locations in the Middle East and Asia, including Japan. . . . She said she enjoyed visiting Asia but was bugged by leering from locals. She attributed it to her being one of very few white girls in the vicinity. People were probably curious, she said. Some would stand too close to her when they hissed, "helloooo." Others would try to take sneaky pictures of her, only to be caught because of their shutter sounds. Street harassment was there to spoil the fun, like always.

Ah, the camera shutters. They were doing something to curb chikan crimes after all. Chikan is a term for a sexual predator and crimes involving one, be it unwanted flashing or groping, in Japan.

In Japan it is impossible to turn off the shutter sounds on camera phones. Women commuters filed complaints that chikans wouldn't stop taking upskirt photos in packed train cars. A bill called the Camera Phone Predator Alert Act, which required all mobile devices to have camera shutter sounds that could not be turned off, was proposed in 2009. The camera shutters were a follow-up to women-only train cars that were implemented in 2001.

I haven't had the experience of owning a camera phone with a mandatory shutter sound or riding a women-only train car since I moved to China, so I am not in a position to say how effective they are in deterring chikans. While I do not oppose the shutter sounds, I am not fond of women-only train cars. First, they are not always women-only. There is a certain number of designated cars on a train with pink signs on the windows. During rush hours in the morning, they become women-only spaces.

I know women-only cars were proposed by well-meaning policymakers. However, limiting women's presence in public spaces is at best reductive and, at worst, downright sexist. It's easy to tell women to ride on designated cars or sign up for self-defense classes. It's easy to blame a victim that she should have known better than to not get on the women-only car. But women-only cars are not dealing with the problem at its roots: men who harass women on trains. I'd like to see "Beware of chikans!" billboards replaced with ones that say, "Don't be a chikan! Make public places safe for everyone!"[26]

Kenya: Harassment and Lost Opportunities

Last week I had an interview with a client for my TV show. I was running late due to heavy traffic, and as soon as I arrived in town, I decided to take the shortest route to the meeting point. As I passed through a bus stage [station], a short middle-aged man who had the responsibility of ensuring the vehicles were quickly boarded said hi to me. I have always believed in responding to greetings from strangers. I mean it is only fair to say hello back to someone since they put in some effort to acknowledge your presence, and as some say, "greetings are from God." So, as usual I said hello back and quickly walked past him. Little did I know he had every intention of following me.

He caught up with me and his comments followed one after the other. "You are very beautiful. Where are you from? Where are you going? Can I escort you?" All this time I was silent[ly] praying to God that this man would just vanish and let me be. As I was about to cross the road, he grabbed my hand and told me "siste si uniwachie hata namba nikutafte kama hutaki kubonga saa hii." This translates to "sister, give me your number so that I can look for you later if you do not want to talk right now."

I quickly shoved him to the side and crossed the road only to find him right behind me. This was getting creepy, and luckily there was a supermarket, and I quickly went in and took the back exit. I looked at my watch, and I was thirty minutes late. Looking at my phone, three missed calls from the client. I found my way to the meeting point, and the receptionist told me that he had left. On trying his phone, he told me he would contact me when he was free again.

I sat down and wondered how this would happen, how many people had lost opportunities because somebody somewhere had delayed their destiny? I blamed myself for having responded to his greetings. If I had not, I would have met the client on time and the interview would be a success. Do people have to mistake other people's kindness for weakness?

I therefore decided that I would never say hello back to anybody in town whom I have no intention of holding a conversation with. Well, that is my way of handling street harassment; stay focused on where I am going. Ignore. Ignore and ignore. This is because some remarks made by these harassers can make you lose your temper and feel the need to exchange words with them in order to justify maybe your way of dressing or in relation to any comment they make about you, and we all know that this can get ugly since most of these harassers you cannot reason with and they would end up getting violent. As we have seen in some countries, they strip our women for talking back at them. Be safe.[27]

Kyrgyzstan: Street Harassment of Transgender People in Bishkek

We get harassed by the police most often. They come up to me or to my friends and start demanding to show identification. After seeing what they consider a discrepancy in the documents between indicated and real gender identity, they take us to the police station, where we are subject to more severe harassment in the form of humiliating interrogations and threats. One of the officers once said that people like me "are perverts and should be killed."

This kind of attitude by the police officers is not only seen as normal, but also encouraged. Even if you call the MIA (the Ministry of Internal Affairs) hotline to report police misconduct and brutality, they hang up on you upon hearing that this was done on the basis of gender identity.

You never feel safe, and you are never protected. Home is not a place where you feel loved and secure for a large part of my friends and myself, and the streets are like a battlefield, where you never know when and who will accost you.

When I or my friends walk down the street, people usually stare at us trying to guess gender identity. Women (mainly) stare at the genital area trying to make out whether the transgender person has male or female genitals. People loudly comment on my appearance, stop, and start giggling or discussing between themselves whether I am a boy or a girl. And this is even worse for people who do not look masculine/feminine enough and thus do not fit into the cis-normative patriarchal gender binary.

Harassment is so normalized that people simply do not consider it as such. It is normal for them to come up to an unknown person and, laughing, start asking whether you are a man or a woman, a boy or a girl. It is also normal for them to start contradicting you, if you choose to reveal your gender identity. They ask incredulously: "Do you really consider yourself a man?! But—just look at yourself!" I get called a hermaphrodite, a faggot, an "it" . . . there are so many insulting names that it won't be possible to list them all here.

However, street harassment is not limited to staring or verbal abuse. Many of my friends have been harassed physically by strangers on the streets who have grabbed their chest to "check whether it is real or not" and have hit and beaten them.

Part of the harassment comes when people confuse transgender people with lesbians and gays, and in such a highly homophobic society as the Kyrgyzstani one is, you have to expect threats, loud insults, hateful and disgusted looks. And just imagine what happens to those who are non-heterosexual or queer transgender people. . . .

This is the society we live in—a discriminatory transphobic, homophobic, biphobic (add your description here) society. I know that tremendous efforts and time are needed to change it. But one thing that any person can do next time he/she has an urge to harass others on the street is to think how it would feel if you were in the place of that person.[28]

United Kingdom: Street Harassment, the Initiative into Adulthood

I remember being jealous of my friend who confessed to being wolf-whistled by the waste collectors she passed on her way to school, regardless of the fact that it clearly distressed her and she was lodging a complaint with the council.

We were 14 or 15 years old then. I had already swallowed whole the idea that street harassment wasn't just something that we had to accept, but it was something that we should appreciate, something that we should want, something that we should envy other victims for. At the same time, these men were harassing a girl in her school uniform. Whether they were behaving in the way they did because they found her sexually attractive, because they wished to intimidate her, or both, they could be fairly safe in the assumption that they were dealing with a child. Clearly, it didn't stop them. Maybe it encouraged them.

As women, we are acutely aware that street harassment is an accepted part of our lives. In many ways, though, it is more than that; it is the rite of passage we must undertake to be considered women. The moment a girl receives her first catcall, her first wolf-whistle, or her first grope, she can consider herself well on the way to adulthood—no matter how unwanted the action was and no matter how uncomfortable it made her. Such is the brainwashing of our society, she feels that she should be grateful because it's a compliment.

If she dares to pluck up the courage and tell someone—a parent, guardian, or teacher, perhaps—she may find her concerns brushed off on the basis that, "It's just something women have to put up with," so she needs to get used to it. If she tells her friends, she might find her complaints rejected because, "You love it really!" They've been taught to view it as a compliment, too.

The entitlement that men perceive themselves to have over women, their bodies, and their lives knows no boundaries, age-related or otherwise. When I tweeted out a request for girls and women to share their earliest memories of street harassment, the majority recalled that it started before they were even teenagers. The 11-year-old catcalled by builders on her way to get ice cream, the 13-year-old beeped and hollered at by men in cars for wearing shorts, and the 16-year-old who can't leave the house for even five minutes in a skirt without a man passing comment all learned that the hard way.

Men began to intimidate them and reduce them to sex objects the moment they hit puberty. That's the initiation into adulthood. One thing above all else sticks out as being universal in the stories I heard, though: from the moment these women had their first experience of childhood street harassment, that harassment immediately became a constant part of their lives and remains so to this day. They graduated into womanhood.[29]

United States: My "Brother" Would Respect Me

I came here today to write about street harassment and race. How my feelings about street harassment are shaped by my identity as a black woman. How the way that I am viewed is tied to a history of excusing violence against black women and dehumanizing black women by portraying us as innately sexual beings with no feelings, virtue, or value. It's a legacy that has been passed down since slavery, and like many perverse tools of subjugation that were created back then, it still affects our everyday. For this reason, I get furious when I am harassed by black men on the street.

I expect better from them, and I cannot shake it. As potential victims of racial profiling and police harassment, I expect black men to be cognizant of what it feels like to be unable to walk down the street without fear or worrying about the way your appearance or body language may be perceived. But I have literally had a black man tell me that I "don't love" myself because I am bothered by street harassment. A strong black woman isn't easily bothered by constant threats and leers and groping from strangers, apparently . . .

I am sometimes accused of "being afraid of brothers," not being attracted to black men out of some fault of my own—usually because I am a light-skinned snob. It's frustrating because the black community became insular out of necessity, and in my mind, using that background to justify harassing black women perverts that history. Pet names like brother, sister, queen, and king were meant to build a sort of fellowship, and now that is distorted to place the blame on me when I am turned off by street harassment.

I expect more from black men because their sexuality has had limitations placed on it by racism, as well. The oversexed man of color is the boogeyman in too many articles that I have read about street harassment. I cannot tell you how many times I have come across comment section standoffs where women of all races swear up and down that they are harassed by men of color at disproportionate rates, unaware of how strongly their comments echo assumptions made about black male sexuality from the "nadir" of American race relations.* Studies and my own personal experiences (I tend to be harassed by black men more frequently, but not exclusively) tell me that that is not true, but perception and reality are two separate animals.

Some feminists who have studied street harassment argue that mistreating women is one of the only spoils of patriarchy in which black men can engage. That may be true. But it does not stop me from shaking my head in disappointment every time I'm accosted by a black, male harasser.

United States: Cultural Machismo in Latino Communities

I was frustrated and nervous walking to and from school as a high school student in the early 2000s. I would best describe myself then as a very conservatively dressed and studious Latina usually wearing a large backpack, casual jeans, my hair tied in a ponytail, and a baggy sweater to hide my large breasts. I would hear catcalls at least twice a day by much older Latino men who took the time to roll down their driver's side window, slow down street traffic, hang out of their truck or car, just to whistle or say, "Hey, Mamasita!"

All I wanted to do was flash my middle finger, but I was honestly too scared to do such a thing, not knowing what that man may do to me and also because I would usually walk by myself. What disgusted me the most was the fact that a Latino man, that could have been my father's age, felt the urge to address me in such a way that was abusive and clearly lacking any human dignity or respect. Because of my experience with constant verbal abuse in public spaces, I felt certain that I would one day get kidnapped and raped. Fortunately, that never happened to me.

I am happy that today I no longer live in southeast Los Angeles, specifically in the city of Cudahy, but I fear for those young girls and women

---

* Usually referred to as the period from 1890 to 1920 when racism was extremely violent and there was a peak of lynchings of African Americans by white Americans.

who continue to interface with (and some who accep)t cultural machismo in Latino communities.

The questions I would pose to all those Latino boys and men are: Why do you think it is OK to catcall or whistle at a female? Would you do that to your sister, mother, tia, grandmother, or family friend?[30]

United States: Love Me Long Time?

I returned home from work on a late afternoon, parked my car on the street, and as I was getting out of my car, a man walked by and said, "Will you suck my dick?" as he passed. The words didn't even register until a few seconds later. He kept walking, and after I realized what he said, I looked in his direction to see who he was. I suddenly realized this man had actually made "suck my dick" comments to me previously, both times on the street by my residence. I felt angry that I was unsafe in my own neighborhood and paranoid that perhaps this man was targeting me and knew where I lived. . . .

I am an Asian-American woman, and I experience street harassment all the time. Sometimes it's just the leering, or just the "Hey babys" or the explicit sexual requests. But more often than not, it turns race-related: "Love me long time?," "Sucky sucky, five dollar," and the "Ni-haos" in my face that sound like meowing. The race-related street harassment is a one-two punch because it thinly veils hatred behind sexual subjugation. It's common, and it happens frequently enough that I'm habitually on edge when I walk outside by myself.

My natural defense mechanism against street harassment and un-wanted attention is to have a scowl on my face. This scowling defense mechanism affects my day-to-day public interactions. A recent example of this is that my husband, an Asian American man, will often recount all the people he encounters when he is out taking the dog for a walk. These encounters, however, consist of friendly hellos to him (and the dog) and remarks about how cute our dog is. Hardly anyone ever greets or tells me how cute my dog is when I take her for a walk. I attribute this difference to my scowl and general "don't bother me" attitude, which I'm not even aware of. Walking the dog while male and walking the dog while female show how street harassment makes a deep impact on seemingly trivial activities.

Speak up about and against street harassment. It's not OK . . . I'd really like to enjoy a walk with my dog sans scowl, the way that it's supposed to be.[31]

United States: Street Harassment 102: When You're Blind and a Woman

I'm walking along the street, minding my own business, scanning the street with my cane for obstacles, when suddenly, from outside of my peripheral vision—I hear a question!

"Hey! Lady! Are you really blind?" . . .

I decide, since I have a person with me, to respond. "Yes. I'm really blind."

"But when you turned the corner, you didn't do it like a blind person does. You did it like you could see!"

Inward groan. "Only 10 percent of blind people are completely blind. Most have some vision. And by the way, it's super impolite to ask people about their disability when you don't know them."

He makes unpleasant noises about the fact that I am apparently being rude to him and scurries away. My friend and I bitch about him when we enter the store.

These interactions are very common in my life. They are the norm. People will ask me this question on the subway. They will do it when I am sitting by myself and reading on my Nook (the greatest thing to happen to me since I got my cane, by the way). I get asked how I could possibly be so hot when I'm disabled—that I dress so well and it's surprising!

There are a lot of reasons why these interactions are startling, for one because it just seems like common sense not to ask people how much they can't see out in the middle of a crowded metropolitan street. What are they going to do, mug me if I'm REALLY blind?

They don't hand white canes out like candy. It's not like I borrowed my cane from somebody in an attempt to make a Helen Keller Halloween costume. I use my cane every single day to traverse the city by myself. Most of the population doesn't notice it, and I have to beat them with it to get them out of my way. A smaller population challenges my right to have the cane, and the last portion of the population politely opens doors and steps out of my way when I need them to.

But there's actually a category even more insidious—the extra helpful people. These are the men who will grab my arm and haul me across the street because they think I can't see and they can help me better than I can help myself. If I don't jaywalk, it irritates them. I once had a man tell me to "come along" and then make it sound like he was calling over a puppy.

These people scare me because they don't see the boundary of asking for help. They don't think that they should ask if I need help—because they know better than I do. They insert themselves uncomfortably into my space, my thoughts, and make the assumption that I need them to make my life easier.[32]

United States: Lesbian Couples and Street Harassment

Before I explored my interest in women (and met the most wonderful girl), I never thought twice about PDA. I knew the politeness around it—holding hands, hugs, and small kisses being okay. Being in complete agreement with these terms, I had no problem following these as a then-identified straight woman. I would go to the mall or a movie and comfortably hold hands with my boyfriend or kiss him goodbye, not once thinking about how much of a privilege that was.

Before I begin, I do have to say I'm lucky to come from [an area] where there is a prevalent LGBTQ community, and for the most part, I feel safe enough to be out in public places. However, with that being said, there is still a certain anxiety I feel when going out with my girlfriend. I want to raise attention to this and ask you all to advocate for change . . .

When I go out in public with my girlfriend, I find myself with one of two paths to take: do not show any PDA and let everyone assume we are friends, or hold her hand and take the chance that someone at any moment may say something to us (which happens more often than not). When I'm with her, I do choose to hold her hand or put my arm around her because, ultimately, she is the one I care about, and I want to show that to her; but this also means that my guard is always up. We've had people on the street direct "positive" and negative comments towards us—and I say "positive" because no street harassment is a comfortable experience. Instead of just being another couple on the street, we are an entity attracting attention. Why are we looked at differently?

We've had comments varying from "how sweet" to "now *that's* what I'm talking about" to even whooping and hollering at a small kiss at a concert. No matter the content, it is demeaning to our relationship. It's been a long-running popular thing for straight women to "act gay" in order to provoke attention from men, and it's that behavior that also demeans the relationship I'm in. When I kiss my girlfriend or hold her hand, it is not for the entertainment of whomever may be passing by; it's a small act of affection for her. Just because you're a witness to it does not entitle you to call out to us and express your enjoyment or dissatisfaction. My relationship's existence is not to fulfill your sexual fantasies. My relationship is just like any other—an emotional connection between two people.[33]

United States: Gay and Bisexual Men Fear Harassment

While waiting for a bus on my way to work, a man approached me and asked about the bus schedule. Then, he asked if I liked him. He said he was on the DL (down-low), that he liked my voice and thought I was sexy. I grew uncomfortable and wasn't sure how to respond. He then questioned whether I liked big black cock and asked if I wanted to see his. His aggression was unwanted, and it took awhile to convince him that I wasn't interested.

Another time while walking through a metro station, I was harassed for holding hands with another boy.

*   *   *

As much as I wish these incidences were rare, they're not—and that's the reality for many men who are perceived to be either gay or bisexual . . . Earlier this year, I conducted research as part of my master's thesis at The George Washington University about the street harassment of gay and bisexual men. I surveyed 331 men around the world about their experiences, and about 90 percent said they are sometimes, often, or always harassed or made to feel unwelcome in public spaces because of their perceived sexual orientation—a figure that is far too high.

But the harassment of gay and bisexual men is complicated. They're targeted because they are men, and they're targeted because their masculinity is, in some cases and to varying degrees, illegible. It's a form of violence that takes place in a heterosexist society, one that tries to enforce traditional gender standards and behaviors on individuals engaged in public interaction.

The types of harassment my respondents experienced tended to vary based on the sexual orientation of the harasser. They reported that it was other gay or bisexual men who whistled at them and touched/grabbed them in a sexual way, while men who they identified as straight were more responsible for other things, like honking, swearing, making homophobic comments, purposely blocking a path, or following.

Many men reported toning down their appearances in public to appear more masculine and avoid harassment. One respondent said he was uncomfortable around guys he referred to as "bros," even though he had little experience being harassed by them.

And this is what I find so unsettling about this form of violence. Though it may happen less often than the gender-based street harassment of women, gay and bisexual men still think about and, at times, agonize over it. In fact, about 71 percent of my survey respondents reported constantly assessing their surroundings when navigating public spaces.

In addition, 69 percent said they avoid specific neighborhoods or areas, 67 percent reported not making eye contact with others, and 59 percent said they cross streets or take alternate routes—all to escape potential harassment.[34]

READING AND LISTENING TO STORIES SPUR ACTION

Street harassment happens in every single country, culture, and community. No region has achieved full gender equality or equal rights for LGBTQ individuals or ended sexual violence, racism, classism, or ableism. So street harassment continues to be a problem everywhere. Research and stories illuminate this reality and provide evidence for its existence and why it must end. Sharing our stories can spur our loved ones and friends to look out for and challenge sexism, homophobia, racism, ableism, and harassment. Of course, though, much more research is needed—particularly on why street harassment happens, the impact it has on individuals and communities, and the best ways to stop it—and more stories from marginalized and under-represented groups will help us understand this issue even more. So we must continue to speak out, collect data, and learn from each other's stories.

What has been especially exciting to see over the past several years is how sharing and reading stories and the increase in data supporting those stories have spurred individuals to say, "Enough!" and to take action together, from organizing tweet chats and rallies to creating art work and youth workshops. Examples of their action locally and globally follow, with more found online at www.stopstreetharassment.org.

Chapter 3

Local Community Activism

Street harassment march in Bucharest, Romania, 2014. (Simona Chirciu)

Street harassment is a global problem, and brave and determined individuals worldwide are doing something about it, whether it's distributing informational flyers, organizing a march, or holding a workshop with youth. In most cases, their actions take place with little to no budget and are carried out largely on volunteered time. These individuals are fueled by a burning desire to be proactive, to make a difference, to create a space that is free from harassment for all. This chapter offers many examples of their creative activities that are regularly taking place worldwide.

TAKING ACTION ON THE STREETS AND TRANSIT LINES

Sidewalk Chalking

Using sidewalk chalk to write messages like "My body is not public space" has become a popular way to quickly raise awareness about street harassment. It is inexpensive, easy, and something an individual or a small group can do, and the impact can be huge. In addition to raising the awareness of people passing by while the chalking happens, dozens, hundreds, or even thousands of people can see it as they pass by—barring rain or other conditions that might wipe out the message. Anti-street harassment chalking parties have taken place all over the world, including in Melbourne, Australia; Ottawa, Canada; Bogota, Colombia; Berlin, Germany; and Dublin, Ireland, as well as in American states like California, Florida, Georgia, Hawai'i, Illinois, Massachusetts, New York, Oregon, Pennsylvania, and South Dakota.

A unique approach to chalking is the Chalk Walk, the group Rebellieus, formerly Hollaback! Brussels, held in 2012. Four young women met at Ribaucourt, Molenbeek in Brussels, Belgium, on a spring morning. Their meeting place was significant because it was where one of the women, Angelika, had been harassed. With a bright-colored piece of chalk, Angelika stooped down and wrote on the sidewalk, "I was harassed here. I Hollaback. I reclaim the street." She proudly stood by her message as her friends hugged her and congratulated her on reclaiming the space. Together, they made a pilgrimage to other spots where they had been harassed: a busy four-lane boulevard for Anna, the sidewalk of a busy bridge for Julie, and the staircase at the Metro stop De Brouckere for Ingrid. At each place, they shared their stories, reclaimed the space with chalk, and hugged. Several people stopped to talk to them, to hear their stories, and to support their message.[1]

"AWESOME is not even a strong enough word to describe it! EMPOWERING comes close!" the women wrote on their Facebook wall. "What we discovered was that writing with chalk on the sidewalk, on the street, on the bridge, telling Brussels: " 'I was harassed here' 'I reclaim the street' is a powerful, liberating ritual and an amazing [experience]."[2] In 2013, they launched a *We Chalk Walk* Tumblr where anyone can submit anti-street harassment chalk messages.

Chalking can be an effective way to start conversations and change minds. In Nassau, the Bahamas, two young women wrote messages such as "Whistle at dogs, not girls" and "Respect girls" on a sidewalk along the beach. They said that among the people who stopped to talk to them was a man "who thought we were writing the message specifically to him. We explained what we were doing to him and told him what he did WAS in fact street harassment. He, of course, did not believe us, and we had to break it down for him. He ended up understanding what we were saying, so we hope we have a converted man in Nassau!"[3] This is exactly the kind of impact they hoped to have. Alicia Wallace, one of the women, told the local newspaper: "Chalk messages are not common here, and we knew it would attract the attention of pedestrians. . . . It is unacceptable, and educating the general public on the definition and everyday examples of street harassment is the first step to combating this problem."[4]

Distributing Anti-Street Harassment Cards

Distributing cards about street harassment to harassers or to educate passersby is a tactic that's been used for years, especially when it became easy to post the cards online for others to download. The Street Harassment Project, for example, has offered cards on its site since the early 2000s and Stop Street Harassment (SSH) has made cards available since 2008. But in recent years, individuals have been creating their own. In 2012, for example, American Mirabelle Jones created "catcalling cards" with a phone number printed on them for women to give to men who won't leave them alone. If the men call the number, they will hear prerecorded messages from women telling harassers exactly what they think of them. On her Tumblr *I Am Not an Object*, she invites women to leave recordings and download the cards.[5]

In Dortmund, Germany, the women in the feminist group ProChange devised another clever way to use cards. Living in a country that is obsessed with football (American soccer), they created "Red Cards" against sexism, "Pink Cards" against homophobia and "Purple Cards" of courage. Individuals can hand out these cards to challenge or commend others' actions without having to directly talk to them. "This can be easier than having any other reaction," the women told me. A group called Avanti had the same idea and had already created cards that they let ProChange adopt. ProChange also created special coasters with information about street harassment for the pubs, bars, and clubs of Dortmund.[6]

One of their first distribution occurred during International Anti-Street Harassment Week 2012 when they handed out 2,000 of these cards and coasters. They have distributed thousands more since, often coinciding with specific days like Equal Pay Day, One Billion Rising (against gender violence), Frauenkampflag (Women's Day), and Fahnentag (the International Day for the Elimination of Violence against Women).

"We get mostly positive feedback regarding the cards," the group members informed me. "Even men approach us to ask for more cards they can give to their partners or daughters. Often people email us to ask for our cards. Our favorite story was when we were in front of the city hall distributing cards. It was too cold and only a few people passed by. An old grumpy-looking man approached us. He took one of the cards and looked at it. Then he shook everybody's hands and thanked us for standing in the cold for women and girls."[7]

In 2014, American Lindsey Middlecamp created the project Cards Against Harassment. The year before, she began verbally challenging street harassers. Sometimes they genuinely listened to her, but a few times they became more confrontational. "I decided that a card would be the ideal middle ground, allowing me to provide feedback that harassment is unwanted without necessarily sticking around for an extended encounter,"[8] she wrote on the SSH blog. The 20 cards she created have messages like "YOUR MOM . . . would be really disappointed to learn that she had raised a street harasser. Be a better man. Don't comment on random people on the street" and "Are you my doctor? I didn't think so. Keep your opinions about me and my body to yourself next time." In just over six months, her site has received 400,000 visitors, and volunteers have translated the cards into Spanish and French with German, Russian, and Portuguese in the works.[9]

Pasting Flyers and Posters on Walls

A simple way to raise awareness about street harassment that one person or a group can do is to hang flyers and posters on bulletin boards, walls, the backs of street signs, and other public places. Take Afghanistan. There, members of the group Young Women for Change, founded by college women, posted flyers about women's rights and street harassment on the walls of Kabul several times, including a day in 2011 when 25 volunteers glued 700 fliers to walls around the city despite the potential danger involved in publicly calling for women's rights. Their acts received a mixture of responses, from anger to support. "I felt like my heart was going to melt down when we posted a poster and a shopkeeper who was there watching us post it couldn't read it [because he was illiterate]," wrote then 20-year-old co-founder Anita Hadiary in a blog post. "He asked another person to read it. When he learned what the poster said, he started fixing the poster and glued it harder on the wall."[10]

In 2013, members of the Zimbabwe Parents of Handicapped Children Association hung signs on trees in their rural community with messages like "It's my right to be in public space. I don't want to be harassed. Leave me in peace not in pieces. It's my world too!" That same year, Ryerson University college students in Toronto, Canada, posted fliers on bulletin boards around their campus. One flier had an image of flat shoes with the words "These shoes do not make me a prude." Another flier showed high-heeled shoes with the words "These shoes do not make me a slut." The larger message was "I do not dress for you."[11]

When a few women in their 20s and 30s formed the STOP Harcèlement de rue in Paris, France, in 2014, one of their first actions was to post 50 fliers against harassment on walls, lamp posts, bar windows, and mailboxes near the Place de la Bastille in Paris, a crowded area well-known for street harassment. The fliers' messages included "Me siffler n'est pas un compliment" and "Ma mini-jupe ne veut pas dire oui" ("Whistling at me is not a compliment" and "My mini-skirt is not a yes"). Throughout the summer of 2014, the women met every Monday night to put up posters around the city.[12]

In the United States, oil painter/illustrator Tatyana Fazlalizadeh launched Stop Telling Women to Smile in 2012. Her own daily experiences with street harassment inspired her to draw her own and other women's faces and add simple anti-harassment messages. She would then photocopy the illustrations and paste them on walls. The messages included "Stop telling women to smile," "Women are not outside for your entertainment," and "Harassing women does not prove your masculinity." During 2013, Fazlalizadeh held a very successful online fundraising Kickstarter campaign so she could travel to more than 10 cities across the United States to meet with women, hear their stories, create portraits, and then paste their portraits in their communities. In 2014, she also went to Mexico City.[13]

Graffiti Art and Murals

A related action against street harassment is painting murals and spray-painting graffiti, a type of political art and communication that has been used in many cultures since ancient times.

During the Egyptian Revolution of 2011, graffiti art and murals were used to voice political opinions. Some women used these to speak out against the sexual harassment and violence many women protesters faced. Artist El Zeft nad Mira Shihadeh, for example, painted a mural called *Circle of Hell* depicting dozens of leering men surrounding one woman like a pack of wolves surrounding its prey.[14] One graffiti stencil from that time period was a blue bra accompanied by the caption "No to the stripping of people" and below it was the outline of a foot that said, "Long live the revolution." It references a 2011 videotaped beating of a female protester by police during which all of her clothes were stripped off, which revealed her blue bra.[15] Some messages were defiant. One graffiti stencil created by Hend Kheera featured a woman with the caption "Warning! Don't touch or castration awaits you!" A stencil created by Mira Shihadeh (featured on this book's cover) showed a woman standing tall and holding a spray can to spray away tiny men. The caption read "No to sexual harassment."[16]

Egyptian anti-street harassment activists with the group HarassMap have also used graffiti to bring attention to sexual harassment in public spaces. In 2013, for example, a team of mostly male volunteers in Giza wrote messages on walls like "Be a man; protect her from harassment instead of harassing her" and "No to harassment" while a team in Alexandria covered up sexist graffiti that promoted violent harassment by painting a mural that said "LOVE."[17]

Anti-street harassment activists in Nepal and the United States painted murals in 2014. In Kathmandu, ten young women and men from the group Astitwa painted a huge mural with a street, a "stop" hand and their logo. The main message in green block lettering was "We Are against Street Harassment," and each person placed her or his hands in red paint and added their handprint below it.[18] On their U.S. mural, People's Justice League (formerly Hollaback! Appalachian Ohio) wrote the messages "Bobcats against cat-calls" and "YOU have the power to end street harassment" (with their logo) and drew a map of uptown Athens with red and green dots showing where people had reported being harassed (red) and where they reported intervening in harassment situations (green).[19]

Holding a Street Demonstration

Initiating a street demonstration by holding signs with anti-harassment messages, asking people to write their own messages, and facilitating impromptu conversations are additional tactics growing in popularity among people wishing to challenge street harassment in their community. These types of actions have taken place in many countries, including Jordan, Egypt, Chile, India, and the United States.

In June 2012, more than 200 people in Amman, Jordan, formed a "human chain" from Al Hussein Sports City to the Interior Ministry Circle to protest various gender-based crimes, including street harassment, the practice of forcing rape survivors to marry their rapists, and honor killings. Women and men of all ages stood in a row, each holding signs that condemned these acts and called for behavioral changes and changes to laws.[20] Weeks later in Egypt, the Nefsi (I Hope) anti-sexual harassment campaign also organized scores of people into a human chain along a busy road in Cairo. Some of the participants' signs read "I wish I could ride a bike without anyone bothering me" and "I wish you would respect me as I respect you."[21]

In 2014, Observatorio Contra el Acoso Callejero en Chile held an open outdoor meeting at a plaza where more than two dozen women and men of all ages discussed street harassment, passed out pamphlets to passersby, and wrote anti-street harassment messages on signs like "Mi cuerpo no es un objeto" ("My body is not an object") and "Yo me visto para mi no para ti" ("I dress for me not for you"). They held the signs for passersby to see and then attached them to strings hung around the plaza. They also attached small ribbons on which they had written their street harassment experiences, and people walking by stopped to read them.[22]

In Bangalore, India, members of the volunteer group Jhatkaa spent a day in 2014 walking around the streets of the city with a whiteboard and asking women to write down their experiences with street harassment. People were eager to participate and wrote statements like, "Lots of times men have pinched my breasts and made passes at me on the buses," "Been whistled and stared at wearing a pair of jeans," and "The creepy stare." The organizers wrote in a summary of their event: "Many women thanked us for doing it and told us they felt lighter after speaking about it and participating in fighting against it. On seeing photos of other women and their experiences, they also felt good knowing that they weren't the only ones. We shared these photos on Facebook and Twitter and received positive comments for the work."[23]

Since 2011, Philadelphia-based groups like FAAN Mail and Feminist Public Works have held a demonstration in the spring. It includes drumming, chalking, and posting flyers and signs and discussing street harassment with passersby. In 2014, they framed it as reclaiming public space at LOVE Park and hosted chalking, street theater, music, art making, and double Dutch jump rope. People could write their answers to complete the phrase "A Safe Street is . . . ," and several chose to publicly share their street harassment stories while standing on a "soap box." Around 50 people participated. "This year's action in Philadelphia was our most dynamic action yet," wrote FAAN Mail co-founder Nuala Cabral in a report of the event. We offered several activities that enabled people to reclaim public space and address this problem in creative ways. Children were a part of the event. Male allies stood with us. It was a beautiful day."[24]

Marching through the Streets

Since the mid-1970s, Take Back the Night and Reclaim the Night marches have occurred annually in many cities worldwide to challenge rape. Starting in 2011, SlutWalk marches spread globally, too, with participants criticizing rape culture and victim blaming. In recent years, there have also been marches in countries like Afghanistan, Colombia, Nepal, Romania, South Africa, and the United States.

On a hot day in 2011, 50 women and men carrying banners and signs with messages like, "We will not tolerate harassment," "Islam forbids men from insulting women," and "I have the right to walk freely in my city" marched together from Kabul University to the Afghanistan Independent Human Rights Commission. Organized by Young Women for Change, marchers handed out fliers to raise awareness about the problem of street harassment in their country.[25] Most of the people they passed on the street stood shocked, staring, since openly supporting women's rights can be dangerous. Despite the presence of a police escort, some men heckled the marchers and called them names. But others were supportive and took fliers or joined the march. Organizer Noorjahan Akbar, then a 20-year-old college student, told me in an interview at the time: "It was so thrilling to see that none of us are alone in this fight and we are willing to stand up for each other."[26]

In 2012, between 3,000 and 5,000 women and men joined together to march through Johannesburg, South Africa, outraged by the sexual assault of two women wearing short skirts at a taxi rank and by the daily street harassment most women face. They carried signs with messages like "I will wear my mini-skirt anywhere!" and "Humiliating women is a sin before God." Lulu Xingwana, the minister of women and children and people with disabilities marched too, and told the local news station: "Through this march, we are reclaiming our streets from those who abuse and terrorize women and children." She also warned she would close down taxi ranks if harassment and assault against women continued there.[27]

In Bogota, Observatorio Contra el Acoso Callejero Colombia held a march against street harassment in the center of the city in 2014. More than 100 people participated, carrying signs with messages like "Nuestros Cuerpos No Hacen Parte Del Espacio Publico!" (Our bodies are not public space!). The group joined forces with a female percussion group called La Tremenda Revoltosa Batucada Feminista and a performance group called Tulpadanza, which both brought extra energy to the march. Also in 2014, with the help of volunteers from the feminist organization Filia, Simona-Maria Chirciu organized a 100-person march through Bucharest, Romania. Women and men of all ages held signs that read, "Harassment is violence," "We don't need your validation," and "It is NEVER ok to harass people! So stop doing it." Numerous women's rights groups participated. Chirciu wrote for the SSH blog: "People on the streets interacted with us, greeted us, and asked questions about our march: 'Hey, do you think a march will solve the problem? Boys need to be educated or legally punished for doing this.' Yes! Maybe a march doesn't solve the street harassment issue, but it can raise awareness and is empowering for the march participants."[28]

Patrolling to Keep People Safe

At various times and places, a spate of well-publicized attacks on women in public spaces has inspired people to set up patrols or volunteer escort services. In recent years, this happened in Norway, the United States, and Egypt.

In 2011, after reading about men raping several young women who were walking home at night in Oslo, Norway, four young women in their early 20s formed Action Against Rape (AAR) and decided they would patrol the city after dark to help make the environment safer. The first weekend they went out, around 200 people joined them. During the next year, AAR organized patrol groups of 4–6 people every Friday and Saturday night from 10 p.m. to 3 a.m. Wearing yellow vests, they fanned out across the city. They rarely encountered harassers, but AAR co-founder Lisa Arntzen felt their very presence deterred harassment and violence. "I was 21 and didn't have the power to make the big changes, so this was something easy I could do," Arntzen told me. "That's why so many people joined us. They realized they could contribute and it wasn't hard at all."[29]

Similarly, in response to numerous sexual assaults of women in Brooklyn, New York, American bike messenger Jay Ruiz reacted by starting the Brooklyn Bike Patrol in 2011. He recruited 10 volunteers, and they began escorting women home from five neighborhood subway stops from 8 p.m. until midnight most nights. People could simply call them to request an escort. Within weeks, they expanded their volunteer base and service area. Wearing fluorescent-yellow T-shirts, the volunteers continue to receive up to a dozen calls each night.[30]

Because many men in Egypt take advantage of crowds at protests and holidays to harass, grope, and commit gang assaults against women, activism groups set up patrols during these times in 2012. Wearing bright-yellow vests, they look for harassment situations and break them up. They also publicize a phone number people can call if they need help. For example, in 2012 during Eid-ul-Fitr, the holiday at the end of the Islamic holy month of Ramadan, volunteers with Bassma (Imprint) interrupted many instances of harassment and helped police arrest several harassers each day. Founder Nihal Zaghloul wrote for the SSH blog, "It is OUR RIGHT as women to walk in the streets safely, and [since] NO ONE will give us this right, we must take it ourselves."[31] Similarly, during political protests, as many as 300 volunteers with groups like Operation Anti-Sexual Harassment wear shirts proclaiming Tahrir Square a "safe square for all" while standing at every checkpoint, atop watchtowers, and throughout the crowd. They pass out hotline numbers and instructions on handling rape trauma victims. After one of their patrols in December 2012, Yasmine Abdelhamid said it was the first time since the uprising that she felt it was safe for her to protest in Tahrir Square.[32]

Transit Campaigns

Harassment on public transportation is a universal problem, and individuals and groups have organized awareness-raising campaigns by distributing literature, performing skits, and sponsoring anti-harassment ads in countries like Colombia, Myanmar, Sri Lanka, India, the United Kingdom, and the United States.

In Bogota, Colombia, the Latin American Women and Habitat Network created a no-groping campaign on the bus system in 2011. They hung posters at every bus stop and station and gave bus drivers shirts with slogans against harassment. They also role-played sexual harassment scenarios on the bus. Women dressed as men performed scenes about groping and then asked passengers what they thought about the behavior. "We generally get positive responses," wrote group member Marisol Dalmazo in a post for *Love Matters*. "More and more, people think sexual harassment should be condemned, that this kind of behaviour mustn't be tolerated."[33]

Whistle for Help is a popular campaign that launched in Myanmar in 2012. Initially, 150 people came together each Tuesday morning for nine months to distribute whistles and pamphlets to women at eight busy bus stops in Yangon. The pamphlets informed women to blow the whistle when they experienced sexual harassment on the bus and advised them to help other women who blow the whistle. The whistle campaign was so popular that riders regularly asked for extra whistles to pass out to their friends and family, and the campaign expanded to other regions, including Burma.[34]

Through their SHOW You Care campaign, Sri Lanka Unites taught hundreds of young men about street harassment in 2012. The men then boarded 1,225 buses on 49 routes in Colombo during a week to apologize to women in the buses for any harassment they had encountered in the past and to provide them with information on legal recourse available to them. They also told men to take responsibility and not harass. "The response from the commuters on buses was astounding. Passengers, both male and female, were very responsive to the campaign," Nadeesh Jayasinghe, one of the organizers of the event, told me in an interview for the SSH blog. "Many encouraged the efforts of the young men . . . and were eager to engage in conversations regarding the issue of harassment on public transportation and were heartened by the efforts of the young men to attempt to resolve this problem in the city of Colombo."[35]

In Lucknow, India, a survey found that 97 percent of women were harassed while riding in auto-rickshaws, and most drivers stayed silent when it happened. Through a Safe Safar campaign launched in 2010 by Zeeshan Mohammad, a man in his 20s who worked on gender and youth issues, the auto-rickshaw drivers received sensitivity training and learned how they can play a proactive role in helping women feel safer. This not only included how to speak out when harassment happened, but they also received instructions to not play offensive music and to remove photos of scantily clad women from their vehicles. In its first four years, the program reached 2,000 auto-rickshaw drivers and has received recognition for its success.[36]

The flash mob approach has been used in a few countries. In Delhi, India, members of the Please Mend the Gap campaign took off their jackets to reveal bright-yellow shirts with anti-harassment messages and create a bright chain against harassment.[37] Upset by a man who pressed his erection against her and ejaculated onto her while she rode the London Tube into work, Ellie Cosgrave returned to the subway line on International Women's Day 2013, held up a sign explaining what had happened, and then danced. "I danced my protest, and it felt right . . . I was responding with my body in the exact place that my body was abused, and while I couldn't sing or shout very loudly, I could dance loudly," Cosgrave wrote in an article for the *Guardian*. Her protest was met with kindness and support from other passengers.[38] Volunteers with Chicago's CTA: Courage campaign[39] and Washington, D.C.'s SSH, Collective Action for Spaces (CASS), and Voices of Men role-played harassment scenarios on subway cars and showed how witnesses can intervene to help stop the harassment. In both cities the groups distributed anti-harassment literature and received support and encouragement.

Working with Nightlife Venues, Campuses, and Young People

While street harassment happens the most in outdoor public spaces, other public spaces, like restaurants, movie theaters, stores, and nightlife venues, are not immune. A few activists and groups have campaigns targeting harassment in some of these venues. Additionally, this section looks at a few campaigns against street harassment that have been initiated by college students on their campuses.

Creating Safe Bars and Nightclubs

Groping, grinding, and verbal harassment are common problems at nightlife venues across the world. Groups in both England and the United States have programs to address and combat this unfortunate reality.

Nightlife harassment stories make up a significant portion of the stories submitted to the Hollaback! London website. Co-Directors Bryony Beynon and Julia Gray wanted to do something about it and lucked out when in 2013, one of London's biggest and most famous clubs, fabric, contacted them acknowledging that it had a harassment problem. Beynon and Gray worked with the club to create the first anti-harassment policy of its kind in the United Kingdom. "The results were amazing," Beynon told me. Kristi Weir, the press officer at fabric, agreed, saying, "We've received some really positive messages from women thanking us for taking this stance and having their backs since we started publicising the campaign."[40]

After their success at fabric, Beynon and Gray created the Good Night Out Campaign and launched it as a London pilot on International Women's Day in March 2014. Only a few months later, it spread across the United Kingdom and Ireland, and within a few more months, 95 licensed premises had signed on to the campaign. The women told me the establishments range from "superclubs to tiny pubs, university union bars, from theatres to pizza joints" and that more are signing up every week.[41]

The women customize the program to meet each establishment's needs and only move forward once everyone there is committed and will sign the pledge, which in part reads: "We want you to have a Good Night Out. If something or someone makes you feel uncomfortable, you can speak to any member of staff, and they will work with you to make sure it doesn't have to ruin your night." The premise must post this pledge very visibly around the venue. This is "so that customers really see them and are aware that they're in an environment that doesn't tolerate harassment."[42]

The staff members of each premise receive an hour-long training session about harassment and handling reports that includes what to say to avoid using victim-blaming language. They also can get other training tools like a hints and tips sheet for the back bar areas. The Good Night Out Campaign is expanding quickly. Through a new partnership with their local council in Southwark, the campaign will soon deliver the training to every venue in the area. Through another new partnership with the national alcohol awareness nonprofit organization Drinkaware, the campaign will "provide training and advice on a pilot project aimed at reducing harassment on nights out by placing hosts in licensed premises to provide help and support."[43]

Similar programs are underway in the United States in Washington, D.C., Arizona, Iowa City, and Boston. Washington, D.C.'s program is a collaboration between grassroots groups Defend Yourself and CASS. In Arizona, the program is run by a sexual violence prevention arm of the Arizona Department of Health and Human Services. The Rape Victims Advocacy Program and Women's Resource and Action Center at the University of Iowa are working with bar staff at venues in downtown Iowa City. The Boston program is run through the Boston Rape Crisis Center in collaboration with law enforcement and the Alcoholic Beverages Control Commission. The reach of each program has been much smaller than the Good Night Out Campaign, but feedback from venues that have used the training has been very positive, and staff members feel better able to address harassment in their establishments.

Making Businesses Safer Spaces

In the United States, a few advocacy groups have worked with businesses to make safer spaces for customers and community members. In 2011 in Arizona, the Southern Arizona Center Against Sexual Assault, for instance, launched Safe Streets AZ to address street harassment, particularly harassment targeted at LGBTQ youth. One component of the campaign is Safe Sites. Staff at restaurants, bookstores, and coffee shops take a 30-minute Safe Sites training, which then allows the establishment to be listed as a place where youth can seek safety if they are facing street harassment or feel unsafe. Nearly 30 businesses have gone through the training, and it is endorsed by the Pima County Small Business Commission, the Southern Arizona Chamber of Commerce Alliance, and the Pima County Public Libraries. Each site is listed on a Google map on the Safe Streets AZ website.[44]

Inspired by the Good Night Out campaign in London, the members of Baltimore's Hollaback! Bmore launched a Safer Spaces Campaign in

2013. They work directly with a business to ensure its current employee guide and/or security policies are comprehensive and sensitive to experiences of gender-based violence. Then Hollaback! Bmore provides a free training workshop on street harassment basics and crisis response that includes role-playing real-life situations. Once a majority of employees have gone through the training, they sign a pledge, hang an informational poster (provided) in plain view, and receive the Hollaback! Employer's Guide to Ending Street Harassment. Hollaback! Bmore then supports and advertises these spaces on its website. So far, eight venues are completely trained, two are being scheduled, and 14 more have expressed interest.[45]

Raising Awareness at Colleges and Universities

A growing number of colleges and universities from Egypt to the United States have been addressing street harassment, often during Sexual Assault Awareness Month or in conjunction with International Women's Day or International Anti-Street Harassment Week. They host workshops and street demonstrations, write sidewalk chalk messages, distribute materials, screen documentaries like the 1998 film *War Zone*, and create their own videos.

In 2012, members of Pennsylvania State University's Triota, the women's studies honor society, held an anti-street harassment demonstration on a busy Friday afternoon in October in downtown State College, Pennsylvania. They held signs proclaiming their anti-harassment message and even included specific remarks that had been yelled at them during their time at Penn State like "Hey girl, you want my big dick?" and "I've always wanted to cross a fat girl off my list." They also held up anti-street harassment messages like "It's not a compliment; it's harassment." Julie Mastrine, one of the organizers, wrote about it for the SSH blog:

Don't be mistaken: these types of incidents aren't rare in this town. Street harassment is a widespread problem in State College, where nearly every woman I know has experienced some form of it: catcalls, taunting, lewd remarks, leering, sexually objectifying remarks, you name it. And this type of harassment functions as part of a larger issue in this town: rape culture. We saw a lot of stares and furrowed brows from passersby. Only a few people approached us to express their support, but it doesn't matter—getting this issue in the eyes and ears of the State College community is important if we want to combat harmful behavior and attitudes toward women.[46]

In Egypt, college student Holly Dagres created the Fight Harassment 101 (FH101) workshop in 2012 to educate female students about harassment and the use of self-defense. For 10 weeks at the American University of Cairo, 15 students took part in FH101 for two hours a week. Dagres wrote for the SSH blog about how the workshop entailed sharing information and stories about street harassment and then practicing self-defense for 90 minutes. She wrote: "It gave them a sense of empowerment to defend themselves in the worst-case scenarios. At first they were shy about sharing their experiences, but once they found it was a common occurrence and learned that it was not their fault, they felt the need to fight against it.[47]

Hosting Youth Workshops

Street harassment begins at a young age for many people. More adults are recognizing this and the importance of creating spaces, like workshops, for youth to talk about their experiences and brainstorm strategies of resistance. Youth workshops have taken place in countries like the United States, Cameroon, and Germany.

In March 2012 in the United States, female youth organizers at the Brooklyn, New York-based nonprofit Girls for Gender Equity (GGE) hosted "Bring Your Brother Day" to talk about street harassment. The young women of GGE "felt strongly about the importance of bringing the young men in their lives into their work to counteract sexual harassment and gender-based violence," wrote community organizer Neferiti Martin and intern Katie Bowers for the SSH blog. "The workshop grew out of youth organizers' concerns that the conversation around street harassment and gender-based violence is taking place primarily among women. By reaching out to the young men in their lives, youth organizers are working to build allies."[48]

The three-hour workshop explored gender stereotypes and how they impacted the lives of young people and included street harassment story sharing and a discussion about how young men can be allies to young women. "The young men were thoughtful, open, and engaged throughout the workshop," wrote Martin and Bowers. "Their comments and opinions added new depth to the conversation and reflected the positive influence of the awesome young women in their lives."[49]

Wearing orange shirts that said "Stop Street Harassment," 25 youth aged 15–19 attended a street harassment seminar in Buea, Cameroon, in December 2013 that was organized by Zoneziwoh M. Wondieh, the leader of Young Women for a Change, Cameroon (WFAC). In small groups, the youth shared their stories of harassment, ranging from whistling to grabbing and touching. "African baby," "Fine ass," "My size," and "Pretty butts" were examples of verbal harassment the girls said they had faced. One boy shared how he had been sexually harassed by a man and how it made him understand better what his female peers experienced on a regular basis.[50]

For six hours the youth listened to guest speakers, learned steps for dealing with harassers, and engaged in role-play and debates with the goal of being ready to mentor others and speak out against harassment in their community. As an outcome of the youth seminar, WFAC launched an SMS text campaign to send educational text messages about street harassment to anyone who wants to receive them on a weekly or bi-weekly basis. Wondieh posts tips and information over social media, too. She estimates that she has reached 1,000 youth through her various efforts, and she's having an impact. For example, a young man recently told her that thanks to the information she shares, he has "reconsidered what he thinks is proper behavior toward women."[51]

In Germany, the women in the group ProChange recognize that the best place to start educating people about street harassment, sexual violence, and sexism is in schools, so in 2014, they created violence prevention and assertiveness workshop trainings for students ages 9–12 years old. So far, they have held one workshop and are working to secure more funding to be able to lead more. "We want to achieve a shift in their mindset so that the youth can be self-confident and free from role models and stereotypes," they told me. "In our view it is important to start at an early age because they are already surrounded by stereotypes and influenced by sexist advertisements and media . . . [We want them] to be empowered to choose their own ways."[52]

Creative Youth Projects

Whether it's by making art or a video or organizing a march, youth from Azerbaijan to the United States are undertaking creative ways to address street harassment.

"What do you get when you annoy girls? They just think you are a bad person," "You shouldn't do it, bro," and "Be a good man," six teenage boys tell their peers in a mixture of Azerbaijani and English in a 2012 YouTube video. Jake Winn, an American youth development Peace Corps volunteer was in Azerbaijan, from 2010 to 2012 and had daily interaction with many young boys and men. He told me he noticed that "street harassment was a learned behavior and most were sincerely ignorant to the dangers and problems with street harassment."[53] When he brought it up with them, there was little resistance to the idea that it needed to stop. It was just something they had never thought about. And for the boys and men who did think there was something wrong, he said, "they didn't know how to bring it up, how to resist, how to convey a message to their peers that it wasn't OK."[54]

After Winn showed the youth an American video of men telling other men to stop harassing women, the boys decided to make their own. "They wrote it, filmed it, edited it. . . . They loved making the video and were proud to show it," Winn said. "Few had ever taken the time to think and reflect. It was great to see how inspired girls were to realize how many allies they had among the young men."[55] To date, it has been viewed more than 6,000 times, and it received a standing ovation when it was shown at a youth film festival in Azerbaijan's capital, Baku. Winn also developed a lesson plan and discussion questions for other Peace Corps volunteers to use with their own students, and more than a dozen volunteers did so. The materials are available on the SSH website in both Azerbaijani and English.

Hey Baby! Art Against Sexual Violence launched in Tucson, Arizona, through the Southern Arizona Center Against Sexual Assault in 2009. Inspired by an art-centric Hey Baby project in North Carolina, up to 50 students and 30 adults participate in the Tucson initiative each spring. Their artwork addresses themes of prevention and support for survivors of homophobia, street harassment, relationship abuse, rape, and child sexual abuse. While the program is currently evolving, in the past, the art has been displayed in public libraries across Tucson during Sexual Assault Awareness Month and online. "I think it is important for youth to engage with troubling social issues in a context where they have control over the processes used to solve that problem," the program's manager (and SSH board member) Manuel Abril told me. "This means that instead of making youth [feel they] have to identify with social issues (social systems dispense blame for social problems affecting them onto marginalized communities) they are able to investigate it, to unravel it aesthetically, and to give it back to society."[56]

The groundswell of individuals and groups choosing to do something is thrilling. From every corner of the globe, people are successfully rising up and taking action to advocate for safe spaces and then sharing what they did to inspire others to do something, too. What will you do?

Chapter 4

Technology-Fueled Efforts

Action Hero Annie Zaidi's sari for the "I Never Ask for It" campaign by Blank Noise in India, 2012. (Blank Noise)

While street harassment—and activism to address it—is not new, today, thanks to the Internet and mobile technology, it's easier than ever to speak out, organize and carry out activism, and collaborate locally and globally.

In 2014, around 40 percent of the world's population—and 84 percent of the U.S. population—had Internet connectivity. That's nearly 3 billion people. Around 1.8 billion have connected since 2004. By region, Africa has the lowest connectivity; it is less than 10 percent in some countries. But even there, mobile access to the Internet has increased from an average of 2 percent in 2010 to 20 percent in 2014.[1] While most social media sites were around before 2010, their use, purpose, and scope have widely expanded over the past five years. In 2014, Facebook had 1.35 billion monthly active users,[2] and Twitter had 288 million monthly active users.[3] YouTube had more than 1 billion unique visitors per month, and 100 hours of video was uploaded every minute in 2014.[4] Instagram reached 200,000 million users that year.[5]

Street harassment awareness and activism have grown as these social media platforms have grown. This is in large part because on a daily basis people are online visibly sharing their stories, running campaigns, and consistently keeping this issue in the news and in our conversations. While it often takes little time or effort to share, the impact can be big. In Delhi, India, for example, out of his frustration that newspapers were blaming women for harassment based on their clothing selection, Dhruv Arora started the Tumblr *Got Stared At* in 2012. It did not take him long to set it up, and soon hundreds of people submitted photos of the clothes they were wearing when they were harassed. Later that year, he received a U.N. Millennium Development Goal's world summit youth award for his awareness-raising effort.[6] In the United States in 2014, California teenager Chloe Parker started an Instagram campaign inviting people to write what their street harasser said to them, how old they were, and where it happened while using the hashtag #WhatMySHSaid. One reads, " 'Hey Sweety, wanna take a ride on this dick?' I turned around and walked away . . . 'Haha fugly ass bitch.' 13 years old, OH, USA." Each post routinely receives at least 1,000 likes, and she has 17,000 followers.[7]

Some of the specific ways people have used these technologies to raise awareness of and challenge street harassment are through Tweet chats, campaigns against companies that support or trivialize street harassment, viral videos, mobile technology programs and phone apps. Discussions about each one follow, as well as information about how harassment and stalking can happen through technology, too.

TWITTER HASHTAGS AND CHATS

Many people use Twitter to share street harassment stories to raise awareness and gain support. They may use #streetharassment, #everyday-sexism, or #Endsh when they do. A study released in January 2015 in the *British Journal of Social Psychology* found that publicly tweeting about sexism can improve women's well-being as it lets them "express themselves in ways that feel like they can make a difference."[8] Twitter hashtags and chats have been an effective way to foster group story sharing and create more awareness about street harassment, and they have been used in many countries for years. For readers unfamiliar with Twitter, a hashtag is a keyword anyone can use in a 140-character tweet, and then when people search for that hashtag, all the tweets that use it will show up. It's a way to add one's voice to a popular topic, and it's a way to create an organized chat on a subject that anyone in the world with a Twitter account can join.

India

Activists in India were among the first to use Twitter to talk about street harassment. #INeverAskforIt was the rallying hashtag of the India-based organization Blank Noise in February 2010 as part of their on- and off-line campaign to combat the victim blaming that women who experience street harassment and sexual abuse often face. They asked people to tweet an image or a description of what they were wearing when they experienced abuse along with the hashtag #INeverAskForIt, and hundreds did. Offline, they also collected the actual clothing people wore when abused for an art exhibit.[9]

At the end of 2012, Blank Noise also launched the #SafeCityPledge campaign in response to the tragedy of the student gang raped by a group of men on a bus in Delhi. The student's death from her injuries sparked global outrage. Fearful that in the aftermath, people might suggest restricting women's access to public spaces as a way to keep them unharmed, Blank Noise encouraged people to think about what other ways they could personally undertake to make their city safer. Across India, people held demonstrations to hold up signs with their pledge and took photos to share on social media, while people in other countries participated online by tweeting their pledges. Examples of the pledges included, "I pledge to fight against patriarchy," "I will stand for women's rights," and "I pledge to defend my sisters and educate my brothers and work for a world without violence."[10] On January 19, 2013, Blank Noise organized a 24-hour #SafeCityPledge tweetathon, and anyone anywhere in the world could share suggestions that encouraged optimism, hope, and personal commitment instead of victim blaming.

Egypt, Lebanon, Sudan, and Syria

On June 20, 2011, activists in Egypt and Lebanon called for a day to blog about street harassment and related gender-based violence. As a companion action, they invited people on Twitter to tweet their stories using the hashtag #EndSH.[11] The following year on June 13, activists in Egypt and other countries in the region like Lebanon, Sudan, and Syria organized another day of action, again calling for people to blog, write Facebook posts, and tweet using #EndSH. The hashtag #EndSH was also used for other campaigns, like HarassMap's "Eid in Egypt is safe everywhere" in 2011. It continued to be tied heavily to campaigns and efforts in Egypt, but activists in the United States and other countries started using it in tweets about street harassment. While other hashtags have been used more times in shorter spurts of time or in specific countries, #EndSH is the tag that is most consistently used across years and countries to talk about street harassment.

England and Germany

In January 2013, activists in England and Germany used hashtags to talk about street harassment and related sexism.

In England, Laura Bates, the founder of the Everyday Sexism Project, invited her 100,000 followers to share their experiences of harassment using the hashtag #ShoutingBack. Within the first five days, 3,500 women had. For example, @VintageRoseJaz wrote: walked home when I was 14. Man said 'hello pretty lady' ignored him and he replied with 'Well fuck you then' #ShoutingBack." @SamanthaIles wrote: "trying to leave train, bloke pushes me back on, grabbing my boobs, saying 'this isn't your stop love' #shoutingback."[12] Bates held other tweet chats on street harassment, such as a chat about being #Followed and #Grabbed in spring 2013 and 2014, respectively. For the #Grabbed chat, within hours, the hashtag had been used more than 6,000 times, and it was the top trending topic in the United Kingdom.[13]

In Germany in January 2013, author and media consultant Anne Wizorek started the hashtag #Aufschrei (#Outcry). She was inspired to do so after a politician sexually harassed a journalist, and when the journalist wrote about her experience, many people minimized what had happened. Wizorek wanted to show that harassment *is* a serious issue. Within 48 hours after #Aufschrei debuted, there were 30,000 tweets about sexual harassment (including street harassment) and other forms of everyday sexism. In just two weeks, there were 60,000 tweets. @KatiKuersch wrote: "Der fremde Mann, der mich im Restaurant auf die nackte Schulter küsste. #aufschrei" (The strange man who kissed me in the restaurant on the bare shoulder.) Nearly two years later, dozens of people per day still use the tag to talk about these issues, like this one from @lililiev in December 2014: "Laufe mit meiner Schwester auf der Straße. Drei Männer gehen vorbei, einer sagt laut: 'Fotzen.' #everydaysexism #aufschrei" (During the course of walking with my sister on the street three men go by and one says loudly "Pussies.")

In January 2014, journalist Von Lisa Caspari wrote about the hashtag's impact and how it had launched discussions on television talk shows, in workplaces, pubs, and homes on a topic that has "previously been regarded as rather outdated: How sexist is our society? What needs to change?"[14] Reflecting on the impact of the hashtag a year later, Wizorek told Caspari, "I think that the discussion and the hashtag have broken a taboo. Many have become so aware of the issue."[15]

United States

2014 was a big year for street harassment-related hashtags in the United States In May, U.C. Santa Barbara student Elliot Rodger ranted about "hot" women who owed him sex before he killed six people and injured 13 more. A follower of the men's rights movement and a member of a pick-up artist community (that teaches men how to cajole and trick women into dating them), his final YouTube post said, "I don't know why you girls aren't attracted to me, but I will punish you all for it."[16] During the course of the discussion about his actions and motivations, some men felt the need to say "not all men" hurt or discriminate against women. In response, Twitter user @Gildespine launched the hashtag #YesAllWomen to give women space to talk about the harassment, sexism, and violence they've experienced. Street harassment was a common topic. There were 1.2 million tweets within the first two days, and the hashtag trended around the world for several days.[17] For example, @leahpickett wrote: "Because every woman I know has experienced some form of sexual harassment, abuse, or assault, myself included. #YesAllWomen," and @katekilla wrote: "Girls grow up knowing that it's safer to give a fake phone number than to turn a guy down. #yesallwomen."[18]

While the conversation brought widespread attention, it also brought criticism, and not just from men who felt defensive or under attack, but also from women, some of whom felt their unique experiences were being silenced or overlooked. A few women with disabilities, for example, felt excluded, as shown in this *Daily Beast* article excerpt: "When Stephanie Woodward blogged about #YesAllWomen, she was excited to join the movement and share her own life experiences as a woman with a disability. She never expected her post to spawn hostile messages from activists scolding [her] for trying to 'detract from the real issue' and instead make it about disability."[19]

Twitter conversations can mirror problems that exist in offline feminism activism, like how middle- and upper-class, educated, white, able-bodied, western, English-speaking (and often heterosexual) women tend to have the biggest voices and their experiences dominate the conversations. But Twitter can also be a place for specific demographics of women to create a space to talk about issues that impact them. During the summer of 2014, a woman with the pseudonym "Feminista Jones" created the hashtag #YouOkSis? to provide space for black women to talk about their street harassment experiences. "A lot of the conversations about street harassment in the mainstream media only show white women as the faces of victims. Rarely do you see black women as the face of the victim,"[20] said Jones in an interview for The Grio. She also started the conversation to inspire people of both genders to intervene in street harassment situations by talking to the victim. "If you just talk to the person who is the focus of the harassment, you're placing yourself in that moment and giving that person an out. It's something that breaks up the situation and diverts attention from the victim,"[21] she said.

Other Twitter conversations about street harassment focused on the types of comments and actions it entails, like #NotJustHello and #DudesGreetingDudes. The latter pointed out how completely unusual it would be for two male strangers to pass each other on the street and say something like "Smile, love" or "Your ass looks great in those jeans." Yet men say things like that to women all the time as a way of "greeting" them and expect women to be OK with it.

Twitter has been an effective platform for bringing more attention to street harassment issues. This is partly because many news outlets will cover popular hashtags and publish powerful Tweets. At the close of 2014, there were many "best of," "most influential," and "most feminist" lists about hashtags used that year. #BlackLivesMatter and #YesAllWomen are two of the hashtags cited the most. Twitter matters.

VIRAL VIDEOS

Despite the thousands of stories harassed persons share online and in person, for those who don't experience harassment or witness it (largely, straight men), videos have been one of the best tactics for proving street harassment is real and what it entails. While many people have made documentaries and short films about street harassment, videos that were at least partially taken with a hidden camera or that candidly capture street harassment have been the most popular. A good example of this is the 1998 film *War Zone* by Maggie Hadleigh-West, which is still screened on college campuses and in communities today. In the early 2000s, people began having access to cell phones that took video footage, and in 2005, YouTube launched and allowed people to easily share their videos with the world.

Films by Bystanders

One of the first camera phone videos about street harassment to go viral was recorded on the New York City subway and posted on You-Tube in September 2010. Unbeknownst to her at the time, a bystander filmed Nicola Briggs, a full-time Tai Chi teacher, confronting a man who pressed his exposed and condom-encased penis against her on the subway. In the video she is shown shouting and calling him out. To the people nearby, she says she wondered why he was standing so close when there was a lot of room, and then she points at him as she says, "And then I see his penis out." Then she tells him directly: "That's it. You're getting arrested. I'm not leaving your side. My plans are done for tonight. I'm escorting you to the police station. . . . I know what I saw. . . ."[22]

Briggs enlisted others to help her detain him until police could arrive. Her attacker—like many are—was a repeat offender who even wore special zipper-less pants to make it easier to violate women. He served four months in jail. After the video was seen by millions of people and was featured in numerous news stories, Briggs gave several interviews, including one for Jezebel, to let women know "you shouldn't stand for these violations," and while acknowledging that everyone has to make the safest choice for themselves, she said she "encourages women to speak up and to go to law enforcement."[23]

Sometimes bystanders film street harassment and assault as it occurs, as has happened in countries like India, Saudi Arabia, and Ukraine. In 2012, a young woman celebrating a friend's birthday at a local bar in Guwahati, India, protested lewd comments by a man. When she stepped outside, he and his friends encircled her, beat her, stripped her, and sexually assaulted her, and a bystander filmed it. During the video, viewers see more men passing by decide to join the attack. For half an hour, 30 men hurt her, and no one did anything. The video sparked numerous news stories and outrage.[24] In 2013 in Saudi Arabia, a bystander filmed a group of men harassing and physically attacking a group of women in a parking lot. As a result, many people called for harsher laws, yet at the same time, former judge and member of the Shura Council Mohammad al-Dahim told the newspaper *Al Arabiya* that "sexual harassment is not a phenomenon that occurs in Saudi Arabia, even if it appears so on social media."[25] In 2012, a Ukrainian news anchor was filming a story during a Dutch parade at Eurocup 2012. Across nearly three minutes, people in the parade interrupted her on live television. While most of the people were clowning around for the video camera in front of her, at around minute 2:25, a group of men surrounded her, rubbed against her, and made her so uncomfortable that she ran away mid-broadcast. Jockular.com, where the video is posted and has been viewed more than 500,000 times, alarmingly dubbed it "The funniest mass street harassment of a sports reporter in European history."[26]

Hidden Camera Videos

As in the 1998 film *War Zone*, a few women have gone out in the streets with hidden cameras—or with someone who has one—to capture their harassers. One of the first of these films to go viral was made in Brussels, Belgium, in 2012.

During a typical 15-minute walk from her office to her apartment in Brussels, 25-year-old graduate film student Sofie Peeters was harassed nearly one dozen times. To channel her frustration with her inability to commute in peace, she produced a short documentary for her culminating school project called *Femme de la Rue* (Woman of the Street). In addition to interviewing other women about their experiences using a hidden camera, Peeters captured men saying "sexy butt" and "naughty slut," leering, and making "pssst" sounds as she walked by. A few men strode alongside her and repeatedly asked for her phone number or a date. When she politely refused, some called her a slut or a whore. The vivid demonstration of street harassment made the film and her story go viral. But there were criticisms, too. Because most of the men were Arab (as were several of the women she interviewed) and Peeters is white, she faced accusations of racism. She responded by saying only a small portion of foreign men are harassers, and her film is a testament to the social situation of some immigrants: there are a lot of foreign men with little more to do than sit in cafes and in parks and bother women.[27] The international discussion her film sparked led to the government of Brussels passing legislation addressing street harassment. For Peeters, just by talking to men in her neighborhood for the film made them think about their behavior and Peeters differently. She said the men respect her now.[28]

In 2014, several videos went viral, like hidden cameras clips showing men harassing a woman in Cairo, Egypt, and one in Minneapolis, Minnesota. Around a million people saw each. A film by Vocativ went viral as well. In their six-minute film about street harassment, they included hidden camera footage of a woman walking in New York City. That video has been viewed nearly 4 million times.[29]

The most-viewed hidden camera film to date was released by Rob Bliss Creative in partnership with Hollaback! in October 2014. "10 Hours of Walking in NYC as a Woman" has been viewed by more than 39 million people so far. The 24-year-old actress Shoshana B. Roberts, who answered a casting call because she wanted another clip for her portfolio, walked around New York City for 10 hours (across a few days) and was harassed more than 100 times. Many of those interactions are captured in the two-minute clip. The film immediately sparked countless debates, was discussed in thousands of articles, and inspired numerous copycat videos ("10 Hours Walking as So-and-so in X Location"). There were a few main reasons for the attention.

First, the fact that Roberts was harassed so many times in 10 hours resonated with a lot of women and upset them. In particular, women and men alike found the physically aggressive harassment shown in the clip to be disturbing. It showed that street harassment really *is* a big problem. But for making this truth visible, Roberts became the target of rape and death threats from men. "I was scared out of my mind. I was really thrust into this. My goal was not to be the face of street harassment,"[30] she said in an interview for the *Guardian*. The unacceptable threats she faced upset many, fueling more attention to the issue and video.

Second, the film caused debates about what constitutes harassment because a few men are shown saying "Bless you" and "Hello." To me, the point of that is to show that compared to men, women often cannot get from Point A to Point B without being needlessly interrupted by men, even if it's "just" to say "hello." And it shows the context for those innocent comments: she's just been harassed by numerous men and is about to be harassed by numerous more, leaving her wary of any man who talks to her. But many people (often men) did not see it that way and wrote comments like "What? We can't say 'hello' now? That's harassment?" Other people felt that the hellos detracted from the more serious forms of harassment.[31] Discussions about what is harassment and whether a hello equals harassment became common points of dispute.

Third, the film depicted a white woman being harassed mostly by men of color, which is unfair and biased. Sexual violence against women and racism against men of color have gone hand-in-hand for centuries in the United States. This is well documented in many places, including

Dr. Estelle Freedman's 2013 book *Redefining Rape: Sexual Violence in the Era of Suffrage and Segregation*. If a black man so much as whistled or leered at a white woman, let alone made a sexual comment or touched her, some white men felt justified attacking, jailing, and lynching him. Today, there is still an unfortunate stereotype that street harassers (and rapists) are primarily men of color and/or men who are working class or homeless. Although of course there are harassers among these demographics, they are also found among all other groups of men, including wealthy white men. However, this video clip suggested that men of color do indeed prey on white women. "The racial politics of the video are fucked up," tweeted Purdue University professor and blogger Roxane Gay. "Like, she didn't walk through any white neighborhoods?"[32]

Soon nearly every article about the film brought up this problem. In response, Rob Bliss wrote on the website Reddit: "We got a fair amount of white guys, but for whatever reason, a lot of what they said was in passing, or off camera [or was ruined by a siren or other noise]." The final product, he said, "is not a perfect representation of everything that happened."[33] Roberts concurred and said in her *Guardian* interview, "That day of filming included a line of white businessmen, who were like, and excuse my language: 'I'd fuck the shit out of you.'"[34]

But, as Hanna Rosin wrote for Slate.com, "That may be true, but if you find yourself editing out all the catcalling white guys, maybe you should try another take."[35] With criticisms accumulating fast, Hollaback! issued a statement on its website that read, in part, "we regret the unintended racial bias in the editing of the video that over-represents men of color. Although we appreciate Rob's support, we are committed to showing the complete picture. It is our hope and intention that this video will be the start of a series to demonstrate that the type of harassment we're concerned about is directed toward women of all races and ethnicities and conducted by an equally diverse population of men."[36]

Due to backlash that included Hollaback! chapters in Boston, Philadelphia, Ohio, and Belgium leaving the organization because they had not been consulted about the film and did not feel it represented their chapter's mission, Hollaback! distanced itself from the video. By December, its name was no longer on the video at all when before it was prominently posted in the first line of the video description with an encouragement from Bliss to donate to the group.

The media already over-represents white women when they depict street harassment and the fact that this video focused on another white woman's experience reinforced the belief that their harassment stories are the only ones that matter. In reality, women of all races, as well as some men, experience it, too. Women of color, especially those who are marginalized due to being young, in the LGBQT community, disabled and/or low-income or homeless, may face more frequent and violent forms. A few days after the video was released, Aura Bogado wrote for the news site Colorlines: "Surveillance video capturing the shooting and killing of a black trans woman in East Hollywood, California, made a few headlines in the Los Angeles area—but remains invisible when compared to the 17 million views (and counting) the Hollaback! video has garnered . . . Thinking and acting upon ways in which to protect trans women of color . . . automatically makes the rest of us safer by default. Doing so means creating narratives that revolve around the most vulnerable among us."[37]

The "10 Hours of Walking in NYC as a Woman" video has done more than anything else to spark discussions about street harassment in the United States, and it also created an important moment for those working to stop street harassment to rethink stances and efforts to make sure everyone, especially the most marginalized and vulnerable to harassment, is recognized and is a leader in creating the solution.

Humorous Videos and Songs

Some viral videos approach street harassment in clever and/or humorous ways. In 2012, for example, when scores of people were making videos about stereotypical things different demographics of people say ("Shit [a particular demographic] say"), a mixture of female and male activists in New York City decided to create their own version for International Anti-Street Harassment Week. "Shit Men Say to Men Who Say Shit to Women on the Street" is a video of men calling out men who harass women. In it, men of different races and ages make comments like, "I don't care how she's dressed; it's not OK," "Come on. That's embarrassing. I can't take you anywhere," "Please stop," "Have you never heard of eHarmony?," and "You're giving all men a bad name."[38]

Fivel Rothberg, who shot, co-edited, and directed the film said in an interview for the *Ms.* blog, "The video encourages men to nonviolently intervene when their friend, for example, is harassing women or others on the street."[39] On making a lighter video about a serious topic, Bix Gabriel, a member of the film-making team who was, ironically, street harassed in the same park the men were being filmed, said in her interview for *Ms.*, "As activists we often need humor to survive. We felt that in a short video, humor was an important entry point into a conversation."[40]

The video was viewed more than 200,000 times in the first week. It inspired similar videos by men in San Jose, California; Cairo, Egypt; and Balakan, Azerbaijan. Additionally, in Philadelphia, Pennsylvania, the activist group FAAN Mail worked with teenage girls of color to produce the "Stuff People Say to Teen Girls" video. Some of their quotes were used in Philadelphia-area transit system ads that Hollaback! PHILLY created and sponsored during Sexual Assault Awareness Month in April 2013.[41]

2014 was a big year for viral videos. In February, Frenchwoman Eléonore Pourriat made the 10-minute film "Majorité Opprimée" (Oppressed Majority). In it, gender roles are reversed, and women belittle, harass, and assault the main character, Pierre. When he seeks help after an assault, he is disbelieved and blamed. In essence, the video shows what everyday life is like for women worldwide. "Sometimes men . . . can't imagine that because they are not confronted with that themselves,"[42] said Pourriat in an interview for the *Guardian*. The film was viewed more than two million times in the first week. In November, Paremos el acoso callejero in Peru teamed up with Natalia Málaga, a former volleyball player who now coaches the Peruvian national women's team, to create the film "Sílbale a tu madre" (Catcall Your Mother). The film was sponsored by the fitness and sporting goods company Everlast. In it, men make sexual comments at women who pass them on the street but then are shocked to find the women are their mothers in disguise! The mothers then chastise them fiercely for being so disrespectful. The film was viewed 4.4 million times in the first month.[43]

Other examples of humorous videos that went viral in 2014 include: "La venganza de la obrera" (The Revenge of the Woman Laborer) when a woman dresses as a construction worker and harasses men in Venezuela; "La revancha de los agarrones" (Revenge of the Touchers) in which a woman touches men on the hand or butt as they walk in Chile; and "What Men Are Really Saying When Catcalling Women," in which American men holler things like, "I'm so lonely" and "I'm uncomfortable talking to women like actual people."[44] All of the video clips have been viewed at least one million times to date.

Using songs and music videos to call out harassment is another way to reach large audiences. Two examples of songs from the 1990s are Queen Latifah's 1993 hit "U.N.I.T.Y" and TLC's 1999 chart topper "No Scrubs" (the lyrics of the latter were spontaneously used by women riding the subway in Chicago to silence a harasser in February 2015.[45]) In recent years, musicians from high-schoolers to nationally known artists have written anti-street harassment anthems. Two that have gone viral are "Stop Looking at My Mom" and "Girl in a Country Song."

In 2010, 14-year-old high school freshman Brian Bradley penned the song "Stop Looking at My Mom," that was directed at street harassers he had seen harass his mom. "I didn't like the way people were staring at my mother when I walked down the street. It was very offending [sic]," he said. "I decided instead of being violent and going about it the wrong way, I'd put it on a record."[46] His song and YouTube video were a hit, and in 2011 his fame rose when he competed on the television music competition *The X Factor* and had the chance to spread his anti-street harassment message far and wide. In 2010, he also testified at the New York City Council hearing on street harassment, saying, "I hope 'Stop Looking at My Mom' will serve as a wake-up call to men and women alike. I wrote it to let men know that vulgar, aggressive language toward women, especially when they are with their children, is highly inappropriate."[47]

In 2014, "Girl in a Country Song" became the number one country song in the nation, and in it, the teenage singers Maddie Marlow and Tae Dye call out harassers and men who disrespect women telling them, "I got a name/And to you it ain't 'pretty little thing,' 'honey,' or 'baby.'"[48] They were inspired to write the song after it dawned on them how poorly women are usually portrayed in country songs.[49] The popularity of Marlow and Dye's song and video (15 million views so far) shows people are ready for a change.

ONLINE CAMPAIGNS AGAINST COMPANIES

Street harassment is a serious problem that limits people's access to public spaces, yet for a long time society as a whole has treated it like a joke, a compliment, or no big deal. This is in part because that's how it's portrayed in the media and in advertisements. While contacting a company with a complaint or suggestion is not new, the ability to do so publicly over social media is, and it has been an effective tactic for pressuring companies, particularly smaller companies, to change. Several anti-street harassment groups have been part of efforts to challenge companies. Stop Street Harassment (SSH) has been involved in around one dozen of these campaigns. While efforts to change large companies like Snickers, YouTube, and Allstate have not succeeded, others campaigns have. A few examples follow.

In 2011, Wendy Stock, PhD, saw a television ad for Togo's, a California sandwich shop chain, that made light of flashing, which she saw as problematic. "This so-called 'edgy' approach is not innocuous—it trivializes the fear women feel from street harassment, including flashers (exhibitionists)," she wrote on the SSH blog. "Thirty percent of exhibitionists also commit acts of direct sexual violence against women. While the clay women in the commercial laughed it off, making this a humorous subject wears down many real women's ability to object, resist, and to stand up to this form of sexual harassment."[50]

She included Togo's contact information in the blog post, and she and several blog readers contacted Togo's. Within a few days, the marketing project manager sent an email: "I am writing with regard to your post regarding Togo's TV commercial on the SSH site. It was never our intent to trivialize sexual harassment. We appreciate your dedication to stopping harassment of women and want you to know that the ad is no longer running."[51]

It was the first time SSH used social media in this way, and it was thrilling to see it work. The next success SSH had was against MarketFair Mall in New Jersey. In June 2012, Elizabeth Harmon spotted and photographed a sign at the mall next to a construction area that read, "We apologize for the whistling construction workers, but man you look good! So will we soon, please pardon our dust, dirt, and assorted inconveniences." SSH reader Katherine Broendel saw the photo on the Feminist Philosophers website and shared the link.[52]

I wrote about the sign on the SSH blog and tweeted about it. Shelby Knox, who worked at Change.org, an online petition site, tweeted back and suggested starting a petition.[53] The petition garnered 1,500 signatures in 24 hours as well as coverage on sites like Huffington Post and Jezebel. I called the company after the 1,000th signature and alerted them to the petition and the negative press. A few hours later, a company representative called back and said they would take it down the next day. Harmon went to the mall and confirmed it was gone. Victory! The successful campaign received media coverage the rest of the week from the Associated Press, NJ.com, ABC News, NYDailyNews.com, and the Sundance Channel blog.

SSH has also collaborated with other people and groups to jointly pressure companies to change. For example, in 2013 after Lisa McIntire tweeted a photo of a Yes to Carrots face wash package that read "Yes to whistling (and yes to getting whistled at!)," she, SSH, Hollaback! and Collective Action for Safes Spaces all tweeted and/or blogged about it. Within hours the company tweeted back, "We're sorry about this offending statement. We're 100 percent going to change this. We only want to be positive!"[54]

Similarly, the Representation Project, a nonprofit social action campaign and media organization, introduced the #NotBuyingIt hashtag on Twitter in 2011 to encourage people to tweet their complaints and frustrations with sexist advertising. During the 2013 Super Bowl alone, there were 10,000 tweets that used the hashtag.[55] Timed for release before the 2014 Super Bowl, the Representation Project created a Not Buying It smartphone app to make it even easier for people to report their complaints.[56]

The SSH blog has also been a place to coordinate complaints against harassing employees. For example, reader EB in New York City submitted a story for the blog about how an employee of a truck company harassed her. Both the harasser and the owner of the company, whom she called and spoke to on the phone, didn't understand how the actions constituted harassment. In her blog post she included the company's phone number. Beckie Weinheimer, a loyal blog reader, called the phone number and talked to the owner. He finally agreed that the behavior was inappropriate and said he would talk to his employees. A few more people who read the whole story on the SSH Facebook page also called the company and left messages urging the owner to do something about harassment.[57]

Online Harassment

There is also a dark side to social media: the growing problem of online harassment. In 2014, the Pew Research Center conducted a study about online harassment and found that 73 percent of U.S. adult Internet users have seen someone be harassed online, and 40 percent have personally experienced it. Among those who had experienced it, 27 percent had been called an offensive name, 8 percent had been physically threatened, 8 percent had been stalked, and 6 percent had been sexually harassed.[58] Women writers and outspoken feminists especially face a lot of criticism, abuse, and threats, as detailed in articles like "Why Women Aren't Welcome on the Internet" by Amanda Hess for *Pacific Standard Magazine*[59] and "Feminist writers are so besieged by online abuse that some have begun to retire," by Michelle Goldberg for the *Washington Post*.[60] Since a lot of it happens on Twitter and to women, it's no surprise that a *Business Insider Intelligence Report* from late 2014 found that Twitter was leaning toward male users. Initially it was a fairly gender-balanced social network, but by late 2014, 22 percent of men used Twitter compared with only 15 percent of women.[61]

Online platforms can also be used to promote offensive messages. Take Facebook. Day after day, men created Facebook pages promoting violence against women, but Facebook would not remove them despite people reporting the pages as offensive. Furthermore, Facebook allowed photographs of violence against women with captions like, "This bitch didn't know when to shut up" and "Next time, don't get pregnant."[62] Facebook has one billion users and should feel a responsibility to those users to not promote or tolerate violence against women. American activist, writer, and former strategic planner for technology companies Soraya Chemaly, Everyday Sexism in England, and the American nonprofit

Women, Action & the Media (WAM!) tried to work directly with Facebook on the issue. However, Facebook told them the pages fell under "humor" and were expressions of "free speech." But since Facebook cracks down on anti-Semitic, Islamophobic, and homophobic speech, it begged the question, why not gender-based hate speech?[63]

When the activists did not receive satisfactory answers from Facebook, they decided to take a strategic and public approach. They created an open letter to Facebook that more than 100 organizations, including SSH, signed. In it they asked that Facebook: "1. Recognize speech that trivializes or glorifies violence against girls and women as hate speech and make a commitment that you will not tolerate this content. 2. Effectively train moderators to recognize and remove gender-based hate speech. 3. Effectively train moderators to understand how online harassment differently affects women and men, in part due to the real-world pandemic of violence against women." They also asked Facebook users to "contact advertisers whose ads on Facebook appear next to content that targets women for violence, to ask these companies to withdraw from advertising on Facebook" until it addresses gender-based violence hate speech.[64]

They took screen shots of pro-rape pages, all of which had automatically generated ads in the sidebar. They set up a program that would allow anyone to tweet the screenshot to the companies whose ads were on the pages and ask them if they support rape. Within a few days, there were more than 60,000 tweets and 5,000 emails to the companies that resulted in 15 companies dropping their advertising with Facebook.

The tactics worked. Facebook invited the activists to meet and agreed to change the policy. Facebook updated its Community Standards around hate speech and trained its moderators on how to appropriately handle complaints.[65] More than a year later, the activists continued to work with and advise Facebook. As there is so much online harassment in general, they began working with the leadership at Twitter and Reddit in 2014 and both companies updated or created anti-harassment policies in early 2015.

MOBILE PHONES

By the end of 2014, nearly 7 billion people had access to a mobile phone.[66] A 2012 U.N. report found that most people with mobile phones only have basic voice, SMS, and low-speed data services.[67] There is a gender gap in many countries, however, with more men than women owning phones. Women with access to a phone often have a shared or borrowed phone, and, overall, women rarely buy their own phones; often they are gifts or hand-me-downs from male family members, husbands, or boyfriends.[68]

As part of its Safe Cities Global Initiative during 2013 and 2014, U.N. Women partnered with Microsoft, with support from U.N. Habitat and UNICEF, to conduct a project titled Mapping Access to and Use of Mobile Phones to Document, Prevent, and Respond to Sexual Harassment and Other Forms of Sexual Violence against Women and Girls in Urban Public Spaces. The main goal of the project was to better understand the role that technology, specifically mobile phones, can play to prevent and respond to violence against women and girls in public spaces. Focus groups, interviews, and other forms of research were conducted in three cities: Rio de Janeiro, Brazil; Delhi, India; and Marrakech, Morocco. The project also included a global review of existing mobile technology tools that I conducted in 2013.

A major project finding was that very few women and girls living in the most disadvantaged communities have access to mobile phones (especially smartphones) that could provide options to prevent, document, or respond to sexual harassment and other forms of violence against women in public spaces. A significant barrier is that harassment is normalized and most people who experience or witness it do not report it or intervene. Other barriers include: gender gaps in mobile phone ownership and the ability to operate a phone; fear that harassers will seek revenge; and concern that an abusive family member may use the device to monitor the victim. Further, few women and girls believe the police will help them if they report an incident.

These barriers can be overcome, however, especially as the number of people who own mobile devices increases annually and as more information spreads about sexual harassment and other forms of sexual violence. A promising key finding was that most of the women and girls in the intervention sites and safe city partners in Rio de Janeiro, Delhi, and Marrakech were eager to learn about innovative solutions that have been or could be developed through the application of mobile phones (and across different models of phones) and gave recommendations for developing new phone features or web-based tools they could envision using.

Some of the tools launched since 2010 include: The SmartWomen App/SOS Mulher app in Brazil that helps women locate and access services near them and learn about their rights; SMS text messages about street harassment sent by the director of Women for a Change in Cameroon to youth who sign up;[69] and the Canadian METRAC's free "Not Your Baby" app that allows users to select their location (for example school, the bus, or work) and the harasser (such as a stranger, classmate, or coworker) to see a list of possible ways to handle the scenario.[70]

In India, Safetipin is an app that allows people to crowdsource and map information about safety in their neighborhoods. Features include posting pictures and comments about issues of concern and recording how safe a user feels while in different places. Users can conduct safety audits and submit the results from the location.[71] The Norwegian company Bipper's bSafe app lets users quickly and discreetly alert designated emergency contacts with a message and their GPS location and create a "Fake Friend" option that causes the phone to ring. There is also a feature that lets a friend follow the user home with live GPS broadcasting.[72] Similarly, the Circle of 6 app, first developed in the United States, allows users to designate six trusted people to join their virtual circle and then they can easily reach them with pre-written messages via text message to let them know if they need help. The app has a section with a list of organizations and resources, too.[73] These apps are gaining popularity as more people become aware that street harassment is not OK or normal and as mobile phones become more accessible to harassed persons.

Of course, mobile phones are also being used to facilitate the harassment of women and girls through stalking, upskirt photos, and men taking photos of body parts without permission. In the United States, the laws have not always kept up with technology, and while taking photos of someone in a locker room or restroom is illegal, in some states it is only illegal to take photos up someone's skirt or down their shirt if they are in a public space. In 2014 states like Massachusetts passed new laws to make it illegal, and Nebraska, Oregon, and New Jersey considered stronger laws.[74] Mobile phones have also been used to persecute LGBTQ individuals. In Egypt in 2014, for example, there were reports of police using dating apps like Grindr to track gays and lesbians and arrest them.[75] So, like all technology, various people choose to use mobile phones for positive and for harmful reasons.

Overall, social media, online videos, and phone apps are helping people raise awareness about street harassment, challenge its normalcy, organize groups worldwide, and provide an outlet for people who want to take some form of action quickly. As issues like online harassment and upskirt photos are better addressed in the coming years, hopefully technology will become a safer space for people to organize, collaborate, and take action to challenge street harassment.

Chapter 5

Global Campaigns

International Anti-Street Harassment Week postcard, 2015. (Holly Kearl)

What makes a city safe, especially for women and girls? How can we create safer cities for them? These are questions that international organizations like U.N. Women, the Huairou Commission, and ActionAid International aim to answer as they work in more than 40 countries across six continents. Building on the work of organizations like Metropolitan Action Committee on Violence Against Women & Children (METRAC) and Women in Cities International (WICI), 2010 was the year these three entities launched or significantly grew their international Safe Cities efforts.

Working in a structured and formal way through existing networks and channels, these Safe Cities campaigns approach street harassment from a framework of women's safety, gender inclusion, and gender mainstreaming. They look at the structure, design, and architecture of a city and think about how to change it so it will be harder for sexual harassment and other forms of gender-based violence to transpire. They also consider how violence intersects with factors like poverty, land rights, disability, and conflict in urban environments. The Safe Cities efforts primarily occur in emerging countries in Africa, Asia, and South America. Through Safety Audits, focus groups, and street surveys, girls and women in these countries, particularly in marginalized communities, discuss what will make the cities safer for them. The suggestions range from more street lamps to sex-segregated public toilets. Then the organizations work with local government and others to address the suggestions. While at first their focus was just on girls and women, in recent years many initiatives have recognized the need for an intersectional approach—recognizing that sexism is interconnected with other oppressions like racism and homophobia—as a more inclusive way to ensure safer cities for all.

At the same time that these more measured and structured efforts to address street harassment grew or launched, individuals who were personally fed up with street harassment started websites to share stories and resources. In 2010, HarassMap launched in Egypt, and Hollaback!, which had existed as a U.S.-based website since 2005, became an international nonprofit organization. In 2012, the Everyday Sexism Project was founded in England, and Stop Street Harassment (SSH), which began as a website in 2008, gained nonprofit status in the United States. These organizations and groups work to end sexual harassment and assault in public spaces by ending its social acceptability. Apart from HarassMap, their audiences and impact are mostly in developed countries, but their overall reach is global. Each entity collects individual stories as a way to understand the issue and raise awareness and uses these stories as a basis for work like community organizing and awareness campaigns.

These two tracks of initiatives and activism do not operate in silos. Members of most groups attend and present at the same international gatherings, like the annual U.N. Commission on the Status of Women. They share tactics and participate together in campaigns like Delhi and Beyond: Global Action for Safer Cities and Meet Us on the Street: International Anti-Street Harassment Week. The collective efforts to address street harassment since 2010 have made this issue a more visible problem and one that an increasing number of local, national, and international leaders are prioritizing and addressing.

SAFE CITIES CAMPAIGNS

Since 2010, U.N. Women, the Huairou Commission, ActionAid International, and other organizations, like the U.N. Human Settlement Programs (U.N.-Habitat) and Plan International, have led Safe Cities initiatives. These are built on decades of related work and are heavily informed by Safety Audits, which were formalized by the Toronto-based nonprofit organization METRAC in 1989. METRAC's communications specialist Andrea Gunraj told me that Safety Audits are so widely used today because they "attend to the unique safety needs of those at highest risk of gender-based violence—diverse women, girls, and transgender individuals. These groups and their safety concerns are rarely considered in policy and practice development and planning processes . . . METRAC's Safety Audit is a tool to help amplify these 'hidden narratives' of those at risk of gender-based violence and increase their chances of being responded to and respected in planning and development."[1]

The Safe Cities efforts also build on the 2002 meeting on women's safety in urban environments organized by the city of Montreal, U.N.-Habitat, the Huairou Commission, and a few other organizations. It was the first time people from different regions of the world came together to talk about best practices and share tools. The Montreal-based organization WICI formed in 2003 as an outcome of that meeting. WICI has served as a connector between organizations doing Safe Cities work ever since and regularly produces reports, provides diagnostic tools, and conducts monitoring and evaluation.[2] In 2004, WICI helped organize a second international conference on women's safety in Bogota, Colombia, and from 2009–2011 conducted the Global Inclusive Cities Programme (GICP) with the support of the U.N. Trust Fund to End Violence Against Women. GICP was a study focused on cities in Argentina, India, Tanzania, and Russia that involved data collection, partnerships, and plan interventions. The purpose was to learn how women can play a key role in creating safer communities and cities and what tools, methodologies, and practices can be used across context and cultures to do so.[3] Most of the current Safe Cities initiatives are informed by the findings from the GICP.

A pivotal moment in the Safe Cities work occurred with the Third International Conference on Women's Safety in 2010.

Third International Conference on Women's Safety

"Sexual harassment in public spaces remains a neglected issue, accepted as a normal part of women's lot and life in the city,"[4] said Ines Alberdi, then executive director of the U.N. Development Fund for Women (which is now U.N. Women), during the opening of the Third International Conference on Women's Safety—Building Inclusive Cities in Delhi, India. Held in 2010 and co-hosted by WICI and the Delhi-based women's organization Jagori, more than 250 participants representing 45 countries and 81 cities attended the three-day conference.[5] I was one of the few Americans who attended and spoke about U.S. anti-harassment transit campaigns.

The purpose of the conference was to "provide an important opportunity to assess some of the current and emerging trends, achievements, and challenges in building safe and inclusive cities for women and girls."[6] The goals were to review and consolidate diverse tools and approaches toward safer and inclusive cities; help build capacities at the local level and mobilize both community and government sections; and assess the lessons learned from practices that aim to enhance women's inclusion and right to the city.[7]

The conference sessions and guided discussions looked at a number of ways (addressing access to land, housing, and essential services like sanitation and water) and tools (like Safety Audits and participatory budgeting) to better ensure women's right to the city and women's safety. Poor women, women living in urban slums, women with disabilities, migrants, immigrants, and refugee women were acknowledged to be groups that face the most barriers to achieving equality and safety in cities, and members of some of these groups were present to share those experiences firsthand. Journalist Brittany Shoot wrote about a few of these women for the *Ms.* Blog. For example, Mary Ikupu represented the Women with Disabilities Network in Papua New Guinea and spoke about the almost complete lack of disability services and accessibility in her country, which had only gained independence 25 years earlier. Shoot wrote: "Ikupu says that she's often asked to speak and advocate for her friends with disabilities because their illiteracy renders them helpless to fight the government and private sector for access to education, transit, and businesses. Because of the stigma surrounding illness and disabilities, many disabled women have been abandoned by their families . . . There is no data [on disabilities] because there are no resources, even to document [it]."[8]

National political leaders, international agency figureheads, and women and girls from communities where programs were underway gave presentations and speeches. In small groups, attendees drew what a safe and inclusive city would look like, such as women walking outside at night, free and safe public toilets, and secure settlement neighborhoods. Collectively, the participants wrote a declaration for the conference that included specific requests for national governments, the United Nations and international agencies, nongovernmental organizations (NGOs), businesses, the private sector, universities, media, and donors. It also summarized hopes for the future, including: "Inclusive cities, in an inclusive state and world, respectful of the diversity and dignity of all. Communities where women and girls are central to the design and leadership of cities and are visible in all aspects of governance . . . Inclusive cities where women and girls are able to live free from violence and the fear of violence in the private, domestic sphere and in all public spaces."[9]

It was incredible to be there, to talk with thought leaders and activists from so many countries, and to learn about the unique problems women in other countries face that differ from those in the United States. A surprising aspect, however, was the lack of attention to men and boys as harassers. More lights or frequent public transportation will have limited utility if boys and men still feel entitled to women's attention and bodies. I was one of the only people to openly talk about male harassment in my presentation on public transportation, which critiqued women-only public transportation as being a Band-Aid solution to the real problem of male harassment. Some women in attendance vocally scoffed or protested at this and voiced their support for sex-segregation. The lack of men at the conference was also noticeable. It meant that, as often is the case, conversations about women's safety were restricted to women, leaving the onus on women to try to keep themselves and other women safe.

Nonetheless, despite its limitations—and every convening has some—the conference was an important turning point for street harassment efforts. More in-depth information about the conference, outcomes, and learnings about Safe Cities can be found in the 2013 book *Building Inclusive Cities: Women's Safety and the Right to the City*. WICI hopes to organize the Fourth International Conference on Women's Safety in 2016.

U.N. Women

In 2010 at the Delhi conference, the United Nations officially launched its Safe Cities Global Initiative with U.N.-Habitat and 50 global and local partners. The initiative is informed by lessons learned from 40 years of women's grassroots organizing and various related efforts and research, such as a 2008 review of women's safety practices by WICI.[10] There are two components to the initiative. The first component, Safe Cities Free of Violence against Women and Girls, focuses on Quito, Ecuador; Cairo, Egypt; New Delhi, India; Port Moresby, Papua New Guinea; and Kigali, Rwanda. In 2011, U.N. Women, UNICEF, and U.N.-Habitat launched the second component, Safe and Sustainable Cities for All, which is a joint program that focuses on Rio de Janeiro, Brazil; San José, Costa Rica; Tegucigalpa, Honduras; Nairobi, Kenya; Beirut, Lebanon; Marrakesh, Morocco; Manila, Philippines; and Dushanbe, Tajikistan. U.N. Women also partners with U.N.-Habitat's Global Network on Safer Cities, which launched in September 2012 to advocate for "gender-responsive urban safety measures and local crime prevention all over the world."[11]

The Safe Cities Global Initiative is "the first-ever global comparative programme that develops, implements, and evaluates tools, policies, and comprehensive approaches on the prevention of, and response to, sexual harassment and other forms of sexual violence against women and girls across different settings."[12] U.N. Women, local authorities, grassroots women's groups, and other United Nations partners are spending five years working to implement comprehensive, human rights- and evidence-based programs to prevent different forms of sexual violence in public spaces. As part of implementation, local partnerships are built and strengthened, and local research partners are hired to work with stakeholders to conduct initial scoping studies to inform the design of the Safe City program, to conduct baseline research, and to develop monitoring and evaluation strategies. Research conducted in several cities has shown that sexual harassment and other forms of sexual violence and fear of sexual violence in public spaces are significant problems. Following this, local governments, women's organizations, and other stakeholders are beginning to implement multi-sectoral interventions (e.g. community mobilization, policy, awareness raising, urban design and planning based on a gender approach, capacity strengthening). End-line studies will be completed before the end of 2017 for the original five cities.[13]

A number of important outcomes have already been achieved in the pilot cities. The municipality of Quito has amended a local ordinance to address street harassment after the local team organized a 10,000-person letter writing effort. The Egyptian Ministry of Housing, Utilities, and

Urban Development "adopted women's safety audits to guide urban planning." Meanwhile in Port Moresby, the National Capital District has taken steps to improve women's safety in local markets by organizing a market vendor association with 50 percent representation of women in the executive leadership positions and a cleaner work environment.[14]

When I spoke with Laura Capobianco, U.N. Women's senior policy specialist for Safe Public Spaces, she explained that unique tools U.N. Women created for developing an evaluable safe city program with women and girls (e.g., step-by-step guidance on how to conduct a scoping study, program design, and baseline with an impact evaluation methodology) are very important contributions to the movement. The methodology emphasizes a "participatory approach first and foremost," and it is important to understand the challenge in addressing the issue since sexual harassment is not named or discussed in many places. Learning how to talk about these sensitive topics with diverse populations has been a major contribution in the field.[15]

Once cities complete the scoping study, they meet with stakeholders in an informed way and make specific requests of them. When it comes to evaluation, Capobianco emphasized that the Safe Cities programs do not solely focus on changes in prevalence. They also look at changes in women's feelings of safety and women's autonomous mobility over time. One way to measure that is by seeing if more women are working in the evenings because they now report feeling safer working in the evening and traveling to their jobs at night. Capobianco said one of the biggest lessons from undertaking a program of this scope is that you need both funding to support multi-sectoral interventions and interdisciplinary expertise (for example, institutions conducting impact evaluation should have team members with a background on gender and the prevention of violence against women). Also, working collaboratively and in a more participatory way is crucial to seeing a program like this succeed.[16]

Over the years, more cities have started to scale tools and approaches in the U.N. Women Safe Cities Global Initiative. As of 2014, there are a total of 19 cities in the Global Initiative, including cities in developed countries, such as Dublin, Ireland; Winnipeg, Canada; and New York City, USA.[17]

ActionAid International

ActionAid International, founded in 1972, is a federation of countries addressing poverty and injustice issues in 45 countries. Using a human rights-based approach with the 15 million people it reaches, the group utilizes mass communication and campaigning, among other activities, to change policies, practices, attitudes, and behaviors. The group focuses specifically on issues like securing women's land rights, sustainable agriculture, education for girls and boys, youth leadership, disaster response, women-centric economic alternatives, and violence against women.[18]

Every five years, ActionAid reviews its strategies and impact and discusses what issues to address. From 2005–2009, the group's work included domestic violence and resulted in many countries passing laws against it. The continuum of violence was a concern as well as the violence connected to increasing urbanization. In this context, ActionAid attended the Third International Conference on Women's Safety in Delhi. Christy Abraham, the Safe Cities programme co-coordinator, told me ActionAid decided expand its work to look at the continuum of violence from the private to the public sphere and voted to add a safe cities focus in 2011. The ActionAid website states that the core belief of the group's Safe Cities for Women movement is "that violence, and fear of violence, restricts women's and girl's access to their cities—including opportunities for employment, health, education, [and] political and recreational facilities."[19]

Similar to U.N. Women, ActionAid began the movement by focusing on five countries: Brazil, Cambodia, Liberia, Nepal, and Ethiopia. The group conducted participatory research like Safety Audits and focus groups with specific groups of women, such as garment factory workers in Cambodia, university students in Liberia, and informal vendors in Ethiopia. ActionAid published its findings in the 2011 report "Women and the City: Examining the gender impact of violence and urbanization." In the following years, interest in the movement grew among other Action-Aid groups. By the end of 2014, Safe Cities for Women campaigns had been launched in Bangladesh, Brazil, Cambodia, Ireland, and Liberia. ActionAid has programming on safe cities in 13 other countries.[20]

ActionAid's Safe Cities for Women movement has four pillars, Abraham told me. The first is to help women and girls understand their right to the city and that the harassment and violence they face is tied to human rights. The group conducts baseline studies using focus groups, Safety Audits, and surveys to find out how prevalent the issue is for women in the communities. In Bangladesh, for example, 87 percent of women said they experienced street harassment in bus terminals and train stations, 80 percent by roadsides, and 69 percent outside of schools and colleges.[21]

The second part is exploring the link between an increase in violence against women and a lack of needed gender-responsive public services like good roads, adequate street lighting, clean and available public toilets, and accessible public transportation. The local ActionAid programs, along with other partners, initiate advocacy and create awareness about how to improve public services, as ActionAid Nepal and its allies did in April 2014 during International Anti-Street Harassment Week. The group's huge banner read "We demand streetlights for women's safety," and nearly 100 men and women marched behind it along a busy road in Kathmandu, Nepal. They asked the government of Nepal to repair and maintain the streetlights around Kathmandu. They carried flashlights to symbolize the lights that were lacking and carried individual signs with messages like "Lights on Insecurity Gone" and "Don't Teach Me What to Wear." Some people also blew whistles to draw the attention of the evening commuters. Once they reached the New Road Gate, several marchers climbed on an overhead bridge and lit traditional Nepali *diyo* (candles) for all the passersby to see. Their action had an immediate impact: community and traffic police stopped and listened to their requests and agreed to consider them.[22]

A specific study on public services and violence against women was conducted in six countries—Brazil, Cambodia, Ethiopia, Kenya, Liberia, and Nepal—and published in the 2013 ActionAid report "Women and the City II: Combating violence against women and girls in urban public spaces—the role of public services."

A third part is addressing community attitudes and behaviors and testing tactics to change the community norms. ActionAid groups use various methods to achieve this, like concerts, radio programs, and public events. The messaging focuses on women's right to mobility and lives free from violence wherever they go, as well as ending victim blaming. For example, in June 2014 in Johannesburg, South Africa, around 50 members of ActionAid South Africa performed a flash mob dance in the center of a busy square. ActionAid's website describes how "the dance moves were choreographed to indicate the solidarity of people around the world, joining together to create safe cities for women," and the dancers gathered 150 names of passersby who wanted to join their campaign.[23] As another example, ActionAid Ethiopia runs a Safe City for Women radio show (Mitchu Lesetoch) and has produced and aired more than 50 programs focused on "the importance of safe working environments for women working in the informal sector [such as street vendors]."[24]

The final step is working with existing entities, like trade unions and youth groups, to raise their awareness about the issues and work to make ending gender violence a common agenda for everyone.

ActionAid country programs regularly produce videos, write blog posts, and update their social media accounts with images from their actions. There is idea sharing among groups, and ActionAid International issues a quarterly newsletter highlighting its work and challenges so the groups can learn from each other. In 2014, ActionAid also released the report "Safe Cities for Women: from reality to rights" to highlight the Safe Cities work with, and the experiences of, women living in poverty in cities in Bangladesh, Brazil, Cambodia, and Liberia, and their respective coalition groups.[25] It provides recommendations like the need for anti-harassment legislation, punishments for perpetrators, safe and gender-responsive public services, and the inclusion of women in decision-making processes. "City authorities must commit to and enter into constructive dialogue with women's groups and advocates for safe cities for women to establish common visions of a city that is safe for women."[26] Abraham said ActionAid International is committed to working on the Safe Cities for Women movement through 2017.[27]

Huairou Commission

The Huairou Commission was established in 1995 at the 4th World Conference on Women in Beijing. It is a global membership and partnership coalition that empowers grassroots (local) women to have a leadership role locally and globally. The commission works with women's networks, NGOs, and grassroots women's organizations in 50 countries. Its members pilot and exchange best practices around specific issues. The four biggest issues are AIDS, community resilience, land and housing, and governance.[28] Most groups also work on domestic violence or rape. After many conversations around gender-based violence, in 2009 the commission began work around safe cities, including street harassment. Huairou uses many of the tools developed by WICI, METRAC, and U.N.-Habitat to empower grassroots women to evaluate their communities and bring their needs forward to government entities.[29]

After the gang rape and death of Jyoti Singh Pandey in New Delhi, India, at the end of 2012, the Huairou Commission organized a global day of action on February 19, 2013, called Delhi and Beyond: Concrete Actions for Safer Cities. One goal of the day was to "consolidate a grassroots women's approach to safer cities by linking the issue of violence against women with making public spaces safer," said Carolina Pinheiro, who was then the commission's governance campaign coordinator. Another was "to shift the discourse around violence against women away from only talking about women as victims and beneficiaries of services and into active agents of change. . . . [and to] focus on concrete actions for safer cities and public spaces, including partnerships with local authorities, public awareness campaigns, and active involvement in policy and budget making" Pinheiro said.[30]

The day of action was extremely successful even though it was organized in just a few weeks with limited funding. People everywhere were dismayed by the Delhi gang rape and felt motivated to channel their frustration into something productive. On the global action day 66 groups in 26 countries held meetings with public officials in 58 cities—from Cordoba, Argentina, to Edinburgh, United Kingdom—to discuss their ideas for localized strategies and to sign agreements to work together to address gender violence.

In Zimbabwe, for instance, members of the Zimbabwe Parents of Handicapped Children Association organized a meeting with advocacy groups and Mayor Muchadeyi Masunda. They asked him to install more streetlights in dark parts of town, to deploy more police officers to monitor for harassment and sexual violence, and to cut the grass in areas where long grass creates a dangerous environment. The director of the grassroots group Theresa Makwara told me, "It was successful because in normal situations it is very difficult to convince the mayor to come for community events." Makwara said that within months: "The streetlights were installed, and municipal police were deployed. The grass-cutting is still in progress." A year later, the grass was cut and, the mayor's office was still working with the grassroots women on initiatives around safer housing and spaces for women to gather. Makwara, a survivor of gender violence and an advocate for girls with disabilities who have faced street harassment in their neighborhoods and outside of their schools, says the meeting led to more partnerships.[31]

As other examples, more than one dozen organizations in Casoria, Province of Naples, Italy, met with the assessors/councillors of equal opportunities from the city of Naples and the city of Casoria to define the priority actions for an action plan against urban violence. ActionAid Ethiopia met with members of the Addis Ababa City Council to present the findings of a new study "Women and the City II: Combating Violence Against Women in Urban Public Spaces—the Role of Public Services." GROOTS Jamaica organized a meeting with the mayors of three cities for which it had previously conducted Safety Audits. The group brought in police officers, church leaders, politicians, and school representatives as well and discussed gender-based violence and harassment. They signed an agreement for concrete actions and have worked collaboratively on several of them.[32]

Rachael Wyant, the Huairou Commission's current governance campaign coordinator, said that in the feedback, community members in every city reported that "being part of a global campaign and showing other groups were involved helped gain legitimacy for our requests to meet with local government."[33] Another effective way to prompt local government to take notice and action, according to Wyant, is when people can show how safer public spaces would allow more women to access jobs, go to school, and gain more economic advancement.[34]

Six months later in August 2013, participating groups submitted a report about outcomes from their global action day meetings. Their successes showed the power of women's organizing, demonstrated the influence of women as experts on the problems and solutions to address safety concerns, allowed for global networking, and showed how much global visibility could pressure local authorities to be accountable and listen.[35] But despite its achievements, the Delhi and Beyond campaign mostly petered out by the end of 2013 due to a lack of funding. Overall, efforts to address safety for women have proven to be the least fundable of the Huairou Commission's work, and it faces the ongoing challenge of finding support. However, at the end of 2014, Wyant said some groups were still holding Safety Audits, continuing the relationships with local leaders, and scaling up the level of partnerships they formed, particularly in countries like Jamaica, Peru, and Zimbabwe.[36]

GRASSROOTS CAMPAIGNS CREATE GLOBAL AWARENESS AND CHANGE

Story-sharing is the core component of organizations and groups like Hollaback!, HarassMap, Everyday Sexism Project, and SSH. This method of activism is informed by the consciousness-raising efforts of the 1970s women's rights movement, 1980s actions like the citywide campaign in Washington, D.C., led by the D.C. Rape Crisis Center, and more recently, in the work of the Street Harassment Project.

Out of a desire to mobilize women on women's issues, community activists Allison Guttu and Fran Luck organized a consciousness-raising session in New York City on International Women's Day in 1998 to allow women to discuss problems they faced that men did not. Around 20 women of all races and ages attended, and street harassment came up several times. After that initial meeting, they gathered once per month at Bluestockings Bookstore, and street harassment came up time and time again in their discussions. Guttu and Luck decided to focus their meetings on street harassment going forward and formed the Street Harassment Project (SHP). At first, only three or four women regularly attended their weekly meetings, but then in 2000, after groups of men sexually assaulted women in Central Park after the Puerto Rican Day parade, the number of women attending the weekly meetings grew. Channeling their anger over the assaults, the SHP members held a rally in Central Park, teach-ins, and discussions in collaboration with a few Latina activist groups. Some women began giving educational programs in high schools while others created anti-harassment squads. For these squads, seven or eight women would walk near each other, and if any of them was harassed or spotted someone who was, she'd signal the others, and they would surround and lecture the man. These women also orchestrated street theater and held more rallies.[37]

They also started the SHP website where they collected women's street harassment stories from around the world. To the knowledge of the organizers, theirs was the first website to do so.[38] It lists suggestions for how to respond to harassers, and the story depository was a rich collection of women sharing what they had tried when harassed and what worked. The consciousness-raising they began offline continued online. Although the group split in 2006 and stopped updating the website, the stories are still accessible at www.streetharassmentproject.org.

Hollaback!

Hollaback! is a nonprofit organization based in New York City that began in 2005 as a website where New York City women posted photos of their street harassers. This was inspired by Thao Nguyen, who had snapped a photo of her harasser, posted it on Flickr, and sparked a citywide conversation about street harassment when the photo was on the front page of the *New York Daily News*. Word about the website spread—largely through news stories—and people in a few other cities set up similar, unaffiliated sites in places like Boston, Chicago, San Francisco, and Toronto. In May 2010, Hollaback! transitioned from being loosely affiliated sites with no consistent central leadership to a 501(c)(3) organization. Now, people who want to start a chapter are trained and officially become part of Hollaback!

"Much of Hollaback!'s power lies in its scalability. To scale effectively, we train young women and LGBTQ leaders throughout the world to use their skills to build a grassroots movement focused on ending street harassment. We train in the application of technology as we also work to ensure that their actions are strategic and high impact,"[39] Emily May and board president Samuel Carter wrote in their first "State of the Streets" report in 2011.

Each trained Hollaback! site leader receives a customizable regional website that displays the stories people submit to the site along with a map that shows the locations of the incidents. Site leaders can write their own blog posts and create their own subsections with various resources. Hollaback! headquarters (or "the mothership," as they call it), focuses much of its efforts on launching and maintaining new sites. By the end of 2011, Hollaback! staff had trained people to lead 46 sites in places like Buenos Aires, Argentina; Santiago, Chile; Croatia; Berlin, Germany; Mumbai, India; Istanbul, Turkey; and several U.S. cities. By the end of

2014, Hollaback! had 79 sites in 26 countries.[40] A challenge Hollaback! faces is that a significant percentage of site leaders turn over and fade out, sometimes within a few months. This may be in part because nearly 80 percent of site leaders are under 30 years old, and while that is important because younger people face the most frequent harassment, it can also mean that life transitions common to young people can disrupt their involvement.

To assist the site leaders as much as possible, Hollaback! provides training and technical assistance, like the website shell, an anti-discrimination policy, and toolkits for taking offline action. In 2014, it released a global Know Your Rights Toolkit. An online resource aimed at site leaders, the toolkit was created in partnership with several law firms that worked pro bono, and it lists the relevant anti-street harassment laws in the countries and cities where Hollaback! has sites. At the end of 2014, the group conducted an opt-in online global survey in partnership with Cornell University researchers targeted to people in regions with Hollaback! sites.

Hollaback! holds monthly trainings for site leaders on topics like rape culture, media interviews, blogging, and managing volunteers, and it facilitates a site leader Listserv and support network. In 2013 and 2014, Hollaback! hosted the Holla:Rev conference on street harassment in New York City that was attended by more than 100 site leaders and members of the public. Through these efforts, site leaders learn from each other and borrow and adapt campaign ideas. Beyond soliciting and posting story submissions on their websites, the site leaders have flexibility to set their own agenda and actions. Many have conducted local opt-in surveys, held workshops, rallies and campaigns, and met with local government representatives. Hollaback! headquarters writes a weekly "In Our Shoes" blog post to highlight the main office's actions and press mentions. During 2014, the 79 sites and the main office organized or participated in 119 rallies and marches, 31 projects and campaigns, and 152 events and received 319 press hits.[41]

The three full-time Hollaback! staff and interns based in New York City also work on other initiatives. They run the I've Got Your Back campaign that allows people to submit stories about being a bystander. In this case, a green dot appears on the map (as opposed to a pink dot for stories by persons who were harassed) and lets people reading harassed persons' stories click a green "I've got your back!" button. They created a guide for employers in social service and related industries to train their staff on how to help clients facing street harassment and a #HarassmentIs guide on how identity impacts people's experiences of harassment. They also address issues beyond harassment in public spaces.

They offer college campus-specific sites and a guide, posters, and pamphlets about sexual harassment for middle and high schools. Currently, they are working on initiatives around online harassment. Hollaback! also works on New York City-specific initiatives. For example, they have worked to improve anti-harassment efforts on transit campaigns, held events and sidewalk chalking, and the Hollaback! phone app allows New York City residents to report incidents directly to their city council member.[42]

From the start, Hollaback! has been a media magnet. By the time the group released its first "State of the Streets" report in 2011, it had received more than 500 media inquiries in the six years since it launched and more than two million website visitors.[43] A 2014 viral street harassment video that has received 39 million views was created with the group's support, and the film's creator, Rob Bliss, named Hollaback! as the beneficiary of the film's proceeds, which led to many donations, press inquiries, and website traffic. For some people in the United States. where the group is most well known, street harassment has become synonymous with "hollaback," which shows the impact of its work.

Stop Street Harassment

SSH grew out of a master's thesis I wrote in 2007 about how women were using websites to talk about street harassment in lieu of societal recognition of the problem. In 2008 the two websites that were the most resources-focused were either not active or gone completely, which led to the birth of www.StopStreetHarassment.org. At the time, there were a handful of localized Hollaback! sites where women posted photos of their harassers. On SSH, anyone in the world could share stories, find resources and suggestions for responding to harassers, and read about activism and campaigns happening globally to stop street harassment.

Through Google alerts for terms like street harassment and Eve teasing, daily searches on social media like Twitter, and research for the 2010 book *Stop Street Harassment: Making Public Places Safe and Welcoming for Women*, I met anti-street harassment activists worldwide. Although SSH initially focused on documenting the work of others, in 2011 SSH began holding initiatives and running programs, too.

To harness the power and voices of people working to address street harassment globally, in February 2011, I declared March 20, the first day of spring, as International Anti-Street Harassment Day in 2011. Groups in 13 countries participated by distributing flyers, holding events, and posting information on social media. The biggest action was a 100-plus-person march in Delhi, India. In Washington, D.C., SSH teamed up with

Collective Action for Safe Spaces (CASS) to hold the city's first-ever Safety Audits.

Based on feedback from the participants of the day, in 2012 the day became a week of awareness and spread to 20 countries. SSH has overseen International Anti-Street Harassment Week annually in April since. In 2015, for example, groups in 41 countries held marches and rallies, handed out flyers, did sidewalk chalking, and more. There were five official tweet chats, as well as webinars, online videos, and nearly 90 media mentions. U.N. Women promotes it, and many regional Action-Aid, Huairou Commission, and Hollaback! sites participate as do groups like HarassMap and Everyday Sexism Project. The week succeeds in gaining increased attention for the topic, and participants find it empowering to join forces with others and not feel so alone.

In 2012, SSH gained nonprofit status with a goal of documenting street harassment, educating people about it, and mobilizing communities to take action to stop it. In 2013, SSH launched the Blog Correspondents program. Ten to fifteen people around the world write monthly articles about street harassment in their communities for four months per cohort. The first cohort of 2015 is the most geographically diverse with 14 members in nine countries on six continents. Also in 2013, SSH started the Safe Public Spaces Mentoring program and works with several groups of activists worldwide on projects they propose. SSH provides mentoring, resources, connections, and a small stipend for expenses. The projects have ranged from workshops in high schools in Afghanistan to surveying women at bus stops in Nicaragua. SSH runs campaigns against companies that trivialize street harassment and collaborates with CASS on Washington, D.C.-specific efforts, like an anti-harassment transit campaign. In 2013, with the assistance of consultants Talia Hagerty, Rickelle Mason, and Whitney Ripplinger, SSH produced a state-by-state Know Your Rights toolkit detailing the relevant laws and reporting process for street harassment for every state and the District of Columbia.

In 2014, after two years of fundraising, SSH was able to commission the largest statistically significant street harassment study in the United States. I self-financed 10 focus groups with under-represented voices, like immigrant Latinas in Florida, queer women of color in New York, Native Americans in South Dakota, college students in Maryland, and gay/bisexual/queer men in Washington, D.C. The report has had more than 125 media mentions and is being used by government agencies, universities, nonprofits, journalists, and activists nationwide.

In addition to documenting the problem and the global activism to stop it, SSH aims to change the social acceptability of street harassment by showing the negative impact it has on people's lives and society as a whole and to facilitate resource and idea sharing among individuals and groups working on the issue. SSH works to achieve these aims through its programs as well as through the more than 250 media interviews and 150 talks SSH board members have given and the more than 60 articles written for outlets like *The New York Times*, the *Washington Post*, and the *Guardian*. The 2010 book and the 2014 study in particular have helped legitimize street harassment as an issue and have provided the context for the thousands of stories people have shared. As of now, SSH is run on the volunteered time of 12 board members and numerous volunteers, interns, and collaborators.

HarassMap

Based in Cairo, Egypt, HarassMap is a social activism project that was founded by four friends in 2010 "because [street harassment] was a problem we were facing every day and we wanted to do something positive about it."[44] Co-founders Rebecca Chiao and Engy Ghozlan previously worked at the Egyptian Centre for Women's Rights (ECWR), which had been addressing street harassment since 2005. After NIJEL, a community mapping project, approached them to offer their services for free to combat street harassment, they tried to incorporate their idea for Harass-Map into their work at ECWR. In the end, the women started something on their own. Advocacy groups like ECWR were focused on passing stronger anti-harassment laws, but the HarassMap founders felt that was not the best approach because the existing laws were not enforced well. Instead, they believed if the community could come together and stand up to make it socially unacceptable, that could help stop harassment.[45] Their approach uses a combination of digital and online technology and traditional offline community mobilization.

For the online component, people anywhere in Egypt can use Frontline SMS and the Ushahidi website mapping platform as well as email, Facebook, and Twitter to make street harassment reports. By the end of 2014, there had been 1,366 approved reports.[46] Once each report is verified, it is placed on the map. This is a way to break the silence on this taboo topic, document it, and help victims by giving them a place to talk about what happened. People who submit a story receive an automated e-mail with resources like information about filing a police report, receiving legal aid and psychological help for the trauma, and finding free self-defense classes.[47]

The online stories inform HarassMap's offline Safe Areas program. Over the years, there have been 1,200 volunteers across Egypt who participate in monthly outreach days. At the end of 2014, there were 250 active volunteers.[48] HarassMap leaders train volunteers to talk to people who have a presence in their neighborhoods—like shopkeepers, police, and people who hang around at cafes and street corners—to ask them to be watchful against street harassment and take action if they see it occurring. The goal is to "embarrass harassers and make them accountable for their actions," said co-founder Sawsan Gad in a 2012 presentation.[49] Volunteers receive a Community Mobilization Guide to assist them.

"It's not a problem in our neighborhood," "It's a compliment," and "It's women's fault because of how they dress" are common responses volunteers hear during the outreach actions. To refute these common misconceptions, volunteers bring printouts of the HarassMap incidents from the area to show it does happen there. They read story submissions to prove the incidents are in no way complimentary. And using past studies, they can disprove victim-blaming assumptions. A 2008 ECWR survey, for example, found that almost 72 percent of women had been veiled when harassed.[50]

The map, stories, and statistics are often effective at changing people's minds. Each volunteer team reports back, and on average, 8 out of every 10 people with whom they speak agrees, by the end of the conversation, to stand up against sexual harassment. Take this man, featured in a HarassMap report:

One microbus driver in Shubra, a Cairo neighborhood where one of our outreach teams has conducted on-the-ground street activities, has started to make a clear statement that sexual harassment is not accepted in his vehicle. He has covered his microbus with stickers from our campaign to dispel myths about sexual harassment, and when witnessing sexual harassment on the street, he makes a point to stop his microbus, even if it is in the middle of the road, get out, and stop the harasser.[51]

In 2012, HarassMap received funding from Canada's International Development Research Centre and went from being an organization led by part-time volunteers with other full-time jobs to having paid full-time staff. At the end of 2014, HarassMap had 20 staff members and was still hiring more. "It's been great in helping us make an impact!" Chaio told me.[52] Now, HarassMap also has the capacity to run a number of awareness campaigns. It has a Safe Schools and Universities program, and in 2014 it helped develop the first-ever policy against sexual harassment at Cairo University. It also conducts research projects, like its 2014 study on the effectiveness of crowdsourcing data.

Throughout its existence, HarassMap has been regularly featured in the media. In 2013, for example, it was profiled on a TV show that has 30 million viewers. Its work has inspired others, and HarassMap leaders have advised groups in 28 countries on starting their own version of HarassMap. Sites have been launched in countries like Algeria, Bangladesh, India, Lebanon, Pakistan, Palestine, Syria, and Yemen.[53] Additionally, HarassMap has advised and partnered with the more than one dozen anti-harassment groups that have sprung up in Egypt since 2010. It has had tremendous success bringing attention to street harassment in Egypt and the Middle Eastern region of the world.

Everyday Sexism Project

After reaching a tipping point in dealing with daily instances of sexism, including street harassment, British journalist Laura Bates began talking to female friends and family members about their experiences. She was surprised to learn they all had similar stories. Their stories—and her own—inspired her to launch the Everyday Sexism Project (ESP), a website where women could submit their stories of sexism, "from the niggling and normalized to the outrageously offensive" in April 2012.[54] Her goal was to allow those who didn't experience the problems firsthand to gain awareness.

In the introduction to her 2014 book *Everyday Sexism*, Bates noted her surprise about the swiftness with which she received story submissions. Within two months, she had more than 1,000 entries from women all over the world. "Hundreds of women and girls wrote to me about their own experiences," Bates wrote in her book. "Stories from the workplace to the pavement, from clubs and bars to buses and trains. Of verbal harassment and 'jokes,' of touching and groping and grabbing and kissing and being followed and sworn at and shouted at and belittled and assaulted and raped."[55]

Soon reporters featured the site in articles and on radio and television programs. Bates began writing regularly about the story submissions for outlets like *The Independent* and the *Guardian*. By the end of 2013, less than two years after the site launched, there were 50,000 entries. By the end of 2014, there were 80,000. Bates has two volunteer coordinators who organize the volunteers who moderate and monitor each story submission before it is published. They also copy and paste entries submitted over Twitter onto the main project website.[56]

When women in other countries asked if there could be a version of ESP in their countries, Bates said yes. Within 18 months there were ESP sites in 18 countries, each run by a team of volunteers who receive moral support from Bates as well as detailed guidelines about how to detect and avoid trolls, what they can and cannot publish (for example, no racism, homophobia, or transphobia), and so on. The volunteers run their sites fairly independently, otherwise, and can even choose to change the platform, as the Japanese volunteers did. Instead of posting stories on a website, they run their version of ESP through a Facebook group. Bates told me there has not been much turnover among the site leaders. "I feel very lucky that there is such a sense of investment and shared ownership in the project and that so many incredible people have come forward and offered to help, and I feel immensely grateful to them for keeping the project going."[57]

Street harassment is a common form of everyday sexism for many women, so street harassment stories feature prominently among the entries and inform one of the chapters of Bates's book. Compared to sites dedicated solely to street harassment, her site clearly shows the context for street harassment and how it is simply one more way women face discrimination over and over again. In a speech she gave in 2014 to the U.N. Commission on the Status of Women, Bates said:

What the testimonies reveal, again and again, is that these varied experiences of sexism, harassment, assault, discrimination, and rape are not isolated incidents, but exist on an interconnected spectrum. The same ideas and attitudes about women that underlie the more "minor" incidents we are often told to brush off or ignore are also at the root of greater inequalities and incidences of sexual violence. For example, the same words and phrases used to a woman who was cat-called in the street were also directed at a victim of sexual assault. A woman who tried to ignore her harasser found that he followed her home and assaulted her on her own doorstep. Women trying to succeed in the male-dominated environment of politics have to contend with a media that objectifies them, reporting on their bodies and clothes instead of their policies.

The treatment of women in one sphere has a clear knock-on effect on behavior toward them in other areas.

So, to reflect an inter-connected set of problems, we also need a joined-up solution. It won't work to take measures to increase the representation of women at the top levels of business and politics unless we also challenge the media's repeated presentation of women as dehumanized sex objects. It won't work to tackle workplace discrimination, if the moment people step outside the office they exist in a public space where sexual harassment continues to be accepted as the norm. Our efforts to tackle gender imbalance will be more effective if they take into account the way that sexism intersects with other forms of prejudice.[58]

Bates continues to write regularly about the topic, to deliver talks nationally and internationally, to run workshops on sexual consent, sexual harassment, and gender stereotypes in schools and at universities, and to give media interviews. She was one of the key players in the campaign to pressure Facebook to change its policies about pro-rape pages and also consulted on both the anti-harassment transit campaign in

London and the current "lad culture" campaign with the National Union of Students that aims to end sexual harassment and violence on university campuses in England. She's working with Women for Refugee Women to start a site focused on refugee women's stories. Bates also represented ESP at a Council of Europe conference that led to the creation of new media guidelines on gender equality for European countries.[59] What started off as one woman's outrage has led to awareness and change at an international level.

From the Safe Cities campaigns to the efforts of grassroots groups, street harassment has gained international recognition, and global collaborations are underway to combat it. The different approaches are complementary in many ways and help ensure a bigger impact. Hopefully, there will continue to be ways to cross-promote, collaborate, and learn from each group's work moving forward.

Chapter 6

Government Initiatives

Touche Pas à Ma Pote, a transit campaign in Brussels, 2012. (Campaign designed by JWT advertising agency. Photographer Charlotte Abramow)

From transit campaigns to laws, from city council hearings to public service announcements, there have been scores of new local and national government efforts to address street harassment since 2010. Many came about because of public pressure and/or internal concern sparked by news stories, studies, or viral videos or from suggestions by grassroots groups and international organizations. Several examples follow.

PUBLIC TRANSPORTATION

From rickshaws to buses, from subways to trains, public transportation is utilized by people everywhere in the world. It is also the site of sexual harassment and assault, especially for women, as a growing number of surveys and individual stories reveal. At least 50 percent of women experience harassment according to various public transit rider studies conducted in Beijing (2002), Tokyo (2004), New York City (2007), Delhi (2009), Chicago (2009), Korea (2010), Pakistan (2011), Sri Lanka (2011), Bogota (2012), and California's San Francisco Bay Area (2012). According to the Association of Urban Buses, in Guatemala City, Guatemala in 2011, "an average of a dozen vehicles per day are attacked by armed assailants who rob passengers and regularly assault female riders."[1] In 2014, a survey of 2,046 people in Hanoi and Ho Chi Minh City, Vietnam, found that 31 percent has been sexually harassed on public buses,[2] and when the French government surveyed 600 female transit riders in 2015, they found every single one had experienced sexual harassment.[3]

The threat of harassment and assault causes some people to feel unsafe while riding public transit systems. A 2012 YouGov survey for the End Violence against Women Coalition found that 28 percent of women and 15 percent of men in London felt unsafe using public transportation.[4] The World Bank conducted a 2013 study in Nepal and found that one in three women and one in six men feel unsafe on public transportation.[5] In 2014, a Los Angeles County Metropolitan Transportation Authority survey found 21 percent of rail passengers and 18 percent of bus passengers felt unsafe during the previous month because of sexual harassment.[6]

The largest study to date on this subject was conducted in 2014 by YouGov, an international Internet-based market research firm based in the United Kingdom. It polled people in 16 major cities worldwide and then ranked the transit systems from safest (New York City, USA) to least safe (Bogota, Colombia). As for experiences of verbal harassment, the top five worst cities were Mexico City, Mexico; Delhi, India; Bogota; Lima, Peru; and Jakarta, Indonesia. The top five worst cities for physical harassment were Mexico City, Bogota, Lima, Tokyo, and Delhi.[7]

Using women-only public transportation, public service announcements, and undercover police, transit agencies in many of these countries, and in others, aim to make their systems safer.

Women-Only Transportation

In 1909, women-only subway cars were proposed for one of the first subway systems in the United States, the Interborough Rapid Transit system in New York, because of the "fearful crushes," "sexual insults," and other types of sexual harassment women riders faced. In the end, they were not instituted.[8] However, in Japan in 1912 they were used for a short time for the same reasons.[9]

Today, major cities in more than 15 countries have implemented women-only subway cars, buses, and taxis as a solution to harassment. Countries with women-only bus services include Bangladesh, Guatemala, India, Indonesia, Mexico, Pakistan, Thailand, and the United Arab Emirates. Women-only subway cars or sections of trains (like women-only sleeper cars) are found in countries like Brazil, Egypt, Iran, Japan, Malaysia, Mexico, Russia, and South Korea. At the time of this writing, women-only buses were going to launch in Kathmandu, Nepal, and women-only buses in Hanoi and subway cars in Beijing were under consideration. There are also women-only taxi services with women drivers in countries like Australia, England, India, Iran, Lebanon, Mexico, Pakistan, Russia, and the United Arab Emirates.

In the 2014 YouGov poll in 16 major cities, nearly 70 percent of women said they would feel safer in single-sex areas on buses and trains. Women in Manila, Philippines, were most in favor of single-sex transport (94 percent) followed by Jakarta, Mexico City, and Delhi. In contrast, women in New York saw the least need for it (35 percent supported it) followed by women in Moscow, London, and Paris.[10] When Malaysia launched women-only carriages on its train, Poovan Kaur, 63, said in an *Inquirer Global Nation* interview, "I will feel safer [on women-only buses], not because I do not trust men, but for someone my age, it's hard to fight for space during peak hours."[11] Women in Delhi reported in a *Globe & Mail* article that the women-only areas can be pleasant places to have conversations together, get advice, and help watch each other's children and that the women-only spaces smell better![12]

No doubt when you face extreme crowds and constant harassment, anything that may offer respite can sound appealing, as I experienced firsthand during a 2012 trip to Cairo, Egypt, when I rode in both the mixed-gender and women-only subway cars. I believe that sex segregation is better than nothing when the alternative is constant harassment in a mixed-sex car. But there are issues with the concept and the execution of it that cause me to advocate for other solutions.

Women-only systems are problematic for several reasons. First, they assume sex and gender are binary and do not consider gender queer and transgender individuals. They also do not account for men's experiences with sexual harassment and assault.

Second, they do not prevent men from harassing women at subway platforms or bus stops (though the government in central Jakarta briefly tried to enforce sex segregated lines at bus stops in 2010[13]). Pallavi Kamat, a 2013 Stop Street Harassment (SSH) blog correspondent, wrote about experiencing and witnessing this in Mumbai, India. "Women continue to face harassment as they board the daily train. This could be in the form of the men's compartment adjacent to the women's compartment from which there is catcalling and verbal harassment. Oftentimes, as a train stops at a particular station, the men on the platform pass lewd comments and whistle at women."[14] Freedom from harassment in the women-only cars is not even guaranteed. In both Delhi and Cairo, it is not uncommon for women to have to shoo away men trying to ride in their space.[15]

Third, they are not offered with enough frequency to allow all women to use them, which leaves some women to fend for themselves in the mixed-sex cars. In 2010 in Japan, women vented during a street harassment workshop that sex-segregation "doesn't solve anything." One woman said, "Women who choose to not travel by ladies-only coaches are seen as fair game sometimes. The 'why are they here if not to be felt up' logic. I once argued with a male cousin about women's seats in buses. I said I would never make a man vacate his seat so I could sit down. He said he would wonder at what kind of woman I was, if I refused to accept the offer of a seat in a crowded bus."[16]

Fourth, they do not address the root issue of why harassment is happening and thus do not solve the problem. Notably, a decade after Tokyo launched women-only subway cars, the 2014 YouGov poll ranked Tokyo in the top five cities in the world for the most physical harassment on public transportation. At the time of the poll's release, Julie Babinard, senior transport specialist from the World Bank, said, "Women-only initiatives are not likely to provide long-term solutions as they only segregate by gender and provide a short-term remedy instead of addressing more fundamental issues."[17]

Various groups have spoken out against women-only options. In 2011, the Egyptian Centre for Women's Rights rejected a project approved by Local Development Minister Mohamed Attiya for women-only taxis. "The project pulls Egypt 100 years backward, isolates women within society, and hinders their freedom of movement," the group said in a statement.[18] In Guatemala that same year, Ana María Cofiño, with the La Cuerda feminist collective, said in an *Inter Press Service* interview: "The problem is that off the bus, harassment is still an issue. Specific actions like this are taken, but violence in other areas like the workplace or the streets, or the fact that women are at risk of being raped at any time, are not addressed."[19] In late 2014, Dinh Thi Thanh Binh, director of the Institute of Transport Planning and Management at the University of Transportation in Hanoi, said in an interview for *Thanh Nien News*: "Female commuters are sexually harassed on numerous routes, and the city can't hope to resolve the problem by segregating the whole system along gender lines. Hanoi should explore other solutions, such as cooperating with the police, raising passenger awareness, and encouraging victims to file reports."[20]

Anti-Harassment Campaigns

What are the alternatives to sex segregation? Since the mid-2000s* and especially since 2010, there have been a growing number of anti-harassment transit campaigns created in partnership with local advocacy groups. They tell people not to harass and provide information about reporting incidents. Several systems use undercover transit police and closed-circuit video recordings to catch more perpetrators. The systems may hold awareness days at stations to pass out flyers and provide information about the campaign at local events.

While certainly these campaigns do not solve harassment and their newness means their effectiveness is not known, they do recognize that changing attitudes about harassment, working in collaboration with advocacy groups, and taking a gender-neutral approach may do more to stop it in the long run than sex segregation. Here are five examples of current transit campaigns.

Bogota

In 2014, Bogota was ranked as the least safe transit system in the world. Nearly 60 percent of women reported verbal or physical harassment on buses.[21] Additionally, a 2012 study found that 64 percent of riders had experienced sexual harassment, and 80 percent of them were women.[22] Other studies have found that one-fourth of men in the city believe there is nothing wrong with grabbing, groping, or fondling a fellow passenger.[23]

---

* My first book looks at anti-harassment transit campaigns in Chicago and New York City.

In response to these findings, Bogota's law enforcement branch created a team of 11 operatives—seven of whom are female—that received special training to recognize and stop sexual assault on the bus system. The undercover squad made several arrests during the first week. The police officer in charge of the squad, Lieutenant Lina Maria Rios, said in a BBC interview, "there has been a slight decrease in the number of reported cases" since the Transmileno Elite Group, as the squad is known, took up its work. "It could be that potential offenders are thinking about it twice because they don't want to risk groping a girl who might be an undercover cop, although I cannot guarantee it," she said. She also explained, "It's about letting women know they're not alone, that the women in the police force have their backs."[24]

While the officers know that under the current legislation, most offenders are unlikely to spend time in jail, they said they hope their job will at least raise awareness: "That's why we're doing this, to make sure these sort of things don't happen again,"[25] one of the female agents said. Time will tell if there is a reduction in incidents.

Brussels

In 2012 Touche Pas à Ma Pote, now a nonprofit focused on street harassment and related issues, launched as an anti-harassment transit campaign in Brussels run by the magazine *ELLE Belgique*. Around that time, Beatrice Ercolini, the magazine's editor-in-chief, found herself advising her daughter to lower her gaze when men harassed her, then thought, "For over a decade, I've edited a leading women's magazine championing women, and encouraged them to be all they can be. Yet here I am, advising my own daughter to keep her mouth shut when men ogle, stare, jeer, and verbally assault her."[26]

She decided she could do something else instead. "Challenging people, getting them talking and thinking, and gently getting things moving, that's where we come in. Which is why we launched [our] campaign inspired by the similarly named 'Touche pas à Mon Pote' effort inaugurated in the '80s by SOS Racisme (a French organization)."[27]

For six months, a public tram on the city's number 4 line was painted pink and carried the slogan "Touching my ass won't help you touch my heart." Billboards with the same slogan were posted in many public transportation vehicles. An advertising agency produced the ads pro bono, four Belgian ministers covered the costs to fund it, and the transit agency supported the campaign by waiving the fee for the ad space.[28]

"We'd barely asked for support and immediately got it. First from Fadila Laanan, Belgium's minister for social equality, then the Council for Francophone Women, and so on," wrote Ercolini. "Our objective is to fight public harassment and step out against everyday rampant sexism. Let's do something about it because it is all around us, in the workplace and in our very city streets. And for goodness' sake, let's stop lowering our gaze."[29]

Periodically, the campaign continues to collaborate with the transit agency to publish more anti-street harassment posters. For example, from December 9–22, 2014, 150 anti-harassment posters were installed around the system. The campaign also has a social media campaign.[30]

London

The British Transit Police (BTP) periodically survey the London transit riders. When a survey revealed that sexual harassment was a fear for a significant percentage of women, BTP leaders created the Project Guardian campaign. Launched in July 2013 as a collaboration between BTP, the Metropolitan and City London police, Transport for London, and three advocacy groups—Everyday Sexism Project (ESP), End Violence Against Women Coalition, and Hollaback! London—it is the first initiative of its size in the world.

Around 2,000 police officers received training enabling them to look for harassers both while undercover and as a visible deterrent. Up to 180 of these officers at a time are deployed at stations. They also learned how to appropriately help transit riders and respond to harassment reports. The campaign includes closed-circuit TV monitoring to deter and catch offenders and messaging to encourage riders to report harassment incidents to transit police officers including via a confidential hotline (0800 405 040). During the spring of 2014, BTP and its partners held outreach days to inform riders about their rights.[31] "Our core aim is to increase confidence and awareness of the victims of these crimes. Only if they come forward can we find out the extent of this problem," said Ricky Twyford, manager of the project, in an interview for the *Guardian*.[32]

BTP took its collaboration with the advocacy organizations very seriously and incorporated their suggestions and ideas for the police training and campaign messaging. Hollaback! London co-director Bryony Beynon said her group was able to successfully "advocate to ensure that LGBTQ people were consulted fully during the research phase, about how unwanted sexual behavior and homophobia can intersect on public transport."[33] ESP founder Laura Bates told me she emphasized the "importance of always believing the victim and of being very specific in public awareness materials with language."[34] The BTP website assures people "you will be always be believed and taken seriously."[35]

From the thousands of story submissions about sexual harassment and assault on public transportation submitted to ESP, Bates was able to show BTP what harassment is like on the system. Bates presented these stories and themes to 50 key officers. Her presentation was filmed and was incorporated into the training that the 2,000 officers received. "It felt immensely valuable that they'd all had that experience of hearing women's own testimonies in their own words,"[36] she said. BTP held focus groups to further understand people's needs and experiences and added campaign components to meet those needs, including the ability to report problems by text message (61016).[37]

About 18 months after the initiative launched, there was a 40 percent increase in both reporting and detection of offenders. While both ESP and Hollaback! London felt more needed to be done to publicize the campaign, they both felt encouraged by the initial results. "What has been brilliant is the extent to which the BTP really put women's rights orgs and their advice right at the center of the campaign from the very beginning," Bates said. Currently, Bates is advising the transit police in West Midlands on a similar campaign called Project Empower. "I'd also love to see the campaign rolled out nationwide as it is so effective and relatively simple and low cost."[38]

Washington, D.C.

Around one-third of the hundreds of harassment stories submitted to the Collective Action for Safe Spaces (CASS) website take place on public transportation. After unsuccessfully trying to meet with the Washington Metropolitan Area Transportation Authority (WMATA) about this issue, in early 2012 CASS leaders decided to testify about the problem during the public portion of WMATA's performance oversight hearing before the Washington, D.C. city council.

On February 22, 2012, CASS co-founder Chai Shenoy, CASS board member Ben Merrion, myself (a CASS board member at the time), and three women survivors, Ami Lynch, Pascale Leone, and Karen Starr, testified about sexual harassment on WMATA's system. When WMATA learned of the group's intentions, it issued statements claiming sexual harassment was not a problem because the reported numbers were very low. The authority tried to dismiss it by saying, "One person's harassment is another person's flirting."[39]

During the hearing, survivors shared their stories of harassment on buses or trains and showed there are serious incidents of unwanted sexual comments, groping, stalking, public masturbation, and assault. WMATA was given three recommendations: (1) Better tracking and reporting of incidents (including verbal harassment); (2) A public service announcement so people know what their rights are and how to report incidents; (3) Better training of Metro employees.

The D.C. city council was disturbed by the testimonies and chairwoman Muriel Bowser (who became mayor in 2015) told WMATA to address the concerns. After extensive local media coverage of the hearing in every major paper and news program, many people sent WMATA their harassment stories and backed up the testimonies. Within two weeks, WMATA began working on the recommendations and invited the group members to meet with its new task force on sexual harassment. Within the month, the authority set up an email address (harassment@wmata.com) and online form (www.wmata.com/harassment) so people could more easily report harassment, and it began tracking verbal harassment for the first time. Everyone who makes a report online receives a follow-up email. Two months later in April, WMATA launched a public service announcement campaign adapted from Boston's successful anti-harassment transit campaign.

In April 2012, CASS and SSH held a community forum on sexual harassment, and WMATA videotaped the stories of willing participants to be incorporated into its new sexual harassment training. During 2013 and 2014, Marty Langelan, who wrote the book *Back Off* on nonviolent direct-action strategies to stop harassers, created and tested a ground-breaking intervention program for bus drivers, station managers, transit police, etc., and began training all 4,000 front-line employees. The training not only teaches them how to help riders facing harassment (including harassment based on race, sexual orientation, gender, nationality, disability, class), but also gives them tools to respond when they themselves are harassed. "Workplace culture at Metro is changing now that people have this intervention toolkit," Langelan told me. "Employees are using it to handle all kinds of harassers, for their co-workers as well as their customers."[40]

Between 2012 and 2014, WMATA held several outreach days with CASS and SSH to hand out flyers, bracelets with the transit police phone number on them, and T-shirts that say "If it isn't yours, don't touch it." WMATA also takes these materials to its events. In February 2015, WMATA released a "phase two" customized public service announcement campaign ("If it's unwanted, it's harassment") with input from CASS and SSH. Caroline Laurin, media relations manager at WMATA, told me: "The greatest outcome from this [campaign] has been the increased awareness we have seen from riders on the system. That sexual harassment, assault, and intimidation is not OK has become part of the dialogue in Washington, and that really is the best way to create lasting and sustainable change."[41]

LAWS AND ORDINANCES

Another way for governments to address street harassment is through laws and ordinances. But since very privileged men are usually the main people who write and pass laws and those laws usually address issues that concern themselves, street harassment, which disproportionately impacts women and marginalized men, is not penalized through the laws of most countries. Former executive director of U.N. Women and current President of Chile Michelle Bachelet lamented this in 2013 saying, "Despite its prevalence, violence and harassment against women and girls in public spaces remains a largely neglected issue, with few laws or policies in place to address it."[42]

In examining laws more closely, some forms of harassment could arguably fall under "disorderly conduct" or "disturbing the peace" ordinances if the harasser is loud and obnoxious. If the harasser repeats his or her actions on more than one occasion or makes threats, then those actions may fall under a general harassment law or a stalking law, if a country has one. Few places, however, have laws specifically acknowledging the most common forms of street harassment: sexist speech, sexual comments, and homophobic/transphobic slurs. Further, the laws and enforcement of them can vary a lot, as detailed in the 2014 *Street Harassment: Know Your Rights* guide commissioned by Hollaback!, the Thomas Reuter Foundation, and DLA Piper and produced by numerous international law agencies. It examines the laws in 22 countries where there are Hollaback! sites.

Over the past few years, there have been some attempts to address street harassment legally. In addition to Egypt (see Chapter 7), another example is the Council of Europe's 2011 convention on preventing and combating violence against women, with signatories including Italy, the United Kingdom, Germany, Denmark, and Belgium. These countries pledged to "take the necessary legislative and other measures to promote and protect the right for everyone, particularly women, to live free from violence in both the public and the private sphere," which includes a section calling on legal sanctions for "unwanted verbal, non-verbal, or physical conduct of a sexual nature."[43] When the United Kingdom signed the convention in 2012, there was an uproar from many men who were concerned that actions like "wolf whistles" and "catcalls" would be illegal.[44] Three years later, there has been no apparent impact on street harassment in the countries that signed the convention.

Another example comes from Bolivia. Because so many female Bolivian politicians were experiencing harassment—more than 4,000 complaints were filed between 2004 and 2012—and even murder, in 2012, the government passed a groundbreaking law making harassment of politicians a crime punishable by up to five years in prison. Physical, sexual, or psychological aggression is punishable by up to eight years. The national women's network Coordinadora de la Mujer and other women's groups advocated for the new law, noting that Bolivian women broke "the glass ceiling for women's political participation" by reaching 35 percent female elected officials, but harassment prevents many from seeking a second term.[45]

Belgium passed a law that mandates fines of up to $1,500 or a prison sentence of up to one year for sexual harassment crimes. The law expands on an existing law against verbal harassment that constituted an "immoral offence" or included obscenities. It states that sexual harassment includes making "a gesture or statement that is clearly intended to express contempt for one or more people of a different gender on the basis of their gender or to make them appear inferior or reduce them to their sexual dimension in a way that constitutes a serious attack on their dignity."[46] The law applies to workplaces, public spaces, and the Internet, but it has been criticized as being too vague and hard to enforce.[47]

There is also a law in Brussels enacted in 2013 that makes sexist, racist, and homophobic insults fineable by up to 250 euros.[48] Within the first three months, 69 fines were imposed for sexual harassment and gay bashing. Hollaback! Brussels, the main anti-street harassment group in the country at the time, published its stance on its blog. The group was "very happy to witness how Belgian politicians are acknowledging the issue and making legislative plans to address sexism and street harassment," but it wished to see a "deeper analysis and research for the problem" to create the most effective solution because it feared some people may have a hard time "proving" the harassment and that a fine may not be enough to deter or reform harassers.[49]

In March 2015, the Peruvian government passed a law against sexual harassment in public spaces. The advocacy group Paremos el Acoso Callejero helped craft it. The law defines sexual harassment as "physical or verbal conduct of sexual nature or connotation by one or more persons against another or others who do not wish or reject such behavior as affecting their dignity and their fundamental rights" and applies to any public space. The penalty for violating the law can be as severe as 12 years in prison.[50]

A few laws were proposed in 2014 and 2015 that have not yet passed. Saudi Arabia is considering fines and jail sentences of up to five years for sexual harassment inspired by a "surge in the harassment of women at workplaces, streets, and shopping malls."[51] In Colombia, Senator Antonio Guerra de la Espriella introduced a bill that would make sexual harassment on public transport a specific and defined crime carrying a prison sentence of two to four years.[52] Activists with the group Observatorio Contra el Acoso Callejero Chile told me in December 2014 they were collaborating with the National Service of Women to expand Chile's current domestic violence act to encompass all kinds of gender violence, including street harassment.[53] In early 2015, laws were proposed in both Argentina[54] and Panama.[55]

In the United States, there is no national law against sexual harassment in public spaces even though pervasive or extreme (e.g., sexual assault) sexual harassment is prohibited in schools, on college campuses, and in workplaces. At the state level, there are laws that apply to some forms of street harassment. In 2013, SSH produced the toolkit *Know Your Rights: Street Harassment and the Law*, which examines the relevant street harassment laws state by state, including disorderly conduct and disturbing the peace laws, laws against indecent exposure and sexual assault in the third degree (groping), voyeurism, and stalking. The toolkit explains the laws as they could apply to street harassment and links directly to the laws on the state websites. A few states, like Iowa and Pennsylvania, have general harassment laws under which repeated or severe harassment falls.

A growing number of cities have anti-harassment ordinances, too. Independence, Missouri, passed an ordinance in 2010 making it illegal for people to harass pedestrians and cyclists from their vehicles.[56] In 2011, the Los Angeles city council made it a crime for drivers to threaten or harass cyclists and permitted victims of harassment to sue in civil court without waiting for the city to press criminal charges.[57] After conducting a survey, lobbying, and testifying at a city council hearing, SSH Safe Public Spaces mentee BikeWalkKC successfully saw the Kansas City, Missouri, city council pass an anti-harassment ordinance to protect pedestrians, bicyclists, and individuals in wheelchairs in fall 2014.[58] It's unclear how often any of the anti-harassment ordinances have been used.

As street harassment continues to gain recognition as a problem and as entities like U.N. Women, ActionAid, and the Huairou Commission make headway promoting safer cities for women and girls, undoubtedly there will be more laws introduced and passed in the coming years.

Challenges with Using Laws

Wording: Even when there are laws against street harassment, they are often challenging to use because of how they are worded. For example, the 2014 anti-harassment law in Egypt requires harassment to be conditional on stalking or following, so if a man makes a comment in passing without also following the woman, it is legal. It also sets burdensome standards for proving harassment such as bringing the harasser to the police or waiting with the harasser until the police arrive and proving that the harasser was motivated by sexual desire and fulfillment.

In Brussels, Belgium, where police say they write an average of two fines per day for verbal abuse targeted at women and LGBTQ-identified individuals, most cases end there. "We forward all complaints to the prosecutor, but perpetrators often go unpunished for lack of evidence," commissioner Christian De Coninck told *Het Laatste Nieuws*. "An officer can only take action immediately if he [sic] happens to overhear something, which has happened 18 times over the past eight months."[59]

In countries like Austria, it is even hard to use laws for assault. Here is an example: When a man grabbed a woman's butt as she was waiting to cross the street, she slapped him, and then he chased her. A police officer intervened, and the woman wanted to press charges of sexual assault. However, the local prosecutor dropped the charges saying, "The incident itself needs to involve physical contact with sexual parts; simply touching the woman on the bottom does not qualify as sexual harassment. That would not have been the case if he had, for example, grabbed her breasts or touched her improperly in the sexual region."[60]

In the United States, most state anti-harassment laws require that the actions be repeated by the same person, which does not often happen, especially in cities. Harassed persons must sometimes prove their harasser had an intent to harass or gain sexual gratification through the harassment, which can be very difficult. The harassed person often must report fearing bodily harm or death at the hands of the harasser, but in reality, most incidents do not rise to this level of immediate threat.

The First Amendment poses another problem. The United States Supreme Court sets a very high bar against government intervention in the case of the First Amendment and only regulates speech that is clearly intimidating or threatening, rather than merely offensive. Lawmakers cannot broadly prohibit speech, even when it is insulting or offensive to some. However, U.S. courts have ruled that the First Amendment does not protect speech that is likely to incite violence because "fighting words" do not contribute to democratic discourse and because society has a collective interest in reducing violence. As such, words or language that would incite a reasonable person to react violently may be legally prohibited. Many of the verbal harassment laws either refer specifically to fighting words or prohibit taunts, insults, or other language that is likely to incite a violent reaction. But women, the typical targets of street harassment, usually do not react violently to men who speak to them on the street, so this caveat rarely applies.

An additional limitation to U.S. laws is the "reasonable man" or "reasonable fear" standards that provide guidance for judges and jurors in interpreting the law. They suggest the harassers' action would have to be something that would cause fear for the average, reasonable person—not *just* the person that was actually made afraid. Because the majority of lawmakers and judges in the United States have been and are today white men and white men don't typically experience street harassment, or if they do, they are rarely afraid as a result, the fear associated with street harassment has not always passed the reasonable man test.

And finally, there is the problematic "homosexual advance as a form of provocation." If a homosexual man makes a sexual advance at a heterosexual man and the heterosexual man kills him, the "homosexual advance defense" will mitigate a murder charge to manslaughter because a "reasonable person" would find the advance so offensive as to respond with a high level of violence. In the context of street harassment, legal scholar Kavita B. Ramakrishnan explains that "women are expected to withstand a higher level of harassment than men before the law may intervene. Queer men who make sexual advances on men risk legal action or even death, whereas heterosexual men who make sexual advances on women can generally expect impunity."[61]

Enforcement: The laws also may be ineffective because they are not enforced. Two years after the anti-political harassment law passed in Bolivia, for example, activists voiced concern that it has not been effective. Reports of harassment rose from 10 to 25 per month. Mercedes Vargas, from the indigenous rights organization Fundacion Machaqa, said in a BBC interview: "These women continue to suffer. We now have a law, but it's not functioning well."[62] Activists say there is a lack of access to justice and lack of protection for complainants, as well as delays in cases brought.

In the United States, there is a concern among anti-street harassment activists and racial justice proponents that anti-harassment laws might be disproportionately applied to men of color, adding to their over-criminalization. While there does not seem to be data on if this has happened in states and cities with ordinances, there are examples of women of color facing charges for defending themselves against harassers that white women likely would not face. This happened to seven African American lesbians who fought back against a sexist and racist street harasser (one taunt he made was that he would "fuck them straight") who became physically violent in Newark, New Jersey. Most of the women sustained injuries, and the harasser was hospitalized from a knife wound. Despite video footage showing that the women were attacked and male bystanders intervened to help them, all but one of the women were convicted and imprisoned. Many believe they were so harshly punished for simply acting in self-defense because they were queer women of color.[63] A 2014 award-winning film *Out in the Night* details their case.

Law Enforcement Agents Do Not Care or Are Harassers: One of the biggest barriers to utilizing laws is that law enforcement agents (from police officers to judges) often do not care to enforce them and they themselves may be harassers. Take a 42-year-old judge who resigned after being accused of harassing a woman on the subway in Korea;[64] the two teenage sisters in Madhya Pradesh, India, who committed suicide after two police officers harassed and assaulted them;[65] and the nearly two-fifths of young women in a survey of 911 New York City teenagers who said that during the past 12 months, "male police officers had flirted, whistled or 'come on to them.' "[66]

Women for a Change, Cameroon founder Zoneziwoh Mbondgulo wrote for the SSH blog about seeing a young woman bullied at the Molyko Junction by two police officers because she wore a short, long-sleeved gown. Mbondgulo was angry:

I went to the police station and asked the officer on duty to show me where exactly in the law it is mentioned that girls should not dress in short clothing and what parameters or what measurement tape do they use to measure what is "short" and what is not. This was the third time I had gone to this police station asking about this mystery clothing law which says what girls/women must and must not wear short clothing in public. The first time I went there, they were not able to show me the document. They referred me to Court. The following day, I went to Court, and there I was referred to the governor's office. And so on. To this date, no office has provided me with any of the documents they claim exist.

It's not just women who are policed. Recently, a young man brought a complaint to my organization. He was on his way home one hot afternoon when a police officer stopped him, bullied him, and dragged him on the unpaved road to a nearby bar in the quarters, asking him to confess that he was gay. This was simply because he had dressed in short demi-jean and had long painted finger nails and shaped eyebrows. There is enough street harassment in my community without police officers doing it, too. Police officers should be security providers, not perpetrators of harassment.[67]

Poor responses by police officers are further evidenced in stories submitted to the SSH blog: "There are a bunch of dudes in my neighborhood who are always street harassing me; yesterday it was worse," wrote Chloe Saavedra. "I was jogging, wearing spandex and my jogging bra, and one guy threw a dollar bill at me and they laughed. I tried to report this at my precinct and the [New York City] police said, verbatim, 'I'd like it if someone threw money at me' and laughed and made fun of the situation.[68]

After Sophie Calas was grabbed, harassed and assaulted by a man at a bar in London, she reported it to the bar's bouncer and a police officer.

She wrote, "I told one of the policeman exactly what happened, and he suggest that as my friend and I are 'both pretty girls' we pretty much had to expect this sort of thing."[69]

In Roanoke, Virginia, Logan Lambert was involved in a fender bender on an interstate, and the police officer asked her and the other driver to move to a gas station. As they all pulled into the gas station, four men in a truck leered at her. One of them made lewd gestures and as they drove off, one yelled, "Hey baby, I want you to choke on my dick!" She looked at the police officer who witnessed it all and asked if he was going to do anything. "He just laughed and said he had to fill out too much paperwork because of the wreck."[70]

P.M was on her way home from a party in France with two female friends when two cars stopped and the drivers "began to call us disgusting names and asked us if we wanted to have sex with them." The men followed them, and the women ran, seeking help from a police officer. The officers checked the men's licenses but then told P.M. and her friends the men "just wanted to 'flirt' and that they saw no reason for further actions against them."[71]

It is not that surprising that these are the attitudes of many police officers. First, most police officers are men. Second, some of them are violent and will not see harassment or violence as a big deal. In the United States, for example, in families of police officers, domestic violence, from stalking and harassment to sexual assault and homicide, is up to four times more likely than in the general population. Cases are under-reported, and when they are reported, officers are rarely fired, arrested, or referred for prosecution.[72] Third, it is very easy for officers to abuse their power and face almost no consequences. In England, for example, the *Guardian* wrote about 56 documented cases from 2008 to 2012 where members of law enforcement abused their positions of power to "rape, sexually assault, harass, groom, and have inappropriate relationships with vulnerable women and young girls, or have been investigated over such allegations."[73]

Police officers in the United States are not only primarily men, but also primarily white and cis-gender. Persons of color and transgender people are other demographics who face high rates of harassment, assault, and murder by police officers with police rarely facing consequences for their actions and brutality. A study by the National Coalition of Anti-Violence Programs that drew on data collected from 15 anti-violence programs in 16 states found that transgender people across the United States experience three times as much police violence as non-transgender individuals. Transgender persons of color experience it at even higher rates. Nearly half were mistreated when seeking help after experiencing hate crimes.

Overall, among LGBTQ-identified people, 48 percent reported incidents of police misconduct.[74]

It is easy to understand why few people decide to report incidents of harassment, sexual assault, and hate crimes given how many police officers do not help, and even hurt, those who seek assistance. Indeed, some of the most common reasons people give for not going to the police include fear that the police will not believe or help them; will engage in victim blaming; will further harass them; will deport them (if they are undocumented immigrants); or will arrest them (if they were engaged in something illegal, like sex work, at the time). Some people may also feel that their communities are already over-policed and fear that the treatment a harasser will face from police or the justice system will be disproportionate to his or her offense.

In other regions, the fact that all police officers are male is enough to deter women from making reports. Police in the Indian state of Odisha launched an innovative method for combating this challenge. In 2014, they created an ATM machine to encourage more reports of sexual abuse by eliminating the practical barrier women face of having to enter an all-male police station. To make a report on the ATM that sits outside a bank, a person clicks on the type of crime she is reporting and then provides further details by typing on the screen, scanning in a written report, or creating an oral report. The complaint is sent to the police station, and the person receives a slip of paper with a number to help her track progress of her case. People can make reports at any time of day. During the year since it was introduced in January 2014, there have been an average of five reports made daily, with harassment the most commonly cited crime. The process seems to work swiftly. One woman interviewed for *The Star* newspaper said that just two days after she filed a complaint against her abusive husband the police came to arrest him.[75]

More creative efforts like this are needed as are more female police officers and officers from marginalized communities, sensitivity trainings, processes to prevent police officers from abusing their power, and methods for better ensuring that police enforce existing laws properly.

OTHER GOVERNMENT RESPONSES

In addition to gender mainstreaming and urban planning efforts and partnering with activists and international entities on Safety Audits and campaigns, there are a few other successful tactics local governments have taken to address street harassment. These examples are from the United Kingdom and the United States.

United Kingdom: Some of the most exciting initiatives in the United Kingdom are government-funded anti-harassment public service announcements (PSAs). In Wales, the Welsh government sponsored a 2010 campaign called One Step Too Far with a website and video PSA showing the connection between sexist and harassing behavior and sexual assault. "The campaign asks individuals to re-assess the impacts of their own behaviour and that of their peers. . . . Sexism falls within a continuum of harm, a slippery slope of ever-worsening behaviours that moves women further and further from where they're entitled to be. Physical violence towards women, sometimes resulting in death, is where that slippery slope ends. Which is why we must all challenge these attitudes."[76] The PSA had hidden-camera footage of street harassment and interviews with harassed women saying how it impacted them. The website—now inactive—listed resources and a discussion board. The PSA aired during the 2010 World Cup.[77]

That same year, with funding from the Scottish government, Rape Crisis Scotland launched a television advertisement and online campaign called Not Ever, focused on ending the prevalent attitude that rape victims are to blame for their perpetrator's crime because of what they were wearing. In the ad, men at a pub look at a woman's skirt and decide that she is "asking for it." The ad then shows the woman earlier in the day shopping for the skirt and saying to the store clerk that she is looking for one that will make men want to rape her. Then she turns to the camera and says, "As if." The ad emphasized this message: "*No woman asks to be raped—ever*. It's as simple as that. Women should not be held responsible for the behaviour of rapists or expected to base their decisions on dress around the possibility that these might lead to an attack." This ad also aired during the World Cup. The website has information on the rape law, quiz questions, and discussion threads.[78]

United States: In the United States, city council hearings have been one way for government and community members to work together. The first city council hearing on street harassment ever held in the world took place in New York City on October 28, 2010. It was organized by the Committee on Women's Issues, which was chaired by council member Julissa Ferreras. She decided to hold it after she read an op-ed about street harassment written by journalist Elizabeth Mendez-Berry in *El Diario* that was inspired by the release of the 2010 *Stop Street Harassment* book. Ferreras couldn't believe harassment was still happening; she remembered being harassed going to and from school. She asked students in her district if they faced harassment, and the girls said yes.

Council member Ferreras decided to call a hearing. Many of her male colleagues tried to dissuade her because they didn't understand the importance of the issue. In a press release, she said, "I hope that this hearing will begin to cast light on this depraved practice and that women and girls will no longer have to adopt a veil of caution when they want to do something as basic as walk down the street."[79] Ferreras's briefing paper for the hearing noted, "Societal attitudes will not be changed without first acknowledging that there is in fact a problem. Today, the committee will start that discussion."[80]

Eighteen women and men—activists, writers, and members of the public—testified about how pervasive the problem of street harassment is in the lives of the girls and women they work with and, for many who testified, in their own lives.* I was invited to open the testimonies and Mendez-Berry spoke as well. Those giving testimony were diverse in age, race, and gender. We each offered suggestions for change and asked the council to take action. By the end of the hearing, Ferreras said the council would. Numerous media outlets were present, which resulted in more than 200 media hits. Since then, Ferreras and other members of the city council have participated in anti-street harassment initiatives, like speaking at International Anti-Street Harassment Week rallies, co-hosting a Safety Audit, and providing funding for the Hollaback! phone app to map reports in New York City. Additionally, in 2011 Manhattan Borough President Scott Stringer took an interest in the topic and spoke out against street harassment, and in 2013, Mayor-elect Bill de Blasio included street harassment in his vision for improving New York City.[81] City council hearings have also been held in Philadelphia (2013), and Kansas City, Missouri (2014).

Government efforts are most effective when they are informed by and run in collaboration with advocacy groups. Initiatives like multi-layered transit campaigns, city council hearings, and campaigns targeting would-be harassers seem to have the potential to do more to stop street harassment in the long run than sex-segregation and ineffective laws. If they want to, local and national government can have a big role to play in addressing and ending street harassment; leaders just need to be smart, strategic, and collaborative in their approach.

---

* You can find most of the testimonies in either audio or print form on the SSH website.

Chapter 7

Egypt and India Case Studies

Men getting ready for the security patrol in Talaat Harb Square, Cairo, during Eid, August 2014. (Nihal Saad Zaghloul)

Severe incidents of street harassment and other forms of sexual violence in public spaces in Egypt and India brought the most international attention to these issues between 2010 and 2015. This section looks at what happened, the public's reaction, and how the combined media attention, on-the-ground efforts of groups and organizations, and public outcry led to concrete changes.

MOB ASSAULTS IN EGYPT RESULT IN
LIMITED GOVERNMENT RESPONSE

On January 25, 2011, Egyptians launched an uprising and revolution to overthrow the 30-year dictatorship of President Hosni Mubarak. They took to the streets and protested daily at Tahrir Square. During the 18 days between January 25 and February 11, the date of the fall of Mubarak, the anti-harassment organization HarassMap received only eight reports of street harassment. In contrast, in the 18 previous days, there were 82 reported cases.[1] On Twitter, many women noted the absence of sexual harassment at Tahrir Square during the political protests.[2]

The reduction in harassment was unusual since street harassment has been a documented problem in Egypt for several years. A 2008 study by the Egyptian Centre for Women's Rights showed more than 80 percent of women had experienced harassment, and more than 60 percent of Egyptian men openly admitted to harassing women.[3] There are numerous video clips and eye- witness reports of male mobs committing mass harassment and sexual attacks on women during Eid holiday celebrations since at least 2006.[4]

Reflecting on the unprecedented low number of reports, HarassMap co-founder Rebecca Chiao said in a speech, "The difference between the low harassment time and now was community engagement. There was no new law, no new police presence; there was no change in women's dress. There was no change except in community engagement . . . people like you and me stopped ignoring harassment and would not stay silent."[5]

This peace abruptly came to an end on February 11. CBS News correspondent Lara Logan was sexually assaulted by a mob of at least 200 men during a 25-minute period while she reported from Tahrir Square on the fall of Hosni Mubarak's government. Months later on a 60 *Minutes* segment, Logan described how she was torn away from her news crew by the mob. Men ripped apart her clothing, raped her with their hands, beat her with flagpoles and sticks, and videotaped it all with their cell phone cameras. She said they also pulled at her hair, "literally trying to tear my scalp off my skull." She was sure they would kill her.[6]

When the mob dragged her near a group of Egyptian women, the women saved her. "The women kind of closed ranks around me," she said.

Around that same time, her news team and soldiers were able to fight through and carry her to safety. She was flown directly back to the United States, where she had to be hospitalized for four days. There were no arrests made, and no police cases were filed against her unknown assailants.[7]

This marked the start of numerous instances of intense harassment and mob attacks on women in public spaces. These violent outbreaks mostly occurred during protests at Tahrir Square and took place during the rule of three different groups: the Egyptian military's Supreme Council of the Armed Forces from February 2011 to June 2012, the elected Muslim Brotherhood-led regime of Mohamed Morsi from June 2012 to June 2013, the return to military rule from June 2013 to June 2014, and then during the inauguration of President Abdel-Fattah el-Sisi, the former defense minister, in June 2014.

Overall, from February 2011 to June 2014, mob attacks routinely occurred during the January 25 anniversary protests. On January 25, 2013, for example, at least 25 women were sexually assaulted by mobs in the square who their used hands and objects like knives to violate them.[8] Some of the worst times for attacks were during political transitions. For instance, an Associated Press reporter witnessed nearly 200 men attack one woman during the June 2012 protests marking a regime change.[9] Across the next regime change, between June 30 and July 3, 2013, nearly 100 women were subjected to mob attacks. On July 3 alone, the night when Egypt's army chief announced the forced departure of Morsi, groups of men attacked more than 80 women.[10] In June 2014, when thousands of people gathered at Tahrir Square to celebrate the election of President el-Sisi, there were at least nine mob attacks on women.[11] These stories were regularly covered in the news and sparked outrage locally and internationally.

But when women and their male allies organized protests against mob attacks at various times between February 2011 and June 2014, men often attacked them to try to silence them. For example, on International Women's Day, March 8, 2011, Egyptian feminist activists called for a million woman march in Tahrir Square to demand "fair and equal opportunity for all Egyptian citizens—beyond gender, religion, or class." Close to 1,000 women and their male allies turned out and marched through Tahrir Square in support of "equality and an end to sexual harassment." Before long, groups of male counter-protesters disrupted the gathering. They shouted: "Men are men, and women are women, and that will never change. Go home; that's where you belong." They also called the women whores and the men faggots. They soon grew bolder and chased the protesters out of the square.[12]

As another example, in mid-June 2012, 50 women and their male allies took to Tahrir Square to march in protest of the mob sexual assaults, but soon after they arrived, men harassed them and swiftly escalated to groping the female participants. The marchers disbursed and fled the area to ensure their safety. Ahmed Hawary, a participant in the march, said in an ABC News interview afterward that he chose to participate because a close female friend was attacked by a mob of men in Tahrir Square on January 25, 2012. She suffered a nervous breakdown and moved from the city. "Women activists are at the core of the revolution," Hawary said. "They are the courage of this movement. If you break them, you break the spirit of the revolution."[13] This might have been precisely the goal.

When I interviewed Sally Zohney, an organizer of that same march, she told me she believed "that the attacks [on women] are systematic and fueled by unknown organized groups" though she was uncertain whether it was by the military regime or others. She saw the assaults as "an attempt to discourage protests by intimidating revolutionaries and painting them in a bad light" and that "many women have avoided Tahrir Square, losing the opportunity to be full participants in the political process."[14]

It turned out that many of the mob attacks were orchestrated to keep women out of the political process and to try to quell the protests, period. A documentary video segment for *Unreported World*, a British television program released at the end of 2012, showed men who said they were paid by sources unknown to them (but likely military leaders) to sexually assault women during protest rallies at Tahrir Square. Some even candidly described using a tactic dubbed "the circle of hell" to achieve their goal. This is when men find a woman alone, form a circle around her, and work together to take off her clothes and assault her.[15]

Instead of helping make Tahrir Square safer for everyone, some military police were directly involved in perpetrating violence against women, particularly during 2011. That year, at least a dozen women protesters were forced to undertake "virginity tests" (a form of sexual assault and torture) by the Supreme Council of the Armed Forces.[16] In November 2011, Egyptian journalist Mona El-Tahawy alleged she was beaten and sexually assaulted by police officers after she was arrested at Tahrir Square. She shared what happened later on Twitter: "@monaeltahawy: 5 or 6 surrounded me, groped and prodded my breasts, grabbed my genital area and I lost count how many hands tried to get into my trousers."[17] In December 2011, military police officers in riot gear swarmed Tahrir Square and beat anyone they could catch. Some of them stripped female demonstrators, tearing off headscarves and clothing. The most publicized incident was one caught on camera: a half-dozen soldiers with batons beat and dragged a woman and tore off her *abaya* (cloak) to reveal a blue bra. They also beat her friend who tried to intervene. After the video and photos of that beating went viral, thousands of outraged Egyptian women marched through the streets demanding safety for women and respect for women in what historians called the largest women's demonstration in nearly 100 years.[18]

First Individuals and Then the Government Responds

With an unstable government, the low prioritization of women's rights and women's safety, and some military police perpetrating or sponsoring attacks, it is not surprising—but still disheartening—that the government did almost nothing to crack down on the assaults until 2014. Individuals took it upon themselves to do something instead. After being attacked by a group of men at Tahrir Square in June 2012, Nihal Saad Zaghloul, for example, founded the group Bassma (Imprint). She and volunteers patrol public spaces wearing neon orange and yellow high visibility jackets, talking to and shaming perpetrators, and forming human chains around attacked women to protect them. While they were most active during political protests, they continue to patrol anytime there are large group gatherings, such as during holidays. Bassma's 40 volunteers halted at least 15 incidents of mob harassment during one of their first big patrols, the October 2012 Eid Al-Adha holiday celebrations.[19]

During fall 2012, a few other groups emerged to address mob attacks. Tahrir Bodyguard and Operation Anti-Sexual Harassment were among the most visible. They both encouraged people in crowds to report attacks, and the groups' volunteers, wearing yellow reflective vests, would enter crowds and encircle women to pull them to safety. They also patrolled crowded sites to look for incidents. Due to safety concerns, men comprise most of the volunteers who patrol while women volunteers assist the rescued women. As word spread about their services, people called these groups for help. During the late June and early July 2013 protests, for instance, Operation Anti-Sexual Harassment received 168 incident reports and was able to rescue the victims of 105 of them.[20]

In the fall of 2012, the group I Saw Harassment formed. It conducts community and campus workshops, provides legal and psychological support to victims, and documents and intervenes in cases of harassment. The group's intervention efforts have been prominent during religious holidays. For example, volunteers patrolled during the four-day Eid al-Fitr holiday in 2013 and handled 65 cases of harassment. They assisted with 17 reported cases of harassment over the 2014 Easter holiday. In contrast to the other patrol groups, this group often has a majority of women volunteers (for example, 63 percent female volunteers for the 2014 Eid al-Fitr patrolling).[21]

Nearly two years after these volunteer patrol groups formed to try to keep women safe, the government finally addressed the issue in a concrete way in June 2014. During the celebration of the election of President el-Sisi that month, there were, as usual, several mob attacks on women, but a bystander recorded one on a mobile phone. In it, men are seen stripping a woman naked, covering her in welts, and pushing, pulling, and groping her. After she was rescued, she was so badly injured that she was hospitalized.[22] The video documenting her attack went viral and prompted el-Sisi to make a publicized visit to her hospital room with flowers and an apology. He said "the incident had shamed the nation."[23] El-Sisi immediately formed a committee tasked with addressing sexual violence. Seven of the 13 men who assaulted the woman were arrested and referred to trial under unusually fast procedures.[24]

Then, quite swiftly, before el-Sisi was sworn into office, Interim President Adly Mansour, a Supreme Constitutional Court judge chosen by el-Sisi to lead the country after Morsi's ejection, approved an anti-harassment law drafted by the interim cabinet. Previously, there had been three different laws under which some forms of street harassment could be categorized. This amended law defined a harasser as anyone who "accosts others in a public or private place through following or stalking them, using gestures or words or through modern means of communication or in any other means through actions that carry sexual or pornographic hints." There is a minimum six-month jail term for convicted offenders.[25]

While certainly the law has been a step forward, its utility has been limited. It requires harassment to be conditional on stalking or following, so if a man makes a comment in passing without also following the woman, it is legal. The law sets burdensome standards for proving harassment such as bringing the harasser to the police or waiting with the harasser until the police arrive. Victims also have to prove that the harasser was motivated by sexual desire and fulfillment. Further, according to Egypt's rape law, rape is defined as only nonconsensual penile penetration of a woman's vagina, which excludes male victims and the most common violations against women during mob attacks: men using their hands or objects to violate women. Two Egyptian organizations, Nazra for Feminist Studies and the Nadeem Center for the Rehabilitation of Victims of Torture, proposed ways to bring Egypt's laws up to international rights standards, but they were ignored.[26]

Still, a few groups voiced cautious optimism. U.N. in Egypt, which is a U.N. Safe Cities Global Initiative site that has undertaken surveying, Safety Audits, and more, issued a statement of support. "The amendment is very encouraging as it defines 'sexual harassment' for the first time in Egypt's history. This law represents a major step toward achieving safety of Egyptian women and girls in public spaces. This law is a concrete result of combined efforts by the Egyptian Government together with civil society and U.N. agencies." The group also urged the law's enforcement.[27] Azza Kamel, the director of I Saw Harassment, said in an interview for *Daily News Egypt*, "The new law brought about a notable increase in awareness about the sexual harassment issue and has encouraged people to report harassment incidents."[28]

HarassMap co-founder Chiao and volunteer Angie Abdelmonem told me during an interview that they feel mixed about the law: "We do applaud increased efforts at creating a safer environment for all individuals in public places. HarassMap's position is that, while new laws are necessary and important to changing the overall structure of gender violence in the country, they do not necessarily change public attitudes. A great deal of work, at multiple levels, is still needed to get people to see sexual harassment as a crime."[29] Absolutely, there is no single way to solve this problem, so it does require all sectors of society to be involved.

The Egyptian government recognized that, too, and, as another step in the right direction, some police officers, primarily women, began receiving training to handle sexual violence reports. They patrolled during Eid Al-Adha celebrations to try to prevent and stop harassment, and they launched a new hotline for reporting incidents. But these efforts, too, are imperfect. "The physical ability of individuals to enter the ministry and access this unit is prohibitive. There are a number of checkpoints that individuals must pass through once inside the ministry," HarassMap volunteer Abdelmon told me. "Also, there has been some public skepticism that people will make use of a hotline while being harassed. Moreover, the need to produce the harasser in order to file a report has similarly created difficulties in allowing the process to move forward."[30]

Harassment and other forms of sexual violence by some police officers pose more problems. There were several publicized incidents of police misconduct at the end of 2014 alone. In November 2014, a woman accused a policeman of beating and detaining her as she was trying to report a sexual harassment complaint against him.[31] In December 2014, two police officers ordered a woman sitting in a car with a man to get out. They drove her to an isolated area and sexually assaulted her. The group I Saw Harassment issued a report in December 2014 about the number of sexual harassment cases 100 days into el-Sisi's term. The list included police officers and law administrators as some of the assailants, including a police officer who raped a university student in his car just five days before the report was released.[32] Samer Fawzy Aziz, an anti-street harassment activist, told me that both the law and new police training are of "limited value and we can't see [their] influence in the streets except in a few occasions." In particular, he feels the law needs revising and more publicizing to the general public. Plus, there must be increased account-ability of police since "we still hear about individual violations that happen from time to time [by] police."[33]

Compared to 2011–2013 when the government did nothing about mob attacks, this amended law and other efforts are important signifiers of progress. And both Chiao and Abdelmonem said they have seen a shift in people's awareness of the issue and more recognition that it needs to be addressed. "The issue is far less taboo in conversation and in the media [compared to a few years ago],"[34] they told me. This is also in large part due to the work of their organization and others. When I wrote about efforts to address street harassment in Egypt in my 2010 book *Stop Street Harassment: Making Public Places Safe and Welcoming for Women*, the Egyptian Centre for Women's Rights was the lone group I found to be working on the issue. Today, there are more than one dozen groups and organizations addressing street harassment, and the topic is regularly in the news and discussed on social media platforms like Twitter.

The Egyptian government needs to continue along the trajectory it began and do even more to address sexual violence in public spaces along-side activists, agencies, and ordinary citizens. Women in Egypt will never achieve equality in political participation or public life without coordi-nated and concerted efforts from every level of society.

OUTRAGE OVER DELHI GANG RAPE LEADS TO COLLABORATIONS IN INDIA

"I want to live," said Braveheart to her mother and brother.[35]

"Braveheart," one of the nicknames given to 23-year-old college stu-dent Jyoti Singh Pandey, was in an intensive care unit after six men brutally gang raped and attacked her on a moving bus in Delhi, India, in December 2012. They targeted her because she was traveling alone with a male friend to whom she was not married or related. The men harassed her at first to punish her, and when her friend stood up to them, they assaulted him and took her to the back of the bus and raped and beat her. More than an hour later, the men threw them, both unconscious, off the bus. A passerby found them and called for help. Soon, Pandey was transported to a hospital in Singapore for a multi-organ transplant because she was suffering from brain injuries and lung and abdomen infections. Candlelight vigils took place outside her hospital.[36]

Her wish, her hope to live, made the news of her death 13 days later that much harder. But in a city where rape—a vastly under-reported crime— is reported every 18 hours[37] and in a country where there were more than

24,000 reported rape cases in 2011,[38] her ordeal is not unusual. Further, research conducted by U.N. Women in 2012 found that 9 out of 10 women in Delhi had experienced some form of sexual violence in their lifetimes, and 6 in 10 had faced it in the previous six months. Nearly 73 percent of women said they feel unsafe in public spaces. Half of men surveyed said they had harassed or physically hurt women and girls in public spaces.[39]

The fact that Pandey died is not that unusual, either. On a weekly basis around that time, there were news stories about Indian women murdered by harassers or, more often, Indian women who killed themselves after being harassed, groped, or raped by men. Within weeks of Pandey's death, a 16-year-old girl committed suicide after a man tried to hold her against her will on her way home from school.[40] A 17-year-old girl set herself on fire and died from the burns after a boy in the area repeatedly harassed her.[41] Another 17-year-old girl killed herself after she was allegedly gang raped and then pressured by police to drop the case and marry one of her attackers.[42]

It's also not unusual that Pandey's male friend was assaulted for standing up for her. Within weeks of the attack on Pandey and her friend, young men attacked a father after he told them to stop harassing and following his daughter.[43] A 30-year-old man stood up to young men he observed street harassing girls, and in retaliation, they stabbed him to death.[44] A 20-year-old man confronted a group of boys who were harassing his female friend, and they stabbed him to death.[45]

What *is* unusual about Pandey's story is the outcry her rape, her fight to live, and then her death sparked. Every day for days after her case became public, hundreds and then thousands of people marched, protested, and held vigils in Delhi and in other cities across India.[46] Even when police prohibited gatherings of more than five people, protestors would not be deterred and stood up to water cannons and attacks.[47] After Pandey's death, even more marches took place day after day, mostly led by young people, both women and men.

Various activist organizations commented on why this particular story struck a nerve. Amitabh Kumar, a leader of the campaign I Stand for Safe Delhi, told me he thought it was because "young India is sick of the hypocritical approach of blaming the victim. . . . This time we were not going to let this happen." He continued, referring to the spontaneous nature of the demonstrations, "Also, there was no 'leader,' hence the common girls and boys felt empowered to speak out loud, to stand against this injustice."[48] Radhika, digital media strategist at the international non-profit organization Breakthrough, said, "[She] was our age, you see. She went to see a movie with a male friend at the cinema, the one that every young person in Delhi has visited at some point in their lives. . . . Young people in Delhi and around the country stood up because they saw themselves, or someone they loved, in her."[49]

The public outcry led officials to speed up the trial of the alleged assailants.[50] It also resulted in meetings between anti-violence groups and the police and government officials to discuss proposed measures for change, including fast-trackinging all future sexual violence cases through the court system.[51] The unprecedented outrage by the public and swift responses by government leaders and police made many people optimistic that this would be a turning point for efforts to prevent gender violence. Kumar said, "This is a milestone for [the] women's movement in India as it has reached the hearts of many."[52] He felt the circumstances of the case sensitized the general public to rape and challenged victim blaming in a significant way. Mallika Dut, the president of Breakthrough, said, "I hope this moment will mark India's transition as a country that is the worst place for women to one which led the charge for serious recognition for women's human rights the world over."[53]

Before the attack and death of Pandey, there were several groups like Breakthrough and I Stand for Safe Delhi working to address street harassment and assault in India. Two others, Jagori and Blank Noise, are among the most well known. Jagori was founded in 1984 to conduct feminist research, support women's leadership initiatives, facilitate networking for feminist movement building, and provide support services for women survivors of violence. In 2009, it launched a Safe City Free of Violence Against Women and Girls initiative in partnership with U.N. Women and the Department of Women and Child Development. From 2009 to 2011, Jagori was also part of the U.N. Trust Fund and Women in Cities International's four-country study called the Gender Inclusive Cities Programme. The group conducts Safety Audits and focus groups, runs a helpline, holds marches, and posts flyers around issues like street harassment.[54] In 2010, Jagori co-hosted the Third International Conference on Women's Safety with Women in Cities International in Delhi. Blank Noise is a volunteer-run group with chapters across India that was started by Jasmeen Patheja in Bangalore in August 2003 as a student project. Blank Noise volunteers across India work to trigger dialogue around street harassment with public demonstrations, art, and campaigns. Volunteers encourage people to be "Action Heroes" by doing something about harassment.[55] After the horrific incident, both groups joined thousands of others in taking action.

Activists and Governments Take Action

The first few months after the attacks saw a flurry of activity from activist groups and ordinary people. Starting January 1, Blank Noise hosted a #SafeCityPledge initiative encouraging people to say what they personally would do to make public places safer. For example, "I pledge to speak up every time I face harassment," and "I pledge to intervene when I see any woman being harassed."[56] Thousands of women marched in Delhi on January 2 to call for an end to sexual violence.[57] More than 100 men in their twenties wearing skirts gathered in Bengaluru in mid-January to challenge victim blaming of women. They said, "I promise that I will be sensitive to gender issues in the way I speak and act. I promise not to be passive. I will step in if I hear offensive speech or views."[58] Blank Noise held a 24-hour Tweet Chat on January 19 and several offline events where people stood in public places holding signs with their pledges.[59] A number of new websites launched around January to encourage women to share their harassment stories, including www.safe city.in, which later turned into an organization named Safe City that holds trainings and workshops on sexual harassment in schools and for corporations across India.

More initiatives occurred in the spring. On March 8, 2013, Breakthrough held a #RingTheBell Tweet Chat about preventing sexual violence.[60] In March 2013, a group of male bikers issued public apologies to "Delhi women" on behalf of "Delhi men."[61] In April, the smartphone safety app Circle of 6 launched a Delhi version.[62]

Thanks to the work of groups like Jagori, the Indian government had already taken a few actions to address street harassment and violence. Notably, in November 2012, a month before the Delhi gang rape, India's Supreme Court acknowledged that sexual harassment is a rampant problem, especially on the streets and on public transportation, and one that negatively impacts the lives of the harassed persons. They issued a countrywide standard for addressing the problem.[63] After the Delhi gang rape, more government leaders were open to and interested in addressing the issue. In Delhi, Jagori held both a local and a regional meeting with police officers during which academics, lawyers, activists, and community members gave their suggestions for what police should do to better address street harassment and sexual assault. Some of these suggestions included: (1) more police night patrols; (2) more investigation of bus drivers and their assistants; (3) banning buses with tinted windows or curtains; (4) posting photos, names, and addresses of convicted rapists on an official website; (5) setting up a committee to speed up trials of sexual assault; (6) sensitization training for the police force; (7) crime mapping in the city; and (8) more female police officers.[64] Anupriya Gosh, the program manager for Jagori's Safer Cities initiative, told me that the first meeting was also the first one ever "where women representatives were part of the police meeting at the local level. It was exciting to see how [local] women, with just a little information and support, [could] demand and claim rights."[65]

The government acted swiftly to implement some of these suggestions. The Delhi police force created a women's help desk in most of the city's 160 police stations, and it began conducting gender sensitization classes for the officers and constables. The Delhi Transport Corporation started holding gender classes for its bus drivers and added GPS systems to the buses to make them easier to monitor and locate.[66] In 2013, police in Delhi began conducting "surprise raids" on public transportation routes to look for harassment.[67] There are now "fast-track courts" to deal with sex crimes as well as "one-stop rape centres" where victims can report the crime and receive medical and psychological support.[68]

The city government of Delhi also established a helpline, and Jagori trained the 17 members of its all-female staff. The government-designated three-digit emergency hotline 181 received more than 138,000 calls in its first six months and continues to receive 250 calls per day on average. The staff members told the *Washington Post* that this was "stark evidence of a newfound courage among Indian women to report crimes that they might have suffered silently just months ago."[69] However, coordinating with police to help callers has been a challenge. For example, when a woman called in to say a group of men were threatening her, the helpline staff members could hear the men, but they could not get the police to track the caller's location in time. Sadly, when they did find her, it was too late. The men had raped and murdered her.[70] Another challenge is that there are already other helplines run directly by police, so there can be confusion about which line people should call for help.[71]

In March 2013, India's Parliament passed a comprehensive bill with almost unprecedented speed that imposed stronger penalties on men who sexually assault women and criminalized offenses like stalking and voyeurism. It expanded the definition of rape, increased the penalty for gang rape, and introduced the death penalty for repeat offenders. A three-member panel that spoke with hundreds of activists and reviewed laws in other countries wrote the law. While many were encouraged by the bill, others, like Sandhya Valluripally, president of the Progressive Organization of Women, felt it fell short. She said in a *New York Times* interview that women's organizations had been advocating for years for a more comprehensive bill, one that also included street harassment. Further, many groups against the death penalty were disappointed that it was included as a possible punishment.[72]

While these were extremely important steps by the government, it will take time to truly reduce incidents of harassment and rape. For example, the December 2014 alleged rape of a woman by an Uber taxi driver almost exactly two years after the Delhi gang rape was widely publicized and sparked outrage. Kamala Bhasin, a prominent feminist who founded Jagori, voiced her thoughts in an interview for Reuters at the two year anniversary: "Laws have become better; there is greater public consciousness, but we need to do much more in terms of addressing the question of why men are doing this and what can be done to stop them behaving like this."[73] Another problem is that many people still do not feel safe seeking help from the police, in part because sometimes police are incompetent or cover up crimes.

On the upside, U.N. Women and Jagori have had more success working with the Delhi government than ever before. In November 2014, U.N. Women Executive Director Phumzile Mlambo-Ngcuka met with the Delhi team members, and they told her about "conducting extensive Safety Audits, spreading awareness, and advocating with authorities for better lighting and pavements."[74] For example, the Ministry of Urban Development used their recommendations to expand the street lighting infrastructure. The Delhi government has adopted the Safety Audit methodology to allow women to have a voice in city planning efforts. "The program has really helped to make women an equal partner in ensuring their safety . . . women are now able to speak of their experiences directly to the police and tell us what is needed to be done,"[75] said Suman Nalwa, additional district commissioner of police, special police unit for women and children, in a U.N. Women article.

During a World Bank interview, Kalpana Vishwanath, who works at Jagori, talked about the improvements she has witnessed. "We began talking about the issues of gender in urban planning in 2005, and today, 10 years later, the government is accepting its importance," Vishwanath said. "In the early days, it was an uphill task to even convince the government that there was any gender dimension to urban planning, design, and governance."[76] Promising. Progress is possible.

News stories spurring public outrage combined with the efforts of established organizations like HarassMap, Jagori, and U.N. Women and new groups like Bassma have helped make street harassment and assault more visible problems that require immediate attention in Egypt and India. Male-led governments with other priorities slow progress and create barriers, as was most clearly evident in Egypt. But public attention, pressure, and response can lower the barriers. Hopefully, the only way to go is forward so that one day Egypt and India will be countries where women and men can ride buses and engage in public dialogue in Tahrir Square together without fearing for their safety or their lives.

Chapter 8

What Comes Next?

Elisabeth Irwin High School junior Shana Fletcher reads her article about street harassment in the 2014 International Day of the Girl assembly in New York City, USA. (Alexandra Clinton)

Not long ago, it felt like an unrealistic dream to believe that street harassment would cease to be viewed as normal, but that dream seems more realistic every day. This is thanks to the tens of thousands of people worldwide who have bravely spoken up and spoken out, the groups that have marched and rallied for safe streets, the international organizations that have used their network connections and resources to advocate for safe cities, the journalists who have centered the issue in headline news stories, and the local and national governments that have taken steps toward ending harassment. In city after city, in country after country, there are now concerted and collaborative efforts to document street harassment, recognize it as a human rights violation, and work to end it.

After taking time to savor and celebrate this progress, the next question is, where do we go from here? Street harassment is a complex and pervasive problem, and ending it requires multi-faceted and multi-layered approaches. We must have entire segments of communities and countries dedicated to thinking about and addressing it in collaborative and strategic ways to truly see change. First, we can move forward with the burgeoning efforts under way. We need to continue to see:

- Research, including more studies to track the prevalence of street harassment in different regions, the types of harassment, who is impacted the most, how specific people and communities are affected, why it happens, and what efforts can stop it. We need government agencies and law enforcement to issue annual reports detailing the recorded number of harassment and sexual violence incidents they receive.
- Stories, both storytelling and story-listening. Currently, certain people's stories are shared and heard the most (namely, young, white, heterosexual, educated, and able-bodied women), and that needs to change. We need privileged people to listen to the stories of people in marginalized communities to better understand their unique street harassment experiences, how harassment impacts them, and their ideas for addressing harassment in their communities in an appropriate and effective manner. Those with the means to do so can create pathways and support systems for other voices to be heard.
- Safety Audits across various regions to empower residents to evaluate their communities and decide what structural changes could be made to reduce the likelihood of harassment and assault. The findings can influence public policy and community planning.
- Awareness-raising events, efforts, and campaigns, particularly ones led by individuals directly affected by street harassment. These can reach community members at a one-on-one level and provide an important outlet for harassed persons after the disempowering experience of being harassed.
- International entities addressing street harassment, like the United Nations, ActionAid, the Huairou Commission, PLAN International, the World Bank,

the World Economic Forum, and more. We need them to continue their commitment to the issue by using their resources and influence to work with affected individuals on campaigns and then to share their findings, recommendations, and best practices with the public.

- Media coverage that portrays street harassment as a serious social ill, not as a compliment or the fault of the harassed person.
- Public service announcements and advertisements, on public transportation systems, billboards, television, and in movie theaters. And not just ads that tell victims to seek help, but also ads that encourage witnesses to do something and would-be harassers to respect others. Overall messages are useful, too, such as the "If it's unwanted, it's harassment" message on 2015 transit ads in Washington, D.C.
- Collaborations between government agencies, NGOs, activist groups, and community members to:
  - Hold city council hearings, community forums, and anti-harassment campaigns.
  - Ensure urban planning and public services are accessible and useful to women and other marginalized groups and do not inadvertently foster or facilitate harassment or assault.
  - Draft anti-harassment policies and create anti-harassment trainings for law enforcement members, transit workers, and other public service providers.
- Community engagement, especially focused on bystanders and witnesses. Everyone is responsible for making public places safer. We need more community-based discussions, dialogues, and strategizing.
- Cross-collaborations to bring street harassment into related issues and related issues into the work of street harassment. For example, street harassment is akin to and overlaps with these issues:
  - Increasing the economic empowerment of women, women in leadership positions, and positive representations of women in the media.
  - Advocating for equal rights and justice for persons of color, LGBTQ-identified individuals, persons with disabilities, homeless people, and youth.
  - Addressing sexual harassment and bullying in schools, campus rape, workplace harassment, online harassment, sex trafficking, rape culture/slut shaming, and harassment by police officers.

On the cross-collaboration point, much more work could be done. For example, within racial justice initiatives, the issues that women and girls of color disproportionately face, like gender-based street harassment and rape, are often overshadowed by issues that disproportionately affect men and boys. As another example, within the LGBTQ rights movement, issues of harassment and violence are often overlooked. During a 2013 focus group with gay and bisexual men in Washington, D.C., as part of the national street harassment study commissioned by Stop Street Harassment (SSH), two men shared these thoughts that illustrate the need for more work on harassment and violence issues: "People think if gay marriage is passed, all the other dominoes will fall into place. I think it's important, but I think violence needs to be addressed right now," and "What good is being able to get married if you're not even safe in your own neighborhood? I think that gets overlooked a lot."[1]

All of the efforts listed above and throughout the book could have more reach, impact, and longevity with more funding. In interviewing various activists and international entities, the lack of adequate funding came up many times. For example, despite the huge success of the Huairou Commission's global day of action on February 19, 2013, after the Delhi gang rape, it could not continue with the campaign due to a lack of funding. Unpaid volunteers run SSH, Everyday Sexism Project, and other groups, and this limits how much they can achieve. Locally, governments may agree to a project or campaign, but without putting funding behind it, the impact is minimal (for example, passing an anti-harassment ordinance but then not providing funding to train law enforcement to handle complaints properly or to advertise that the ordinance exists) and likely short-lived. Funding is needed from foundations, governments, corporate sponsors, and community fundraisers to see sustainable and long-term programs put into place and succeed.

What else do we need?

BETTER LAWS AND ORDINANCES

Should there be more laws and ordinances against verbal street harassment? There is no consensus among groups working to stop street harassment. Usually, on one side are entities like U.N. Women and Action-Aid who advocate for laws, and on the other are grassroots anti-street harassment activists and others who fear the laws would not be properly enforced and may lead to the over-incarceration of young men, low-income men, and men of color.

On the one hand, laws can help shape attitudes and foster cultural shifts, and one can question the stance of throwing out laws completely because of an imperfect system (with that logic, should we do away with rape laws or those against robbery or murder?). On the other hand, by and large the existing laws against both physical and verbal forms of harassment are underutilized and largely ineffective due to a variety of factors. Factors include: poor wording that excludes common forms of harassment or makes it difficult to report harassers (such as in Egypt where the harasser must be present at the time of the report); people fearing repercussions from harassers or their family for reporting; the long and draining prosecution process that may not seem worth the effort; and a lack of advertising about the law. Further, law enforcement can be a barrier if the officers engage in victim blaming, harassment, or misconduct or act indifferent toward harassed persons.

Any new laws against verbal harassment should be written only after conducting thorough research on street harassment in the community or country, holding community discussions, and working with advocacy groups and a coalition of survivors of harassment from a range of backgrounds and experiences to craft the language of the law. Then it must be mandated that law enforcement agents receive training about the law and street harassment in general (and why the issue even matters). There also needs to be more checks and balances in place to hold law enforcement officials accountable if they fail to act appropriately and/or if they harass or assault someone.

In sum, without input and buy-in from diverse community groups and the reform of law enforcement, a new law likely will not make a significant difference. What would be more useful than government officials passing a poorly written law just to appease public pressure or because that is what they best know how to do in the face of a problem? A government committing to comprehensive initiatives that aim to create cultural change and are carried out in collaboration with advocacy groups. Entities like ActionAid, HarassMap, Jagori, U.N. Women, and Women in Cities International have reports and guides on their websites that can assist groups that want to work with government agencies in this kind of comprehensive and meaningful way.

MORE FOCUS ON PREVENTION, ESPECIALLY WITH YOUTH

The most important next step for the movement as a whole and any individual who wants to stop street harassment is to focus on prevention. A number of people with whom I spoke talked about the need to emphasize preventing street harassment now that it has been articulated and documented as a problem. "The instinct is to be more reactionary and punitive (with laws and law enforcement), but that misses the mark," Kathryn Travers, executive director of the Montreal-based organization Women in Cities International, told me. "We need to look at the underlying issues."[2]

Instead of taking the easier but less effective risk-reduction approach (which also limits people's mobility and equal access to full public engagement) of telling harassed persons to change how they dress, where they go, and what they do and instead of having initiatives like women-only public transportation or public service campaigns that are only directed at harassed persons, we need to look at what societal factors and messages foster a culture of harassment and work to prevent harassment from occurring in the first place. Policies and laws will have limited utility otherwise. Marty Langelan, past president of the D.C. Rape Crisis Center and the "godmother" of citywide anti-harassment campaigns, agrees. She told me: "We need to work to prevent harassment from occurring in the first place. Any policies or laws we enact—even if they are written well and properly enforced—will have a limited impact unless we also change the underlying culture of male entitlement."[3]

How do we address underlying issues and create a cultural shift? There are many ways, but two of the most important are speaking out and educating youth.

Speak Out: Something anyone and everyone can do is speak out against sexism (and homophobia, racism, etc.) to end its social acceptability. Tell people what they said is neither cool nor OK and why. If you consume media that promotes or condones these attitudes and behaviors, use it as a teachable moment or discussion point with friends and family.

Speak out when harassment occurs to deter harassers from acting that way in the future and to show others that the behavior is socially unacceptable. Creating a distraction or disruption, or directly intervening are all possible tactics. Doing something that surprises harassers (such as asking them to repeat themselves or asking them to show some respect) is often effective and seems to be the least likely to escalate the situation because the harasser is too shocked or thrown off to respond. The "fake friend" approach is a good one for witnesses of harassment to use: pretend to know the person being harassed and engage them in a friendly conversation. Simply asking a harassed person if he or she is OK is also important; many people share stories about being shocked and humiliated that no one witnessing them being harassed said or did anything. Reporting people who harass in clubs, bars, stores, restaurants, transit systems, and events to the person in charge is a possibility as is reporting employees to their employers if they are visibly engaged in street harassment while on the job. Langelan shared why speaking out can be so important:

While the barrage of constant harassment can keep us silent, unsafe, and excluded, nonviolent direct-action is even more powerful. The cumulative effect of consistent, continuing intervention makes it first difficult, then impossible, for harassers to persist. Every time we use calm, clear direct-action to interrupt a sexist bully, we're changing the cultural dynamics—making harassment fail. How do you end a social practice? You make it stop working; you remove the rewards; you interrupt and de-normalize the behavior, again and again, with a toolkit of nonviolent tactics that works. Many harassers fold immediately. Imagine a global spark, a movement, a million women, kids, dads, and grandmothers calmly, consistently interrupting harassers on every street corner on the planet.[4]

More on strategies—and the theories behind them—are found in Langelan's book *Back Off!* In addition to trainers like Langelan, organizations like the Collective Action for Safe Spaces, Defend Yourself, Green Dot, hu-MAN Up, Men Can Stop Rape, Men Stopping Violence, and the National Sexual Violence Resource Center offer resources, tools and/or workshops on how to call out and intervene in instances of sexism, homophobia, racism, or harassment.

Speaking out could also include calling out sexism in advertising, media, or the comments of politicians by using social media, petitions, and boycotts. SSH blog correspondent Lea Goelnitz wrote about an interesting initiative in Germany that could be modeled in other countries.

In 2014 in Berlin, 15 women from various women's rights projects founded a working group against sexist, discriminatory, and misogynistic advertisement. They developed a catalog of criteria to define sexist ads, which was presented in front of the city senate and subsequently approved. In some areas of Berlin, it is now illegal to put up ads that violate the criteria. The working group also serves as a platform to which people report sexist ads. The aim is to have a dialogue with the companies that launch the ads and to explain alternatives to their problematic [messaging]. The role model for this initiative is Austria, where the official advertisement council established an elaborate catalogue and intervenes in discriminatory ads.[5]

Educate Youth: Sexism, homophobia, racism, and other forms of discrimination are learned behaviors. This means they can be unlearned or never learned in the first place. Dr. Agustin Fuentes wrote a 2014 article for *Psychology Today* "busting the myth" that human male aggression toward females is natural or genetic. Instead, Fuentes wrote, it is learned. "Most men aren't sexual predators. But we need to be more active when someone is—especially with regard to sexual harassment, coercion, and assault on women," he wrote. "Society needs to own up to the fact that sexual aggression is not inevitable—but it *is* predictable, explicable, and, in most cases, avoidable."[6]

How can we make it avoidable? Groups that work with youth—and schools in particular—can play important roles in helping children become empathetic and respectful citizens. They can do so by hiring teachers and administrators who treat students with respect and by enforcing policies that do not disproportionately punish students of color or LGBTQ-identified youth (as happens currently in the United States) and that do not enforce harmful gender stereotypes on children.

Indeed, how educators talk to students about gender and how students feel about gender roles impacts their tolerance and actions of gender-based violence. Vanita Sundaram, a senior lecturer in education at the University of York conducted research with 14- and 15-year-olds in northern England and found that young people have a nuanced understanding of gender violence. More of them said male violence against females was OK if it was being used to enact or reinforce expected gender behavior. "Given that gender appears to be a primary influence on young people's views on violence, schools should prioritize teaching about equality between the genders in order to effectively challenge the acceptance and justification of some forms of violent behavior," Sundaram wrote in a 2015 *Washington Post* article. "This could include cross-curricular teaching about gender stereotypes, sexism, sexual and gender pressures, and gender-based harassment and violence."[7]

This education needs to start at a very young age. Researchers at the University of Illinois and the U.S. Centers for Disease Control and Prevention found in 2014 that adolescent boys who bully peers and engage in homophobic teasing in middle school are more likely to perpetrate sexual harassment later on in life. Researcher Dr. Dorothy L. Espelage said this association "warrants greater prevention and intervention efforts in schools . . . even earlier than in middle school . . . that focus on gender-based aggressive acts that precede sexual harassment perpetration, especially homophobic name-calling."[8]

Educators report witnessing this among elementary school students. One teacher in Philadelphia told me after a street harassment talk that he has seen first-grade boys harass women walking by their school playground. They were mimicking the masculinity they had seen older boys and men display. Children pick up on social norms, and it is up to us to make sure they pick up on the right ones.

Every time I speak with young people—whether elementary school, high school, or college students—they have been aware of and extremely receptive to discussing street harassment. Usually it has been the first time they have had the opportunity to talk about these issues and share their stories. In mix-gender rooms, the boys have always been shocked to hear the stories of their female peers. For example, during a visit to a Virginia high school classroom, nearly every 16-year-old female student in the room volunteered a recent street harassment story, and many of their male peers voiced their surprise and dismay. They all had the opportunity to create art work afterward, and one of the young men drew a piece of meat walking past wolves who were harassing her and wrote the caption "You are not a piece of meat."

Relando B. Thompkins, program coordinator for the Future Public Health Leaders program at the University of Michigan and a former SSH board member suggests: "Help young men recognize their role in it. Talk with them about sexism. Talk about male privilege and violence against women (not just physical, but emotional, sexual, and other methods). Find ways to help them recognize patterns in themselves and among those around them."[9]

Young people are often more willing than adults to change their behavior. While adult men know they are being creepy and inappropriate, some young men do not realize that their behaviors toward their female peers are harassment because it is what they have been taught and had modeled for them by peers, family members, and celebrities. During a fall 2014 visit to a classroom of first-year students at Shenandoah University in Winchester, Virginia, I shared several of my experiences of harassment as did a few female students during the Q&A. Following the talk, students had to write essays on my talk. Later, their professor sent me one of the essays, and the student gave permission for part of it to be shared here:

What men like me see as trying to get a girl's attention (catcalling) can be seen as street harassment. I myself have not witnessed any instance of anyone being street harassed personally, but I have been the harasser before. When I'm with my boys riding around and see a fairly attractive female, I would yell out the window at them saying comments like 'AYEEE CUTIE!' without thinking twice of it. Then I didn't think anything of it, and I was just doing it for fun, without thinking about how the girl felt about some random guy yelling out the window at her.

Now that I listened to Ms. Kearl's presentation, I see that my actions could be a form of street harassment. Even though I had no intentions of trying to harass anyone, I see that my actions could have made those girls uncomfortable, and that was the last thing I was trying to do. Now that I am well informed about the topic, I will not be doing anymore catcalling out of the window of a car to girls walking down the street. I do not want any woman feeling uncomfortable toward me, so a different approach will be made if I am interested in a woman. I learned what was harmless fun to me could make someone else uncomfortable, and that is not what I am trying to do.[10]

What if every young man had the chance to hear women's street harassment stories in a safe, non-judgmental environment? Peer-to-peer discussions and story-sharing sessions can be really powerful ways to stop boys from growing into harassers. Here are several examples of what this can look like:

The Sara Communication Initiative was developed by the Pearson Foundation's Digital Arts Alliance and UNICEF, and through it, 200 girls in Tanzania, Zambia, South Africa, and Namibia have used Nokia mobile phones and laptops with film-making software to create short films about topics like sexual harassment, HIV, and early marriage. Their videos have been shown all over their countries to their peers as prevention and education pieces.[11]

In Bangladesh, after many publicized suicides by harassed girls, the local UNICEF office organized a rally of 600 people in the Narsingdi district to protest street harassment. They worked with other local groups, parents, and youth to hold community workshops about street harassment that included role-playing and to support youth groups called Kishori Clubs to allow girls and boys to learn to socialize in positive, consensual ways.[12]

The International Center for Research on Women (ICRW) launched a Parivartan program in India in 2010. It teaches boys about healthy masculinity, respect for girls/women, and anti-violence through the unifying sport of cricket. Cricket coaches and role models on community cricket teams attend workshops on gender issues, and then because the others on the team look up to them, they expose large groups of boys to healthy definitions of manhood and respect for women. It has been successful. Take Rajesh, who used to be a harasser who liked to "make fun of [girls'] existence" but then "learned to respect them and gain the confidence to speak out against mistreating women and girls." He said in an ICRW article, "I know now that [harassment] is harming someone's dignity."[13]

In Belgium, since turning the Touche Pas à Ma Pote transit campaign into a nonprofit, the leaders have been able to collaborate with schools to host street harassment workshops. On March 8, 2013, for example, every school in the Uccle district held a sexism awareness effort for International Women's Day, and they received "Touche Pas à Ma Pote" flyers and pins. In fall 2014, Touche Pas à Ma Pote received funding to hold street harassment role-playing and discussion-based workshops in all 5th and 6th grade classrooms in their city. The group plans to continue to host them in 2015.[14]

In 2010, the Toronto-based nonprofit METRAC launched an online and mobile-accessible interactive game called "What it is" to teach youth about sexual violence. Through interactions at varying levels, players learn about what sexual abuse is, what consent is, and what some of the myths and realities of sexual violence are. The game also includes resources to help victims. High-scoring players win a song track. Youth helped design the game, and focus groups of youth gave feedback on it before it officially launched. In a survey of 136 users, 95 percent felt they knew more about issues of sexual violence after playing the game.[15]

Also in Canada, after eight years of activism and lobbying by the Miss G Project (a group of women in their twenties), the Ontario Minister of

Education approved all schools in the province to offer women's and gender studies as an elective starting with the 2013–14 school year. Eight schools immediately chose to do so.[16]

New York City high school teacher Ileana Jiménez runs the blog *Feminist Teacher*. She teaches a feminism elective that is widely popular and successful and always includes discussions about street harassment. "For me, stopping street harassment is a part of my work in making the lives of my students safer, just, and whole," she told me. "Designing courses that address issues of gender-based violence from street harassment to sexual harassment to rape and assault to sex trafficking are critical for making these issues visible to students."[17]

Jiménez has launched a movement to promote gender and feminism courses in K-12 schools, and her blog is a wealth of information. She connects with, features, and collaborates with teachers across the United States and in countries like Canada, India, Norway, and the United Kingdom, where there are also burgeoning efforts to teach gender in schools. In 2013, in partnership with the American Association of University Women (I was the primary contact) and the University of Missouri, St. Louis, Jiménez organized a one-day symposium "Creating Classrooms of Justice: Teaching Gender Studies in Schools." Fifty educators and activists from both public and private schools from the United States and Canada came together to discuss how to teach gender, not only in feminist or women's studies classes, but also in history, English, and sex education courses. Much idea sharing took place, and several teachers who were not yet incorporating gender into their classrooms began doing so during the 2014–15 school year.

Resources and Ideas

In the United States, organizations like Girls for Gender Equity, A Long Walk Home, Gay, Lesbian & Straight Education Network (GLSEN), Men Can Stop Rape, Men Stopping Violence, Futures without Violence, and STEPS to End Family Violence work with young people on issues of sexism, homophobia, racism, harassment, and gender violence, often in the context of both schools and public spaces. Many of them offer programming or resources that other groups can use in their schools or communities. For example, the 20-minute film *Hey . . . Shorty!* created by Girls for Gender Equity is available for purchase on the group's website (www.ggenyc.org). The group's book *Hey, Shorty! A Guide to Combating Sexual Harassment and Violence in Schools and on the Streets* is also available for purchase online. Three specific examples of resources in addition to what these groups offer are the following:

- The award-winning four-minute film *Walking Home*. The film and a companion discussion guide, created by the filmmaker, Nuala Cabral, is available on the International Anti-Street Harassment Week website (www.meetusonthes treet.org). The film is also available on YouTube.
- A comic book about street harassment directed at youth created by Feminist Public Works (formerly Hollaback!PHILLY). It can be ordered online at www .feministpublicworks.org/
- Rogers Park Young Women's Action Team's "Where Our Boys At?" toolkit for engaging young men as allies to end sexual harassment and violence. It is available for free at www.rogersparkywat.org

There are also examples on the SSH website and in the International Anti-Street Harassment Week reports of youth-oriented activities, such as youth making their own PSA videos, as did high school students in New Mexico and Illinois, or creating art work, as did high school students in New York, Virginia, and Arizona. Youth groups in Azerbaijan, San Jose, California, and Egypt each made videos calling out harassers—there is even a lesson plan available in English and Azerbaijani for the Azerbaijan video on the SSH website. In Chicago, the teenage members of A Long Walk Home organized an anti-street harassment march around their school and brought anti-harassment T-shirts, posters, and flyers they designed.

When working with youth, it is important to create the space for them to safely and respectfully talk about these issues, to provide them with age-appropriate and informed resources, and to offer them ways and methods for taking action should they choose to do so. Examples include setting up a blog where they can share their stories or providing them with art supplies to create art related to the topic.

The movement to stop street harassment has come a long way. Compared to 2010, there has been a huge increase in the number of people sharing stories, conducting research, organizing on- and offline activism, launching international initiatives, and working with local government on campaigns and ordinances. Yet, in many places, street harassment is still a cultural norm, but it doesn't have to be normal forever. In addition to moving forward with the efforts underway, expanding them, modeling them, and funding them, focusing on educating and engaging youth is the best way to help break the cycle of harassment so that it becomes abnormal and socially unacceptable behavior. We are well on our way toward realizing the dream of a world that is free from street harassment. What will you do to make that dream a reality?

Appendix: Further Reading on Street Harassment

Bates, Laura. *Everyday Sexism*. London: Simon & Schuster UK, 2014.

Drucker, Susan J., and Gary Grumpert, eds. *Voices in the Street: Explorations in Gender, Media, and Public Space*. Cresskill, NJ: Hampton Press, 1996.

Freedman, Estelle. *Redefining Rape: Sexual Violence in the Era of Suffrage and Segregation*. Cambridge: Harvard University Press, 2013.

Gardner, Carol Brooks. *Passing By: Gender and Public Harassment*. Berkeley, CA: University of California Press, 1995.

Huppuch, Meghan, Joanne Smith, and Mandy Van Deven. *Hey, Shorty!: A Guide to Combating Sexual Harassment and Violence in Schools and on the Streets*. New York: The Feminist Press at CUNY, 2011.

Kearl, Holly. *50 Stories about Stopping Street Harassers*. CreateSpace, 2013.

Kearl, Holly. *Stop Street Harassment: Making Public Places Safe and Welcoming for Women*. Santa Barbara, CA: Praeger, 2010.

Langelan, Martha J. *Back Off: How to Confront and Stop Sexual Harassment and Harassers*. New York: Fireside, 1993.

McGuire, Danielle L. *At the Dark End of the Street: Black Women, Rape, and Resistance—A New History of the Civil Rights Movement from Rosa Parks to the Rise of Black Power*. New York: Vintage, 2011.

Nielsen, Laura Beth. *License to Harass: Law, Hierarchy, and Offensive Public Speech*. Princeton, NJ: Princeton University Press, 2006.

Phadke, Shilpa, Sameera Khan, and Shilpa Ranade. *Why Loiter? Women & Risk on Mumbai Streets*. Gurgaon: Penguin Books, 2011.

Richards, Amy, and Cynthia Greenberg, eds. *I Still Believe Anita Hill*. New York: Feminist Press, 2012.

Segrave, Kerry. *Beware the Masher: Sexual Harassment in American Public Places, 1880–1930*. Jefferson, NC: McFarland & Company, 2014.

Spain, Daphne. *Gendered Spaces*. Chapel Hill, NC: The University of North Carolina Press, 1992.

Stanley, Liz and Sue Wise. *Georgie Porgie: Sexual Harassment in Everyday Life*. London: Pandora, 1987.

Whitzman, Carolyn et al. *Building Inclusive Cities: Women's Safety and the Right to the City*. New York: Routledge, 2013.

Wilson, Elizabeth. *The Sphinx in the City: Urban Life, the Control of Disorder, and Women*. Berkeley, CA: University of California Press, 1991.

Notes

INTRODUCTION

1. United Nations, "World's Population Increasingly Urban with more than Half Living in Urban Areas," United Nations, July 10, 2014, http://www.un.org/en/development/desa/news/population/world-urbanization-prospects-2014.html.

2. Susan J. Drucker and Gary Grumpert, "Voices in the Street: Explorations in Gender, Media, and Public Space," in *Voices in the Street: Explorations in Gender, Media, and Public Space*, ed. Susan J. Drucker and Gary Gumpert (Cresskill, NJ: Hampton Press, 1996), 3.

3. Ibid., 6.

4. Joan Fayer, "Changes in Gender Use of Public Space in Puerto Rico," in *Voices in the Street*, 213.

5. Drucker and Grumpert. "Shopping Women, and Public Space," in *Voices in the Street*, 122.

6. Holly Kearl, "Part 2: Redefining Rape and Street Harassment: 1880s–1920s," *Stop Street Harassment*, October 3, 2013, http://www.stopstreetharassment.org/2013/10/redefiningrape2/.

7. Ibid.

8. Fayer, "Changes in Gender Use of Public Space in Puerto Rico," 215.

9. Ibid., 223.

10. Clare Olivia Parsons, "Reputation and Public Appearance: The De-Eroticization of the Urban Street," in *Voices in the Street*, 65–66.

11. Kerry Segrave, *Beware the Masher: Sexual Harassment in American Public Places, 1880–1930* (Jefferson, NC: McFarland & Company, 2014), 4.

12. Fayer, "Changes in Gender Use of Public Space in Puerto Rico," 218.

13. Kearl, "Part 2: Redefining Rape and Street Harassment: 1880s–1920s," *Stop Street Harassment*, October 3, 2013, http://www.stopstreetharassment.org /2013/10/redefiningrape2/.

14. Library of Congress, "Miss Alice Reighly, President of the Anti-Flirt Club," *Library of Congress*, Call 12295, v.1, February 27, 1923, http://www.loc.gov /pictures/item/2002695741/.

15. Cynthia Gordy, "Recy Taylor: A Symbol of Jim Crow's Forgotten Horror," *The Root*, February 9, 2011, http://www.theroot.com/articles/culture/2011/02 /recy_taylor_a_symbol_of_jim_crows_forgotten_horror.html.

16. Danielle L. McGuire, "About the Book," *At the Dark End of the Street*, n.d., accessed January 5, 2015, http://atthedarkendofthestreet.com/.

17. Ash M. Richter, "The Wall Street Ogle-In of 1970," All Day, November 2014, http://allday.com/post/1619-the-wall-street-ogle-in-of-1970.

18. Marty Langlean, e-mail message to the author, February 8, 2015.

19. Kathryn Travers, phone interview with the author, December 9, 2014.

20. METRAC, "Safety," *METRAC*, n.d., http://www.metrac.org/what-we -do/safety/.

21. Margaret Shaw, Caroline Andrew, Carolyn Whitzman, Fran Klodawsky, Kalpana Viswanath, and Crystal Legacy, "Introduction: Challenges, Opportunities and Tools," in *Building Inclusive Cities: Women's Safety and Their Right to the City*, ed. Margaret Shaw, Caroline Andrew, Carolyn Whitzman, Fran Klodawsky, Kalpana Viswanath, and Crystal Legacy (New York: Routledge, 2013), 4.

22. Google, "Street Harassment," Google Trends, http://www.google.com /trends/explore#q=%22Street%20harassment%22.

CHAPTER 1: A HUMAN RIGHTS VIOLATION

1. Hindustan Times, "Bangladeshis Raise Voice Against Sexual Harassment," *Hindustan Times*, June 19, 2010, http://www.hindustantimes.com/world-news /bangladeshis-raise-voice-against-sexual-harassment/article1-560011.aspx.

2. Salim Mia, "Bangladesh 'Eve Teasing' Takes A Terrible Toll," *BBC*, June 11, 2010, accessed January 5, 2015, http://www.bbc.co.uk/news/10220920.

3. Mia, "Bangladesh 'Eve Teasing' Takes a Terrible Toll," *BBC*, June 11, 2010, http://www.bbc.co.uk/news/10220920.

4. Holly Kearl, "Unsafe and Harassed in Public Spaces: A National Street Harassment Report," *Stop Street Harassment*, June 3, 2014, http://www.stop streetharassment.org/our-work/nationalstudy/.

5. Anonymous, "Harassed 17 times in 7 Minutes," *Stop Street Harassment*, February 10, 2014, http://www.stopstreetharassment.org/2014/02/7minutes/.

6. Anonymous, "First Harassed at Age 7 on the Streets," *Stop Street Harassment*, June 11, 2014, http://www.stopstreetharassment.org/2014/06/harassed age7/.

7. Susan Popkin and Robin Smith, "Girls in the 'Hood—What Violence Means for Girls," Urban Institute, September 14, 2011, http://blog.metrotrends .org/2011/09/what-violence-means-for-girls/.

8. Ibid.

9. Ibid.

10. Kathryn Stamoulis, " 'Hey Baby' Hurts," *Psychology Today*, August 19, 2011, http://www.psychologytoday.com/blog/the-new-teen-age/201108/hey-baby-hurts.

11. Kearl, "Our Streets, Our Rights," *Stop Street Harassment*, December 10, 2012, http://www.stopstreetharassment.org/2012/12/our-streets-our-rights/.

12. Frustrated and Disgusted, "Harassers at Work and in the Parking Lot Prompt Move," *Stop Street Harassment*, August 6, 2010, http://www.stopstreet harassment.org/2010/08/harassers-at-work-in-the-parking-lot-prompt-move/.

13. Anonymous, "Constant Harassment at California Bus Stop," *Stop Street Harassment*, June 20, 2011, http://www.stopstreetharassment.org/2011/06/cons tant-harassment-at-california-bus-stop/.

14. Sisonke Msimang, "The Backlash Against African Women," *The New York Times*, January 10, 2015, http://www.nytimes.com/2015/01/11/opinion /sunday/the-backlash-against-african-women.html&assetType=opinion&_r=0.

15. CNN, "Pakistan's Educational Challenges," *CNN*, October 10, 2014, http://www.cnn.com/2013/10/09/world/asia/infographic-pakistan-education/.

16. Nathan Hodge and Jenny Gross, "Pakistani Girls' Education Activist Malala Yousafzai Rose to Global Prominence after Taliban Shooting," *The Wall Street Journal*, October 10, 2014, http://www.wsj.com/articles/pakistani-girls -education-activist-malala-yousafzai-rose-to-global-prominence-after-taliban-shooting-1412942763.

17. U.N. Women, "Bolivia Approves a Landmark Law Against Harassment of Women Political Leaders," UN Women, June 11, 2012, http://www.unwomen .org/en/news/stories/2012/6/bolivia-approves-a-landmark-law-against-harassment -of-women-political-leaders; see also "Bolivian Women Battle Against Culture of Harassment," *BBC*, March 11, 2014, http://www.bbc.com/news/world-latin -america-26446066.

18. Emel Armutçu, "Turkish Mayor Advises Women to 'Stay Home' to Avoid Harassment," *Hurriyet Daily News*, May 25, 2011, http://www.hurriyetdaily news.com/default.aspx?pageid=438&n=sit-in-your-homes-unless-you-want-to -be-sexually-harassed-2011-05-25.

19. Dofa Fasila, "Women Should Not Wear Miniskirts on Angkot: Jakarta Governor," *The Jakarta Globe*, September 16, 2011, http://thejakartaglobe .beritasatu.com/archive/women-should-not-wear-miniskirts-on-angkot-jakarta -governor/.

20. The Jakarta Globe, "Indonesian Women Don Miniskirts in Rape Protest," *The Jakarta Globe*, September 18, 2011, http://thejakartaglobe.beritasatu.com /archive/indonesian-women-don-miniskirts-in-rape-protest/466109/.

21. Raymond Kwan, "Don't Dress Like a Slut: Toronto Cop," *Excalibur–York University's Community Newspaper*, February 16, 2011, http://www.excal .on.ca/dont-dress-like-a-slut-toronto-cop/.

22. Terry Davidson, "Cops: School Uniforms May Attract Pervs," *Canoe News*, October 8, 2011, http://cnews.canoe.ca/CNEWS/Canada/2011/10/07 /18799506.html.

23. Indian Express, "Swaziland Bans 'Rape-Provoking' Mini-skirts, Low-rise Jeans," *Indian Express*, December 31, 2012, http://archive.indianexpress.com /news/%22swaziland-bans-rapeprovoking-miniskirts-lowrise-jeans%22/1049615/.

24. A Cappella, "Shanghai Subway Tells Scantily Clad Women to Expect Sexual Harassment," *Tea Leaf Nation*, June 25, 2012, http://www.tealeafnation .com/2012/06/shanghai-subway-tells-scantily-clad-women-to-expect-sexual-ha rassment/.

25. Ian Millhiser, "Judge to Woman Sexually Assaulted by Cop: 'When You Blame Others, You Give Up Your Power to Change," *ThinkProgress*, 7 September 2012, http://thinkprogress.org/justice/2012/09/07/809861/judge-to-woman-sex ually-assaulted-by-cop-when-you-blame-others-you-give-up-your-power-to -change/?mobile=nc.

26. BBC News, "Nigeria Anti-gay Law: Fears Over New Legislation," *BBC*, January 14, 2012, http://www.bbc.com/news/world-africa-25728845.

27. Economic and Social Council, Commission on the Status of Women: Report on the Fifty-seventh Session, United Nations, April 2, 2013, http://www .un.org/ga/search/view_doc.asp?symbol=E/2013/27.

28. Kearl, "Unsafe and Harassed in Public Spaces: A National Street Harass-ment Report," *Stop Street Harassment*, June 3, 2014, http://www.stopstreet harassment.org/our-work/nationalstudy/.

29. Aaron Feis, "Woman's Throat Slashed after Rejecting Man's Advances," *New York Post*, October 8, 2014, http://nypost.com/2014/10/08/womans-throat -slashed-after-rejecting-mans-advances/.

30. Michael Harthorne, "Police: Men Threaten to Shoot Woman who Ignored Their Advances," *Komo News*, November 17, 2014, http://www.komonews .com/news/crime/Police-Men-threaten-to-shoot-woman-who-ignored-their-ad vances-282938701.html?mobile=y.

31. Eleanor Harding, "Student Suffers Horrific Injuries after She is Punched in the Face at Notting Hill Carnival for Telling Men to Stop Groping Her," *The Daily Mail*, August 27, 2014, http://www.dailymail.co.uk/news/article-2735612 /Horrific-injuries-woman-punched-face-Notting-Hill-Carnival-telling-man -stop-groping-her.html.

32. Dyana Bagby, "Trans Women Brutally Attacked on Atlanta's MARTA," *GA Voice*, May 26, 2014, http://thegavoice.com/trans-women-attacked-atlantas -marta/.

33. Danielle Young, "Shot Down: Mother of Three Killed Because She Said No to a Man's Advances," *Michigan Chronicle*, October 8, 2014, http://michro nicleonline.com/2014/10/08/shot-down-mother-of-three-killed-because-she-said -no-to-a-mans-advances/.

34. Ujwala Shenoy Karmarkar, "No More Roadside Romeos: Is Stalking a Tragedy in the Making?" *Women's Web*, September 3, 2014, http://www.womens web.in/2014/09/no-more-roadside-romeos-is-stalking-a-tragedy-in-the-making/.

35. Associated Press Staff, "Serial Killer on Motorcycle may be to Blame for 12 Slayings: Police," *Global News*, August 5, 2014, accessed January 5, 2015, http://globalnews.ca/news/1492999/serial-killer-on-motorcycle-may-.

36. Rebecca Rose, "Man Stabbed for Asking Someone to Stop Catcalling His Girlfriend," *Jezebel*, November 20, 2014, http://jezebel.com/and-this-is-why -more-men-men-who-are-pissed-off-at-str-1661480851?utm_campaign=social flow_jezebel_facebook&utm_source=jezebel_facebook&utm_medium=social flow.

37. David Chang, "Man Knocked Unconscious After Defending Women from Catcallers: Police," *NBC Bay Area*, August 13, 2014, http://www.nbcbayarea .com/news/national-international/Man-Punched-Knocked-Unconscious-Du ring-Rittenhouse-Square-Attack-270588441.html.

38. Rosemary Regina Sobol, Meredith Rodriguez, and Steve Schmadeke, "Father Dies Shielding Daughter, 15: 'I'm Going to Make Him Proud,'" *Chicago Tribune*, March 21, 2014, http://articles.chicagotribune.com/2014-03-21/news /chi-father-died-protecting-teenage-daughter-her-mother-says-20140320_1_dau ghter-disability-benefits-chest.

39. Egyptian Streets, "Teenager Killed in Egypt While Defending Women from Sexual Harassment," *Egyptian Streets*, October 6, 2014, http://egyptianstreets .com/2014/10/06/teenager-killed-in-egypt-while-defending-women-from-sexual -harassment/.

40. Alison Smale, "A Student's Death Exposes German Struggle for a Multi-cultural Ideal," *New York Times*, December 2, 2014, http://www.nytimes.com /2014/12/03/world/europe/tugce-albayrak-death-rattles-germany.html?_r=1.

41. Elizabeth Arveda Kissling, "Street Harassment: The Language of Sexual Terrorism," *Discourse Society* (1991), http://das.sagepub.com/content/2/4/451 .abstract.

42. AH, "Street Harassment is a Trigger for Rape Survivors," *Stop Street Harassment*, July 6, 2010, http://www.stopstreetharassment.org/2010/07/why -street-harassment-is-a-big-deal/.

43. Haley Miles-McLean, Miriam Liss, Mindy J. Erchull et al. (2014). "'Stop Looking at Me!' Interpersonal Sexual Objectification as a Source of Insidious Trauma," *Psychology of Women Quarterly*. http://pwq.sagepub.com/content /early/2014/11/03/0361684314561018?papetoc.

44. Laurel B. Watson, Jacob M. Marszalek, Franco Dispenza, and Christo-pher M. Davids, "Understanding the Relationships Among White and African American Women's Sexual Objectification Experiences, Physical Safety Anxiety, and Psychological Distress," *Sex Roles* (2015), http://link.springer.com/article /10.1007/s11199-014-0444-y/fulltext.html.

45. Kimberly Fairchild and Laurie A. Rudman, "Everyday Stranger Harass-ment and Women's Self-Objectification." *Social Justice Research*, 21 (2008): 348.

46. Heather R. Hlavka, "Normalizing Sexual Violence: Young Women Account for Harassment and Abuse," *Gender & Society* (2014), http://gas.sagepub.com /content/early/2014/02/28/0891243214526468.full?keytype=ref&siteid=spgas &ijkey=1zjS.dsfVDs32.

47. The Grio, "Rape on the Rise in Aftermath of Haiti Quake," *The Grio*, March 16, 2010, http://thegrio.com/2010/03/16/rape-on-the-rise-in-aftermath -of-haiti-quake/.

48. Judie Kaberia, "Somali Women Raped Enroute to Kenya," *Capital-News*, August 8, 2011, http://www.capitalfm.co.ke/news/2011/08/hungry-somali-women-raped-enroute-to-kenya/.

49. Agence France Presse, "Rape Another Risk for Somali Drought Refugees," *Capital News*, August 17, 2011, http://www.capitalfm.co.ke/news/2011/08/rape-another-risk-for-somali-drought-refugees/.

50. Kim Lewis, "Somali Women Face Rape, Sexual Assault as They Flee Famine," *Voice of America*, August 1, 2011, http://www.voanews.com/content/somali-women-face-rape-sexual-assault-as-they-flee-famine----126598458/160072.html.

51. Jamie Dettmer, "Libya Women Report Increased Harassment," *Voice of America*, November 1, 2013, http://www.voanews.com/content/libya-women-report-increased-harassment/1781596.html.

52. Ibid.

53. BBC, "What is At Stake in the Colombian Peace Process?" *BBC*, January 15, 2015, http://www.bbc.com/news/world-latin-america-19875363.

54. ABC Colombia, *Colombia: Women, Conflict-Related Sexual Violence and the Peace Process* (London: ABColombia: 2013), 1.

55. Adriana Pérez-Rodríguez, "Colombia: Harassment and Armed Conflict," *Stop Street Harassment*, February 13, 2013, http://www.stopstreetharassment.org/2013/02/colombiaarmedconflict.

56. Andrew Willis Garcés, "Ruta Pacífica: Colombian Women Against Violence," Upside Down World, February 4, 2009, http://upsidedownworld.org/main/colombia-archives-61/1699-ruta-pacifica-colombian-women-against-violence.

57. ACLU, "Racial Profiling," *ACLU*, n.d., accessed January 8, 2015, https://www.aclu.org/racial-justice/racial-profiling.

58. Robert Brame, Shawn D. Bushway, Ray Paternoster, and Michael G. Turner, "Demographic Patterns of Culmative Arrest Prevalence by Ages 18 and 23," *Crime & Delinquency*, January 6, 2014, http://cad.sagepub.com/content/early/2013/12/18/0011128713514801.full.pdf+html.

59. The Sentencing Project, "Report of The Sentencing Project to the United Nations Human Rights Committee Regarding Racial Disparities in the United States Criminal Justice System," The Sentencing Project, August 2013, http://sentencingproject.org/doc/publications/rd_ICCPR%20Race%20and%20Justice%20Shadow%20Report.pdf.

60. NYCLU, "Stop-and-Frisk Data," NYCLU, n.d., http://www.nyclu.org/content/stop-and-frisk-data.

61. Joseph Ax and Marina Lopes, "New York City Ends Legal Defense of Stop-and-Frisk Police Tactic," *Reuters*, January 30, 2014, http://www.reuters.com/article/2014/01/30/us-usa-newyork-stopandfrisk-idUSBREA0T1JY20140130.

62. Dr. L'Heureux Dumi Lewis-McCoy, "Parallels of Street Harassment & Police Harassment," *Stop Street Harassment*, May 5, 2011, http://www.stopstreetharassment.org/2011/05/parellels-of-street-harassment-police-harassment/.

63. National Coalition of Anti-Violence Programs, "National Report on Hate Violence Against Lesbian, Gay, Bisexual, Transgender, Queer, and HIV-Affected Communities Released Today," *National Coalition of Anti-Violence Programs*,

June 4, 2013, http://www.avp.org/storage/documents/2012_mr_ncavp_hvre
port.pdf.

64. Mike Ludwig, " 'Walking While Woman' and the Fight to Stop Violent
Policing of Gender Identity," *Truthout,* May 7, 2014, http://www.truth-out
.org/news/item/23551-walking-while-woman-and-the-fight-to-stop-violent
-policing-of-gender-identity.

65. Chase Strangio, "Arrested for Walking While Trans: An Interview with
Monica Jones," ACLU, April 2, 2014, https://www.aclu.org/blog/lgbt-rights
-criminal-law-reform-hiv-aids-reproductive-freedom-womens-rights/arrested
-walking; see also James Nichols, "Monica Jones, Transgender Woman, Convicted of 'Manifesting Prostitution," *Huffington Post,* April 16, 2014, http://www
.huffingtonpost.com/2014/04/16/monica-jones-transgender_n_5159638.html.

66. Melanie Poole, "When We Talk about Police Shootings, We Need to Talk
about Gender," *Feministing,* December 17, 2014, http://feministing.com/2014
/12/17/when-we-talk-about-police-shootings-we-need-to-talk-about-gender/.

67. Ryan Gabrielson, Ryann Grochowski Jones, and Eric Sagara, "Deadly
Force, in Black and White," *ProPublica,* October 10, 2014, accessed January 7,
2015, http://www.propublica.org/article/deadly-force-in-black-and-white.

68. Mike Males, "Who are Police Killing?" *Center on Juvenile and Criminal
Justice,* August 26, 2014, http://www.cjcj.org/news/8113.

69. Joanne Smith, "Young Women of Color Break the Silence. Now What?"
Women's eNews, December 4, 2014, http://womensenews.org/story/equality
women%E2%80%99s-rights/141203/young-women-color-break-the-silence
-now-what#.VIDWGaTF-VZ.

70. Sara Boboltz, "#AliveWhileBlack Highlights the Ugly Discrimination
Black America Knows Too Well," *Huffington Post,* December 4, 2014, http://
www.huffingtonpost.com/2014/12/04/alivewhileblack-hashtag-twitter_n
_6271820.html.

71. Nuala Cabral and Mari Morales-Williams, "Black Women Activists Talk
Back: How We Can End Street Harassment Through Transformative Justice,"
Black Youth Project, October 31, 2014, http://www.blackyouthproject.com
/2014/10/black-women-activists-talk-back-how-we-can-end-street-harassment
-through-transformative-justice/.

72. Sarah Colomé, "USA: Our Oppressions are Intertwined," *Stop Street
Harassment,* October 20, 2014, http://www.stopstreetharassment.org/2014/10
/intertwinedoppressions/.

CHAPTER 2: RESEARCH AND PERSONAL STORIES

1. Carol Brooks Gardner, *Passing By: Gender and Public Harassment*
(Berkeley, CA: University of California Press, 1995), 89–90.

2. Oxygen/Markle Pulse Poll, "Harassment of Women on the Street Is Rampant; 87% of American Women Report Being Harassed on the Street By a Male
Stranger," June 22, 2000, http://www.thefreelibrary.com/Oxygen%2FMarkl
e+Pulse+Poll+Finds%3A+Harassment+of+Women+on+the+Street+Is...-a0628
70396.

3. Marija Stanković, "Serbia: Street Harassment Survey has an Impact," *Stop Street Harassment*, December 29, 2014, http://www.stopstreetharassment.org/2014/12/serbiaspsmfinalreport/.

4. World Economic Forum, *The Global Gender Gap Report: 2014*, 2014, http://www3.weforum.org/docs/GGGR14/GGGR_CompleteReport_2014.pdf.

5. Steve Crabtree and Faith Nsubuga, "Women Feel Less Safe than Men in Many Developed Countries," *Gallup*, July 6, 2012, http://www.gallup.com/poll/155402/women-feel-less-safe-men-developed-countries.aspx.

6. Patrick McNeil, "Street Harassment at the Intersections: The Experiences of Gay and Bisexual Men," *The George Washington University Dissertation*, 2014, http://gradworks.umi.com/15/50/1550487.html.

7. "LGBT Persons' Experiences of Discrimination and Hate Crime in the EU and Croatia," *European Union Agency for Fundamental Rights*, 2013, http://fra.europa.eu/sites/default/files/eu-lgbt-survey-factsheet_en.pdf.

8. Sherele Moody, "Research reveals 90% of women have been harassed in public," *The Observer*, March 8, 2015, http://www.gladstoneobserver.com.au/news/Research-reveals-90-of-women-have-been-harassed-i/2567007/.

9. Zyman Islam, "Not Safe Even Among People," *The Daily Star*, January 29, 2014, http://www.thedailystar.net/not-safe-even-among-people-8895.

10. Sandra Segall, "Three in Four Chilean Women Regularly Harassed in Public, Study Finds," *Santiago Times*, May 5, 2014, http://santiagotimes.cl/three-four-chilean-women-regularly-harassed-public-study-finds/.

11. U.N. Women, "In Brief: Safe Cities Global Initiative," UN Women, 2014, http://www.unwomen.org/~/media/headquarters/attachments/sections/library/publications/2014/un%20women%20safe%20cities%20brief-us-web.pdf.

12. Huong Dang-Vu and Thomas Le Jeannie, "Femmes agressées au domicile ou à l'extérieur : une analyse des risques," National Institute of Statistics and Economic Studies, 2013, http://www.insee.fr/fr/ffc/docs_ffc/ES448G.pdf.

13. Shabana Ansari, "80% of women in Mumbai face sexual harassment," *DNA India*, March 3, 2012, http://www.dnaindia.com/mumbai/report-80-women-in-mumbai-face-sexual-harassment-1657755.

14. Ilan Lior, "Vast Majority of Tel Aviv Women Report Sexual Harassment, Survey Finds," *Haaretz*, November 23, 2011, http://www.haaretz.com/print-edition/news/vast-majority-of-tel-aviv-women-report-sexual-harassment-survey-finds-1.397163.

15. U.N. Women, "In Brief: Safe Cities Global Initiative."

16. Elizabeth Vallejo Rivera and Maria Paula Rivarola Monzon, "La violencia invisible: acoso sexual callejero en Lima Metropolitana y Callao," El Instituto de Opinion Publica de la PUCP, December 2013, http://textos.pucp.edu.pe/texto/Cuadernos-de-Investigacion-N-4—La-violencia-invisible-acoso-sexual-callejero-en-Lima-Metropolitan.

17. U.N. Women, "In Brief: Safe Cities Global Initiative."

18. Noura bint Afeich, "Saudi Women Turn to Social Media to Combat Harassment," *Al-Monitor*, March 26, 2012, http://www.al-monitor.com/pulse/culture/2014/02/sexual-harassment-rise-saudi-arabia.html#.

19. "4 in 10 Young Women in London Sexually Harassed Over Last Year," *End Violence Against Women*, May 25, 2012, http://www.endviolenceagainst women.org.uk/news/20/evaw-coalition-in-the-media.

20. Crosby Burns and Philip Ross, "Gay and Transgender Discrimination Outside the Workplace: Why We Need Protections in Housing, Health Care, and Public Accommodations," *American Progress*, July 19, 2011, https://www .americanprogress.org/issues/lgbt/report/2011/07/19/9927/gay-and-transgender -discrimination-outside-the-workplace/.

21. Andrew Dugan, "In U.S., 37% Do Not Feel Safe Walking at Night Near Home," *Gallup Poll*, November 24, 2014, http://www.gallup.com/poll/179558 /not-feel-safe-walking-night-near-home.aspx.

22. Holly Kearl, "Unsafe and Harassed in Public Spaces: A National Street Harassment Report," *Stop Street Harassment*, June 3, 2014, http://www.stop streetharassment.org/our-work/nationalstudy/.

23. Noorjahan Akbar, "A Letter to My Harasser," *World Pulse*, November 24, 2012, https://worldpulse.com/node/61735. Used by permission.

24. Tara Ashford, "Australia: Was #IllRideWithYou Worth It?" *Stop Street Harassment*, January 18, 2015, http://www.stopstreetharassment.org/2015/01 /illridewithyouworthit/.

25. Pallavi Kamat, "India: Festivals and Street Harassment," *Stop Street Harassment*, September 9, 2013, http://www.stopstreetharassment.org/2013/09 /india-festivals/.

26. Kasumi Hirokawa, "Phone Camera Shutters and Women-Only Cars: Japan's Answer to Chikan," *Stop Street Harassment*, July 10, 2014, http://www .stopstreetharassment.org/2014/07/phone-camera-shutters/.

27. Linnet Nyawira Mwangi, "Kenya: He Mistook My Kindness for Weakness," *Stop Street Harassment*, January 15, 2015, http://www.stopstreetharassment .org/2015/01/kindness-for-weakness/.

28. Aikanysh Jeenbaeva and the BFCSQ team, "Kyrgyzstan: Street Harassment of Transgender People in Bishkek," *Stop Street Harassment*, October 20, 2013, http://www.stopstreetharassment.org/2013/10/kyrgyzstantransgender/.

29. Tilly Grove, "UK: Street Harassment, the Initiation into Adulthood," *Stop Street Harassment*, September 26, 2013, http://www.stopstreetharassment .org/2013/09/adulthood/.

30. Nathalie Sanchez, "Cultural Machismo in Latino Communities," *Stop Street Harassment*, March 30, 2011, http://www.stopstreetharassment.org/2011 /03/cultural-machismo-in-latino-communities/.

31. Sarah Chang, "Street Harassment in Boston," *Stop Street Harassment*, July 2, 2014, http://www.stopstreetharassment.org/2014/07/street-harassment -in-boston/.

32. Elsa S. Henry, "Street Harassment 102: When You're Blind and a Woman," *Feminist Sonar*, September 7, 2012, http://feministsonar.com/2012/09/street -harassment-102-when-youre-blind-and-a-woman/. Used by permission.

33. Seanna Pratt, "Lesbian Couples and Street Harassment," *GERM Magazine*, September 3, 2014, http://www.germmagazine.com/lesbian-couples-and -street-harassment/.

34. Patrick McNeil, "Harassing Men on the Street," *Feministe*, October 15, 2012, http://www.feministe.us/blog/archives/2012/10/15/harassing-men-on-the-street/. Used by permission.

CHAPTER 3: LOCAL COMMUNITY ACTIVISM

1. Hollaback! Brussels, "Chalk Walk: Women in Brussels Reclaim the Places Where They Were Harassed," *Stop Street Harassment*, March 25, 2012, http://www.stopstreetharassment.org/2012/03/chalkwalk/.

2. Ibid.

3. Holly Kearl, *International Anti-Street Harassment Week 2014 Report* (*Stop Street Harassment*, 2014), 14.

4. Tribune 242, "Taking Harassment Off The Streets," *Tribune 242*, April 1, 2014, http://www.tribune242.com/news/2014/apr/01/taking-harassment-off-the-streets/?news.

5. Mirabelle Jones, "Catcalling Cards," *I am Not an Object*, September 14, 2012, http://iamnotanobject.tumblr.com/post/31544486531/catcalling-cards.

6. ProChange, e-mail message to the author, December 6, 2014.

7. Ibid.

8. Lindsey Middlecamp, "Talk Back to Your Harassers with these Cards!" *Stop Street Harassment*, June 10, 2014, http://www.stopstreetharassment.org/2014/06/cardsagainstharassment/.

9. Middlecamp, e-mail message to author, December 21, 2014.

10. Kearl, "700 Anti-Violence Posters Pasted Throughout Kabul, Afghanistan," *Stop Street Harassment*, December 26, 2011, http://www.stopstreetharassment.org/2011/12/posterskabul/.

11. Kearl, "*International Anti-Street Harassment Week 2013 Report*," *Stop Street Harassment*, 2013, http://issuu.com/stopstreetharassment/docs/endshweek2013report.

12. Emmanuelle Fenice, Claire Larrieux, and Héloïse Raslebol, e-mail message to the author, December 11, 2014.

13. Rigoberto Hernandez, "'Stop Telling Women to Smile': Denouncing 'Jackals' and Catcalling in Mexico," *NPR*, February 10, 2015, http://www.npr.org/blogs/codeswitch/2015/02/10/384994475/stop-telling-women-to-smile-denouncing-jackals-and-catcalling-in-mexico.

14. Anny Shaw, "Artists fight violence against women in Egypt," *The Art Newspaper*, August 20, 2014, http://www.theartnewspaper.com/articles/Artists-fight-violence-against-women-in-Egypt/33419.

15. Nama Khalil, "Blue Bra Graffiti (Bahia Shehab)," *Design and Violence*, September 3, 2014, http://designandviolence.moma.org/blue-bra-graffiti-bahia-shehab/.

16. Suzee in the City, "Women in Graffiti: A Tribute to the Women of Egypt," *Suzee in the City*, January 7, 2013, http://suzeeinthecity.wordpress.com/2013/01/07/women-in-graffiti-a-tribute-to-the-women-of-egypt/.

17. Kearl, *International Anti-Street Harassment Week 2013 Report*, 27–28.

18. Kearl, *International Anti-Street Harassment Week 2014 Report*, 64.

19. Ibid., 118.

20. Nadine Toukan, "Jordan: Women's Basic Rights for Dignity and Social Cohesion," *Global Voices Online*, June 27, 2012, http://globalvoicesonline.org /2012/06/27/jordan-womens-basic-rights-for-dignity-and-social-cohesion/.

21. Kearl, "Egypt: Protests Against Harassment This Week," *Stop Street Harassment*, July 6, 2012, http://www.stopstreetharassment.org/2012/07/egypt2 protests/.

22. Kearl, *International Anti-Street Harassment Week 2014 Report*, 27–28.

23. Ibid., 45.

24. Ibid., 124–126.

25. Kearl, "Interview with Organizer of Afghanistan Anti-Street Harassment March," *Stop Street Harassment*, July 16, 2011, http://www.stopstreet harassment.org/2011/07/interviewnoorjahanakbar/.

26. Ibid.

27. News24, "Minister to take part in miniskirt march," *News24*, February 16, 2012, http://www.news24.com/SouthAfrica/Politics/Minister-to-take -part-in-miniskirt-march-20120216.

28. Simona-Maria Chirciu, "Romania: Organizing a Street Harassment March," *Stop Street Harassment*, January 14, 2015, http://www.stopstreetharass ment.org/2015/01/romaniashmarch/.

29. Lisa Arntzen, Skype communication with the author, December 3, 2014.

30. Sumathi Reddy, "A Thin Line on Skirts," *Wall Street Journal*, September 30, 2011, http://www.wsj.com/news/articles/SB10001424052970204226 2045766011742409 52328?mod=ITP_newyork_1&mg=reno64-wsj&url =http%3A%2F%2Fonline.wsj.com%2Farticle%2FSB100014240529702 0422620457660117424095 2328.html%3Fmod%3DITP_newyork_1; see also Jamie Feldmar, "Following Sexual Assaults, Cyclists Rally to Escort Park Slope Women Home," *Gothamist*, September 20, 2011, http://gothamist.com/2011/09 /20/following_sexual_assaults_cyclists.php.

31. Kearl, "Patrols Against Harassment in Egypt," *Stop Street Harassment*, August 22, 2012, http://www.stopstreetharassment.org/2012/08/patrols -against-harassment-in-egypt/.

32. Ghazala Irshad, "Attention Men: If You Attack a Woman In Tahrir Square, You Might Get Your Ass Kicked, Finally," *Gawker*, December 6, 2012, http:// gawker.com/5966368/attention-men-if-you-attack-a-woman-in-tahrir-square -you-might-get-your-ass-kicked-finally.

33. Love Matters, "'No Groping' on Bogota's Buses," Love Matters, April 22, 2011, http://lovematters.in/en/news/no-groping-bogotas-buses.

34. Cherry Thein, "Whistle Campaign a Hit on City Buses," *Myanmar Times*, February 27, 2012, http://www.mmtimes.com/index.php/national-news/yangon /1161-whistle-campaign-a-hit-on-city-buses.html; see also Yola Verbruggen, "Yan gon's Women Start to Fight Sexual Harassment," *Bangkok Post*, October 19, 2014, http://www.bangkokpost.com/print/438372/.

35. Kearl, "Sri Lanka Campaign Reached 30,000 Commuters in One Week," *Stop Street Harassment*, August 9, 2012, http://www.stopstreetharassment.org /2012/08/30000/.

36. Samhati Mohapatra, "Yellow-and-Green Gender Revolution on 3 Wheels," *New Indian Express*, October 25, 2014, http://www.newindianexpress.com /magazine/Yellow-and-Green-Gender-Revolution-on-3-Wheels/2014/10/25 /article2491608.ece.

37. Kuber Sharma, "I Flashed a Mob and I Liked It," *Stop Street Harassment*, June 2, 2011, http://www.stopstreetharassment.org/2011/06/i-flashed-a -mob-and-i-liked-it/.

38. Ellie Cosgrave, "I Danced Against Sexual Assault on the Tube to Reclaim It for Women," *The Guardian*, July 23, 2013, http://www.theguardian .com/commentisfree/2013/jul/23/danced-sexual-assault-tube-women.

39. Sarah Colomé, "USA: Flash Mob Against Harassment on CTA," *Stop Street Harassment*, November 7, 2014, http://www.stopstreetharassment.org /2014/11/flashmobcta/.

40. Bryony Beynon and Kristi Weir, e-mail message to the author, December 2, 2014.

41. Beynon, e-mail message to the author, December 2, 2014.

42. Ibid.

43. Ibid.

44. Manuel Abril, e-mail message to the author, December 9, 2014.

45. Shawna Potter, e-mail message to the author, January 6, 2015.

46. Julie Mastrine, "Penn State Students Conduct Anti-Street Harassment Demonstration," *Stop Street Harassment*, October 22, 2012, http://www.stop streetharassment.org/2012/10/pennstate/.

47. Holly Dagres, "Workshop Idea: Fight Harassment 101," *Stop Street Harassment*, July 10, 2013, http://www.stopstreetharassment.org/2013/07/fh101/.

48. Katie Bowers and Nefertiti Martin, "'Bring Your Brother Day' Workshop on Street Harassment," *Stop Street Harassment*, March 30, 2012, http:// www.stopstreetharassment.org/2012/03/bring-your-brother.

49. Ibid.

50. Zoneziwoh Mbondgulo Wondieh, "Cameroon Workshop to Raise Awareness and Build Allies with Adolescents," *Stop Street Harassment*, December 14, 2013, http://www.stopstreetharassment.org/2013/12/cameroon16daysworkshop/.

51. Wondieh, e-mail message to the author, December 30, 2014.

52. ProChange, e-mail message to the author, December 6, 2014.

53. Jake Winn, e-mail message to the author, November 27, 2014.

54. Ibid.

55. Ibid.

56. Abril, e-mail message to the author, December 9, 2014.

CHAPTER 4: TECHNOLOGY-FUELED EFFORTS

1. Salvador Rodriguez, "60% of World's Population Still Won't Have Internet by the End of 2014," *LA Times*, May 7, 2014, http://www.latimes.com/business /technology/la-fi-tn-60-world-population-3-billion-internet-2014-20140507 -story.html; see also Robert A. Ferdman, "4.4 Billion People Around the World Still Don't Have Internet. Here's where they live," *Washington Post*, October 2,

2014, http://www.washingtonpost.com/blogs/wonkblog/wp/2014/10/02/4-4-billion-people-around-the-world-still-dont-have-internet-heres-where-they-live/.

2. Caitlin Dewey, "Almost as many people use Facebook as live in the entire country of China," *Washington Post*, October 29, 2014, http://www.washington post.com/news/the-intersect/wp/2014/10/29/almost-as-many-people-use-facebook-as-live-in-the-entire-country-of-china/.

3. Twitter, "About," Twitter, n.d., https://about.twitter.com/company.

4. YouTube, "Statistics," YouTube, n.d., https://www.youtube.com/yt/press/statistics.html.

5. Samuel Gibbs, "Instagram Reaches 200 Million Users," *The Guardian*, March 26, 2014, http://www.theguardian.com/technology/2014/mar/26/instagram-200-million-users-facebook-mobile-photo-sharing.

6. Holly Kearl, "Male Allies Win Awards!" *Stop Street Harassment*, September 11, 2012, http://www.stopstreetharassment.org/2012/09/male-allies-win-awards/.

7. Rebel.grrrl, Instagram, http://instagram.com/rebel.grrrl, accessed February 17, 2015.

8. Kathryn McCullagh, "Tweeting about Sexism may Improve a Woman's Wellbeing," *British Psychological Society*, EurekaAlert!, January 30, 2015, http://www.eurekalert.org/pub_releases/2015-01/bps-tas013015.php.

9. Kearl, "Tweet #INeverAskforIt" *Stop Street Harassment*, February 17, 2010, http://www.stopstreetharassment.org/2010/02/tweet-ineveraskforit/.

10. Kearl, "India: New Reporting Site and #SafeCityPledge Events," *Stop Street Harassment*, January 1, 2013, http://www.stopstreetharassment.org/2013/01/indiajan1/.

11. Kearl, "June 20: Lebanese Day of Blogging against Sexual Harassment," *Stop Street Harassment*, June 17, 2011, http://www.stopstreetharassment.org/2011/06/june-20-lebanese-day-of-blogging-against-sexual-harassment/.

12. Kearl, "#ShoutingBack Stories Flood Twitter," *Stop Street Harassment*, January 8, 2013, http://www.stopstreetharassment.org/2013/01/shoutingback/.

13. Kearl, "Stories about Being #Grabbed Trended on Twitter," *Stop Street Harassment*, May 18, 2014, http://www.stopstreetharassment.org/2014/05/grabbed/.

14. Von Lisa Caspari, "Der #aufschrei und seine Folgen," *Zeit Online*, January 23, 2014, http://www.zeit.de/politik/deutschland/2014-01/sexismus-debatte-folgen.

15. Ibid.

16. Roxanna Bennett, "Yes, All Women," *Gender Focus*, May 26, 2014, http://www.gender-focus.com/2014/05/26/yes-all-women/#sthash.TG5ZIHJW.dpuf.

17. Pete Pachal, "How the #YesAllWomen Hashtag Began," *Mashable*, May 26, 2014, http://mashable.com/2014/05/26/yesallwomen-hashtag/.

18. Nolan Feeney, "The Most Powerful #YesAllWomen Tweets," *Time*, May 25, 2014, http://time.com/114043/yesallwomen-hashtag-santa-barbara-shooting/.

19. Elizabeth Heideman, "#YesAllWomen, but Not Really: How Feminism Leaves the Disabled Behind," *The Daily Beast*, November 24, 2014, http://

www.thedailybeast.com/articles/2014/11/24/yesallwomen-but-not-really-how
-feminism-leaves-the-disabled-behind.html.

20. Demetria Irwin, "#YouOkSis: Online Movement Launches to Combat Street Harassment," *The Grio*, August 2, 2014, http://thegrio.com/2014/08/02/youoksis-online-movement-launches-to-combat-street-harassment/.

21. Ibid.

22. Asafoetida, "Then I See His Penis Out!" YouTube, September 4, 2010, https://www.youtube.com/watch?v=iIlObKYwUyI.

23. Irin Carmon, "How to Shout Down a Perv: Tips and Tricks from the Subway Badass," *Jezebel*, December 17, 2010, http://jezebel.com/5714562/tips-on-how-to-handle-pervs-from-subway-badass-nicola-briggs.

24. NDTV, "Outrage in Assam after Mob Publicly Strips, Molests Girl in Guwahati," YouTube, July 13, 2012, https://www.youtube.com/watch?v=vGW2HL92VEw&feature=related.

25. "Saudi Arabia Sexual Harassment Video Sparks Social Media Outrage," *Al Arabiya*, October 24, 2013, http://english.alarabiya.net/en/News/middle-east/2013/10/24/Saudi-Arabia-sexual-harassment-video-sparks-social-media-outrage-.html.

26. Телеканал ОНТ, "EURO-2012: Holland Fans and Ukranian Reporter, Funny Video, Kharkiv," YouTube, June 15, 2012, https://www.youtube.com/watch?v=XmQlb_N-K64.

27. Kearl, "Street Harassment Fuels a Viral Documentary," *Ms. Blog*, August 7, 2012, http://msmagazine.com/blog/2012/08/07/street-harassment-fuels-a-viral-documentary/.

28. Ibid.

29. Kearl, "2014: The Year of the Tipping Point (Part 2)," *Stop Street Harassment*, December 29, 2014, http://www.stopstreetharassment.org/2014/12/2014-part-2/.

30. Hermione Hoby, "The Woman in 10 Hours Walking in NYC: 'I Got People Wanting to Slit My Throat,'" *The Guardian*, December 17, 2014, http://www.theguardian.com/lifeandstyle/2014/dec/17/the-woman-in-10-hours-walking-in-nyc-i-got-people-wanting-to-slit-my-throat.

31. Akiba Solomon, "On that Street Harassment Video and Race," *Colorlines*, October 30, 2014, http://colorlines.com/archives/2014/10/on_that_street_harassment_video_and_race.html.

32. Roxane Gay, Tweet, October 29, 2014, https://twitter.com/rgay/status/527470600261218304.

33. Hanna Rosin, "The Problem with that Catcalling Video," Slate.com, October 29, 2014, http://www.slate.com/blogs/xx_factor/2014/10/29/catcalling_video_hollaback_s_look_at_street_harassment_in_nyc_edited_out.html.

34. Hoby, "The Woman in 10 Hours Walking in NYC: 'I got people wanting to slit my throat.'"

35. Rosin, "The Problem with that Catcalling Video."

36. Emily May, "Statement about Recent Street Harassment PSA," Hollaback! October 30, 2014, http://www.ihollaback.org/blog/2014/10/30/statement-about-recent-street-harassment-psa/.

37. Aura Bogado, "De-Centering Whiteness is Essential to Thinking About Street Harassment," *Colorlines,* October 30, 2014, http://colorlines.com/archives/2014/10/decentering_whiteness_is_essential_to_thinking_about_street_harassment.html.

38. Anti-Harassment, "Shit Men Say to Men Who Say Shit to Women on the Streets," YouTube, March 19, 2012, https://www.youtube.com/watch?v=5P4eVjwVd_U.

39. Shira Tarrant, "Shit Men Say to Men about Street Harassment," *Ms. Magazine Blog*, April 4, 2012, http://msmagazine.com/blog/2012/04/04/sht-men-say-to-men-about-street-harassment/.

40. Ibid.

41. Kearl, "Buses and Metros Carry Messages Against Harassment," *Women's Media Center*, April 12, 2013, http://www.womensmediacenter.com/feature/entry/buses-and-metros-carry-messages-against-harassment.

42. Paula Cocozza, "Oppressed Majority: The Film about a World Run by Women that went Viral," *The Guardian*, February 11, 2014, http://www.theguardian.com/lifeandstyle/womens-blog/2014/feb/11/oppressed-majority-film-women-eleonore-pourriat.

43. Gabriela Garcia Calderon Orbe, "3 Videos Turn the Tables on Street Harassment of Women in Latin America," *Global Voices*, December 11, 2014, http://globalvoicesonline.org/2014/12/11/3-videos-turn-the-tables-on-street-harassment-of-women-in-latin-america/.

44. Orbe, "3 Videos Turn the Tables on Street Harassment of Women in Latin America."; See also BuzzFeedYellow, "What Men Are Really Saying When Catcalling Women," YouTube, August 7, 2014, https://www.youtube.com/watch?v=lUJ24mblCLY.

45. Alan Trotter, "@RantingOwl has a Great Train Harassment Story to Tell," Storify, February 6, 2015, https://storify.com/alantrotter/commuter-harrassment.

46. Michael J. Feeney, "Teen Rapper Astronomical Kid Angry with Guy Ogling His ma, so He Makes a YouTube Hit," *Daily News*, October 14, 2010, http://www.nydailynews.com/new-york/teen-rapper-astronomical-kid-angry-guys-ogling-ma-youtube-hit-article-1.187010.

47. Stop Street Harassment, "The Astronomical Kid Testifies at NYC Council Hearing on Street Harassment," YouTube, October 29, 2010, https://www.youtube.com/watch?v=awwzjnxicQo.

48. MaddieandTaeVEVO, "Maddie & Teo–Girl in a Country Song," YouTube, July 24, 2014, https://www.youtube.com/watch?v=_MOavH-Eivw.

49. Kelsey McKinney, "Maddie & Tae Top the Charts with Feminist Country Music," *VOX*, December 11, 2014, http://www.vox.com/2014/8/7/5966739/country-music-feminist.

50. Dr. Wendy Stock, "Togo's Restaurant Trivializes Street Harassment," *Stop Street Harassment*, November 4, 2011, http://www.stopstreetharassment.org/2011/11/togos/.

51. Kearl, "Way to go Togo's," *Stop Street Harassment*, November 21, 2011, http://www.stopstreetharassment.org/2011/11/togos3/.

52. "Check It Out—A Sign Made Entirely of Fail," Feminist Philosophers, June 15, 2012, https://feministphilosophers.wordpress.com/2012/06/15/check-it-out/.

53. Kearl, "Take Down Pro-Harassment Sign!" Change.org, June 2012, https://www.change.org/p/take-down-pro-harassment-sign.

54. Kearl, "Yes to Carrots: It's Not a Compliment," *Stop Street Harassment*, February 25, 2013, http://www.stopstreetharassment.org/2013/02/yestocarrots/.

55. Elizabeth Plank, "#NotBuyingIt App Could Put an End to Sexist Advertisements," *Mic*, March 21, 2013, http://mic.com/articles/30592/notbuyingit-app-could-put-an-end-to-sexist-advertisements.

56. Clare O'Connor, "New App Launched in Time for Super Bowl Lets You Call Out Brands for Sexist Ads," Forbes.com, January 27 2014, http://www.forbes.com/sites/clareoconnor/2014/01/27/new-app-launched-in-time-for-super-bowl-lets-you-call-out-brands-for-sexist-ads/.

57. Kearl, "Call Them Out, Literally," *Stop Street Harassment*, January 30, 2012, http://www.stopstreetharassment.org/2012/01/callthem/.

58. Maeve Duggan, "Online Harassment," Pew Research, October 22, 2014, http://www.pewinternet.org/2014/10/22/online-harassment/.

59. Amanda Hess, "Why Women Aren't Welcome on the Internet," *Pacific Standard Magazine*, January 6, 2014, http://www.psmag.com/health-and-behavior/women-arent-welcome-internet-72170.

60. Michelle Goldberg, "Feminist Writers are so Besieged by Online Abuse that Some Have Begun to Retire," *Washington Post*, February 20, 2015, http://www.washingtonpost.com/opinions/online-feminists-increasingly-ask-are-the-psychic-costs-too-much-to-bear/2015/02/19/3dc4ca6c-b7dd-11e4-a200-c008a01a6692_story.html.

61. Thiago Guimares, "REVEALED: The Demographic Trends for Every Social Network," *Business Insider*, December 12, 2014, http://www.businessinsider.com/2014-social-media-demographics-update-2014-9#ixzz3MYu0wMNL.

62. Soraya Chemaly, Jaclyn Friedman, Laura Bates, "An Open Letter to Facebook," *Huffington Post*, May 21, 2013, http://www.huffingtonpost.com/soraya-chemaly/an-open-letter-to-faceboo_1_b_3307394.html.

63. Chemaly, Friedman, and Bates, "Take Action to End Gender-Based Hate Speech on Facebook," Women, Action & the Media, n.d., http://www.womenactionmedia.org/facebookaction.

64. Chemaly, Friedman, Bates, "An Open Letter to Facebook."

65. Chemaly, Friedman, Bates, "May 28, 2013," WAM!, http://www.womenactionmedia.org/fbagreement/.

66. International Telecommunication Union, "ITU releases 2014 ICT figures," ITU, May 5, 2014, http://www.itu.int/net/pressoffice/press_releases/2014/23.aspx.

67. International Telecommunication Union, "Measuring the Information Society," 2013, Pg 1, http://www.itu.int/en/ITU-D/Statistics/Documents/publications/mis2013/MIS2013_without_Annex_4.pdf. See also Astrid Zweynert, "More than 4 billion people forecast to remain unconnected online–UN report," Thomas Reuters Foundation, October 8, 2013, http://www.trust.org/item/20131008152926-w1xfd/?source=hpeditorial&siteVersion=mobile.

68. Kearl, "Cross-Regional Report: Mapping Access to and Use of Mobile Phones to Prevent, Document, and Respond to Sexual Violence Against Women and Girls in Urban Public Spaces," UN Women, June 2015.

69. Zoneziwoh Mbondgulo Wondieh, Facebook message communication to the author, December 31, 2014.

70. METRAC, "Not Your Baby," iTunes, n.d., https://itunes.apple.com/us/app/not-your-baby/id545191859?mt=8.

71. Safetipin, "Our Vision," n.d., http://ww.safetipin.com/our-vision; see also Ayesha Vemuri, "Meet Safetipin: A Mobile Application That Tells Exactly How Safe Any Locality is For You," Youth Kiawaaz, 20 November 2013, http://www.youthkiawaaz.com/2013/11/meet-safetipin-mobile-application-tells-exactly-safe-locality/.

72. Mike Butcher, "Clever bSafe Panic Alarm App Launches in U.S. with Free Offer to New Yorkers," *TechCrunch*, 26 June 2013, http://techcrunch.com/2012/06/26/clever-bsafe-panic-alarm-app-launches-in-us-with-free-offer-to-new-yorkers/; see also Google Play, "bSafe Personal Safety Alarm," August 14, 2013, https://play.google.com/store/apps/details?id=com.bipper.app.bsafe&hl=en.

73. Lindsay Rosenthal, "Eliminate Violence Against Women and Girls? There's An App for That," *Science Progress*, March 8, 2013, http://scienceprogress.org/2013/03/eliminate-violence-against-women-and-girls-worldwide-there%E2%80%99s-an-app-for-that/; see also Nancy Schwartzman, "Harnessing Mobile Tech to Prevent Sexual Assault," *Huffington Post*, April 2, 2013, http://www.huffingtonpost.com/nancy-schwartzman/circle-of-6-app_b_2999887.html.

74. Kearl, "Laws Protecting Women from Upskirt Photo Assaults Fall Short," *The Daily Beast*, March 12, 2014, http://www.thedailybeast.com/witw/articles/2014/03/12/tighten-laws-on-upskirt-photos.html.

75. Conor Sheils, "Egyptian Cops Using Grindr to Hunt Gays," Cairoscene, August 31, 2014, http://www.cairoscene.com/ViewArticle.aspx?AId=13967-Egyptian-Cops-Using-Grindr-To-Hunt-Gays.

CHAPTER 5: GLOBAL CAMPAIGNS

1. Andrea Gunrai, e-mail message to author, December 10, 2014.

2. Kathryn Travers, phone interview with the author, December 9, 2014.

3. Kalpana Viswanath, "Gender Inclusive Cities Programme–Implementing change for women's safety," in *Building Inclusive Cities: Women's Safety and Their Right to the City*, ed. Margaret Shaw, Caroline Andrew, Carolyn Whitzman, Fran Klodawsky, Kalpana Viswanath, and Crystal Legacy (New York: Routledge, 2013), 76–78.

4. NTV, "Delhi Joins UN Initiative to make Urban Areas Safer for Women," NTV, November 22, 2010, http://www.ndtv.com/article/cities/delhi-joins-un-initiative-to-make-urban-areas-safer-for-women-67905.

5. Women in Cities International, "Third International Conference on Women's Safety–Building Inclusive Cities," Women in Cities International, n.d., http://www.femmesetvilles.org/index.php/en/conferences/third-international-conference-on-women-s.

6. Women in Cities International and Jagori, "Third International Conference on Women's Safety: Building Inclusive Cities—Conference Programme," Women in Cities International and Jagori, November 22, 2010 (print copy).

7. Ibid.

8. Brittany Shoot, "Resilience in Slums a Lesson for Cynical Western Feminists," *Ms*. Blog, November 24, 2010, http://msmagazine.com/blog/2010/11/24/resilience-in-slums-a-lesson-for-cynical-western-feminists/.

9. Women in Cities International, "Third International Conference on Women's Safety," http://www.femmesetvilles.org/index.php/en/conferences/third-international-conference-on-women-s.

10. Laura Capobianco, phone interview with the author, December 7, 2014.

11. UN Women, "Joining Forces with UN-Habitat to Promote Women's Voice, Access and Safety in Sustainable Urban Development," UN Women, June 11, 2013, http://www.unwomen.org/en/news/stories/2013/6/joining-forces-with-un-habitat.

12. UN Women, "Creating Safe Public Spaces," UN Women, n.d., http://www.unwomen.org/en/what-we-do/ending-violence-against-women/creating-safe-public-spaces.

13. Capobianco, e-mail message to the author, February 18, 2015.

14. U.N. Women, "In Brief: Safe Cities Global Initiative," UN Women, n.d., http://www.unwomen.org/~/media/headquarters/attachments/sections/library/publications/2014/un%20women%20safe%20cities%20brief-us-web.pdf.

15. Capobianco, phone interview.

16. Ibid.

17. Capobianco, e-mail message to the author.

18. ActionAid, "Our New Strategy for Ending Poverty," ActionAid, n.d., http://www.actionaid.org/who-we-are/our-new-strategy-ending-poverty.

19. ActionAid, "Violence against Women," ActionAid, n.d., http://www.actionaid.org/what-we-do/womens-rights/violence-against-women.

20. ActionAid, "Safe Cities for Women," ActionAid, n.d., http://www.actionaid.org/safe-cities-for-women.

21. *Safe Cities for Women: From Reality to Rights,* ActionAid, May 2014, http://global.safecitiesforwomen.org/wp-content/uploads/sites/5/2014/02/safe-cities.pdf.

22. Kearl, *International Anti-Street Harassment Week 2014 Report* (*Stop Street Harassment*: 2014), 60–61.

23. ActionAid, "ActionAid South Africa Flashmob," ActionAid, June 19, 2014, http://www.actionaidusa.org/south-africa/videos/actionaid-south-africa-flashmob.

24. ActionAid, "Safe Cities Programme: Women's right to the city" ActionAid, September 2014 newsletter, PDF emailed to the author by Christy Abraham.

25. *Safe Cities for Women: From Reality to Rights*, http://global.safecitiesforwomen.org/wp-content/uploads/sites/5/2014/02/safe-cities.pdf.

26. Ibid., 34.

27. Christy Abraham, phone interview with the author, December 18, 2014.

28. Huairou Commission, "Mission and Description," Huairou Commission, n.d., http://huairou.org/mission-and-description.

29. Rachael Wyant, phone interview with the author, December 4, 2014.

30. Carolina Pinheiro, e-mail message to the author, June 6, 2013.

31. Kearl, "Street Lights and Short Grass: Local Strategies Help Improve Global Women's Security," *Ms*, Summer 2013, 23.

32. Huairiou Commission, "Delhi and Beyond: Concrete Action for Safer Cities" Google Map, Huairiou Commission, n.d., https://www.google.com/maps /d/viewer?oe=UTF8&ie=UTF8&msa=0&mid=zHkzk8nfZBkI.kYRnz3LaV FmY.

33. Wyant, phone interview.

34. Ibid.

35. Pinheiro, e-mail message.

36. Wyant, phone interview.

37. Fran Luck, phone interview with the author, January 12, 2015.

38. Ibid.

39. Samuel Carter and Emily May, "Hollaback! State of the Streets Report, 2011," Hollaback! December 2011, http://issuu.com/hollaback/docs/finalstate _of_the_streets_12.19?e=4099169/3126329.

40. May and Allison Sesso "Hollaback! State of the Streets Report, 2014," Hollaback! December 2014, http://issuu.com/hollaback/docs/sots14v4.

41. Ibid.

42. Information about these activities are found in their annual State of the Streets reports and monthly newsletters.

43. May and Carter, "Hollaback! State of the Streets Report, 2011."

44. IDRC, "Rebecca Chiao—HarassMap: Social Mapping Sexual Harassment and Violence in Egypt," YouTube, February 11, 2013, https://www.youtube.com /watch?v=hLq7fCUQANM.

45. Ibid.

46. Rebecca Chiao and Angie Abdelmonem, e-mail message to the author, January 4, 2015.

47. IDRC, "Rebecca Chiao—HarassMap: Social Mapping Sexual Harassment and Violence in Egypt."

48. Chiao and Abdelmonem, e-mail message.

49. Stop Street Harassment, "Sawsan Gad–Street Harassment Talk," You-Tube, March 20, 2012, https://www.youtube.com/watch?v=dwwa0qqsDfw.

50. HarassMap, "Sexual harassment myths," HarassMap, n.d., http://harass map.org/en/resource-center/harassment-myths/.

51. HarassMap, "IDRC Write-Up on Impacts" document e-mailed to Holly Kearl by Rebecca Chaio, January 4, 2015.

52. Chiao and Abdelmonem, e-mail message with author.

53. HarassMap, "Around the world," HarassMap, n.d., http://harassmap.org /en/what-we-do/around-the-world/.

54. Laura Bates, *Everyday Sexism* (Simon & Schuster UK Ltd: 2014), 16.

55. Bates, 18.

56. Bates, e-mail message with author, January 2, 2015.

57. Ibid.

58. Bates, "Everyday Sexism Speech to the UN: 'Sexism and Sexual Harass-ment is not a 'Women's Issue'—It is a Matter of Human Rights," New Statesman,

March 13, 2014, http://www.newstatesman.com/2014/03/everyday-sexism-speech
-un-sexism-and-sexual-harassment-not-womens-issue. Used by permission.

59. Bates, e-mail message with author.

CHAPTER 6: GOVERNMENT INITIATIVES

1. AQ Online, "Guatemala Debuts 'Women Only' Buses," *Americas Quarterly*, June 16, 2011, http://www.americasquarterly.org/node/2589.

2. Thai Son, "Vietnam Capital Plans All-Female Buses Following Reports of Sexual Harassment," *Thanh Nien News*, December 25, 2014, http://www.thanhniennews.com/society/vietnam-capital-plans-allfemale-buses-following-reports-of-sexual-harassment-36725.html.

3. Sarah Elzas, "On French public transit, '100 per cent' of women have been sexually harassed," *RFI English*, April 16, 2015, http://www.english.rfi.fr/france/20150416-french-public-transit-100-cent-women-have-been-sexually-harassed.

4. End Violence Against Women Coalition, "Poll Reveals 1/4 Women do not Feel Safe on London Public Transport," End Violence Against Women, March 30, 2012, http://www.endviolenceagainstwomen.org.uk/news/14/poll-reveals-14-women-dont-feel-safe-on-london-public-transport.

5. The World Bank, "Riding a Bus in Kathmandu: Gender and Transport in Nepal," *The World Bank*, March 17, 2014, http://www.worldbank.org/en/news/feature/2014/03/17/riding-a-bus-in-kathmandu-gender-and-transport-in-nepal.

6. Laura J. Nelson, "Survey: Sexual Harassment makes 20% of Metro Riders Feel Unsafe," *LA Times*, May 7, 2014, http://www.latimes.com/local/lanow/la-me-ln-passengers-feel-unsafe-20140507-story.html.

7. Thomas Reuters Foundation, "Most Dangerous Transport Systems for Women," Trust.org, October 31, 2014, http://www.trust.org/spotlight/most-dangerous-transport-systems-for-women/.

8. Dorothy Schulz and Susan Gilbert, "Women and Transit Security: A New Look at an Old Issue," Proceedings of the Women's Travel Issues Second National Conference, October 25–27, 1996, Baltimore, MD, 551.

9. Daniel Krieger, "Why Women-Only Transit Options Have Caught On," *The Atlantic*, Februrary 8, 2012, http://www.theatlanticcities.com/commute/2012/02/why-women-only-transit-options-have-caught/1171/.

10. Karrie Kehoe, "Exclusive Poll: Does Single-Sex Public Transport Help or Hinder Women?" *Reuters*, October 29, 2014, http://uk.reuters.com/article/2014/10/29/women-poll-carriages-idUKL6N0S42MD20141029.

11. Agence France-Presse, "After Pink Train Coaches, Malaysia Launches Women-Only Buses," *Inquirer Global Nation*, December 2, 2010, http://globalnation.inquirer.net/cebudailynews/news/view/20101202-306599/After-pink-train-coaches-Malaysia-launches-women-only-buses.

12. Stephanie Nolen, "Finding Solace in Delhi's Women-Only Subway Car," *The Globe & Mail*, February 23, 2012, http://www.theglobeandmail.com/news/world/worldview/finding-solace-in-delhis-women-only-subway-car/article548716/.

13. Indah Setiawati, "Men, Women have Separate Busway Queue Lines," *The Jakarta Post*, June 10, 2010, http://www.thejakartapost.com/news/2010/06/10/men-women-have-separate-busway-queue-lines.html.

14. Pallavi Kamat, "India: Public Transport, Private Harassment," *Stop Street Harassment*, August 15, 2013, http://www.stopstreetharassment.org/2013/08/mumbaitransport/.

15. "MetroEgy," YouTube, n.d., https://www.youtube.com/user/MetroEgy?feature=watch; see also Stephanie Nolen, "Finding solace in Delhi's women-only subway car," *The Globe & Mail*, February 23, 2012, http://www.theglobeandmail.com/news/world/worldview/finding-solace-in-delhis-women-only-subway-car/article548716/.

16. Holly Kearl's talk at the 3 International Conference on Women's Safety in Delhi, India, November 23, 2010.

17. Kehoe, "EXCLUSIVE POLL: Does Single-Sex Public Transport Help or Hinder Women?"

18. Staff, "Egyptian Rights Group Rejects 'Women-Only' Taxi," *Egypt Independent*, July 27, 2011, http://www.egyptindependent.com/news/egyptian-rights-group-rejects-women-only-taxis.

19. Danilo Valladares, "GUATEMALA: Women-Only Buses Against Sexual Harassment," *Inter Press Service*, June 2011, http://www.ipsnews.net/2011/06/guatemala-women-only-buses-against-sexual-harassment/.

20. Son, "Vietnam Capital Plans All-Female Buses Following Reports of Sexual Harassment."

21. Anastasia Moloney, "Colombia Steps Up Campaign to Combat Sexual Harassment on Buses," Thomas Reuters Foundation, November 5, 2014, http://www.trust.org/item/20141105160728-yro0i/.

22. Noticias RCN, "Preocupantes cifras de acoso a mujeres en Transmilenio," Noticias RCN, May 9, 2014, http://www.noticiasrcn.com/nacional-bogota/preocupantes-cifras-acoso-mujeres-transmilenio.

23. Arturo Wallace, "Colombian Anti-Groping Squad Goes to Work," BBC, August 25, 2010, http://www.bbc.com/news/world-latin-america-28925622.

24. Ibid.

25. Ibid.

26. "Project Summary in English," Touche Pas a MA Pote, n.d., e-mailed to the author by Pauline Pourtois on December 16, 2014.

27. Ibid.

28. Pauline Pourtois, e-mail message to the author, December 18, 2014.

29. "Project Summary in English," Touche Pas a MA Pote.

30. Ibid.

31. British Transit Police, "Project Guardian," British Transit Police, n.d., http://www.btp.police.uk/advice_and_information/how_we_tackle_crime/project_guardian.aspx.

32. Jane Martinson, "Police Act to Halt Sex Harassment on London Buses and Trains," *The Guardian*, July 21, 2013, http://www.theguardian.com/uk-news/2013/jul/22/sexual-harassment-london-transport.

33. Bryony Beynon, e-mail message to the author, December 2, 2014.

34. Laura Bates, e-mail to the author, January 2, 2015.

35. British Transit Police, "Project Guardian," British Transit Police, n.d., http://www.btp.police.uk/advice_and_information/how_we_tackle_crime/project _guardian.aspx.

36. Bates, e-mail message to the author.

37. Ibid.

38. Ibid.

39. WUSA 9 Staff, "Is Sexual Harassment a Problem on Metro?" *WUSA 9*, February 21, 2012, http://www.wusa9.com/story/local/2012/02/21/3933 809/.

40. Marty Langelan, phone interview with the author, December 7, 2014.

41. Caroline Laurin, e-mail message to the author, April 2, 2013.

42. Nicole Elphick, "Belgium to Ban Sexist Comments," *Daily Life Australia*, March 17, 2014, http://www.dailylife.com.au/news-and-views/news-features /belgium-to-ban-sexist-comments-20140317-34w68.html.

43. Ibid.

44. Amelia Hill and Juliette Jowit, "Sexist Remarks and Wolf-Whistles could Become Criminal Offences," *The Guardian,* March 7, 2012, http://www.the guardian.com/society/2012/mar/08/sexist-comments-to-become-criminal -offence.

45. U.N. Women, "Bolivia Approves a Landmark Law against Harassment of Women Political Leaders," UN Women, June 11, 2012, http://www.unwomen .org/en/news/stories/2012/6/bolivia-approves-a-landmark-law-against-harassment -of-women-political-leaders; see also "Bolivian women battle against culture of harassment," *BBC*, March 11, 2014, http://www.bbc.com/news/world-latin -america-26446066.

46. Ludovica Iaccino, "Belgium: Sexual Harassment Punished with Imprisonment Under New Law," *International Business Times*, March 17, 2014, http://www.ibtimes.co.uk/belgium-sexual-harassment-punished-imprisonment -under-new-law-1440582.

47. Eugene Volokh, "Belgium Bans a Wide Range of Sexist Speech," *The Washington Post*, March 21, 2014, http://www.washingtonpost.com/news/volokh -conspiracy/wp/2014/03/21/belgium-bans-a-wide-range-of-sexist-speech/.

48. RT, "Filming Insults: Street Harassment Prompts New Brussels Law," RT, September 5, 2012, http://rt.com/news/law-fines-insults-brussels-421/.

49. Hollaback Brussels, "Who Wants to Know!? The Government Responds to 'Femme de la rue,'" Hollaback Brussels, August 8, 2012, http://brussels.ihol laback.org/2012/08/08/government-responds-Hollaback-replies/.

50. Hillary Ojeda, "Peruvian Gov't enacts sexual harassment prevention law," Peru This Week, March 26, 2015, http://www.peruthisweek.com/news -peruvian-govt-enacts-sexual-harassment-prevention-law-105671.

51. Anastasia Moloney, "Colombia Steps up Campaign to Combat Sexual Harassment on Buses," Thomas Reuters Foundation, November 5, 2014, http:// www.trust.org/item/20141105160728-yro0i/.

52. Observatorio Contra el Acoso Callejero Chile, e-mail message to the author, December 2, 2014.

53. Eli Vallejo, Facebook message with the author, January 27, 2015.

54. "Anti-Street Harassment Bill Proposed in Argentina," *PanAm Post*, April 27, 2015, http://panampost.com/panam-staff/2015/04/27/anti-street-harass ment-bill-proposed-in-argentina/.

55. George Rodriguez and Jill Replogle, "Panama Congresswoman's anti-sexual harassment bill faces ridicule," The Tico Times, March 24, 2015, http://www.ticotimes.net/2015/03/24/panama-congresswomans-anti-sexual-harassment -bill-faces-ridicule.

56. Kearl, "Car Harassers Can Go to Jail in Missouri!" *Stop Street Harassment*, September 22, 2010, http://www.stopstreetharassment.org/2010/09/car -harassers-can-go-to-jail-in-missouri/.

57. Kate Linthicum, "Bicyclist Harassment Outlawed by Los Angeles City Council," *LA Times*, July 21, 2011, http://articles.latimes.com/2011/jul/21/local /la-me-bicycle-law-20110721.

58. Kearl, "Kansas City, MO, Passes Anti-Harassment Ordinance," *Stop Street Harassment*, October 3, 2014, http://www.stopstreetharassment.org/2014 /10/shordinance/.

59. Robyn Boyle, "Two Complaints a Day in Brussels for Street Harassment," *The Bulletin*, October 14, 2014, http://www.xpats.com/two-complaints -day-brussels-street-harassment.

60. Austria Independent, "Bum Groping is not Sexual Harassment in Austria," *Austrian Independent*, November 22, 2012, http://austrianindependent.com/news /General_News/2012-11-22/12686/Bum_groping_is_not_sexual_harrasment_in _Austria.

61. Kavita B. Ramakrishnan, "Inconsistent Legal Treatment of Unwanted Sexual Advances: A Study of the Homosexual Advance Defense, Street Harassment, and Sexual Harassment in the Workplace," *Berkeley Journal of Gender, Law & Justice* 26 (2011): 354.

62. BBC, "Bolivian Women Battle Against Culture of Harassment."

63. Laura S. Logan, "The Case of the 'Killer Lesbians,'" *The Public Intellectual*, July 18, 2011, http://thepublicintellectual.org/2011/07/18/the-case-of-the -killer-lesbians/.

64. The Korea Herald, "Judge Resigns Over Subway Sexual Harassment," *The Korea Herald*, April 23, 2011, http://www.koreaherald.com/view.php?ud =20110423000008.

65. NDTV Correspondent, "MMS Scandal: Molested and Harassed, Sisters Driven to Suicide," *NDTV*, May 28, 2010, http://www.ndtv.com/article/cities /mms-scandal-molested-and-harassed-sisters-driven-to-suicide-28192.

66. Michelle Fine, Nick Freudenberg, Yasser Payne, Tiffany Perkins, Kersha Smith, and Katya Wanzer, "'Anything Can Happen with Police Around': Urban Youth Evaluate Strategies of Surveillance in Public Places," *Journal of Social Issues* 59, no. 1 (2003): 141–158.

67. Zoneziwoh Mbondgulo Wondieh, "Cameroon: Safe Cities Walk," *Stop Street Harassment*, October 30, 2013, http://www.stopstreetharassment.org/2013 /10/cameroon-safe-cities-walk/.

68. Chloe Saavedra, "Woman Reports Street Harassment, NYPD Officer Laughs," *Stop Street Harassment*, October 6, 2013, http://www.stopstreetharas sment.org/2013/10/nypdlaughs/.

69. Sophie Calas, "Hey Police Officer, What does Being 'Pretty' have to do with Assault?" *Stop Street Harassment*, January 19, 2012, http://www.stop streetharassment.org/2012/01/revolutionbar/.

70. Logan Lambert, "Harasser Uses Sexually Violent Language in Front of Cop, Cop Laughs," *Stop Street Harassment*, July 18, 2011, http://www.stop streetharassment.org/2011/07/harasser-uses-sexually-violent-language-in-front -of-cop-cop-laughs/.

71. P.M. "No, Officers, Harassment, Following and Assault does not Equal 'Flirting,'" *Stop Street Harassment* Blog, April 9, 2011, http://www.stopstreet harassment.org/2011/04/no-officers-harassment-following-and-assault-does -not-equal-flirting/.

72. Marcie Bianco, "One Group Has a Higher Domestic Violence Rate Than Everyone Else—And It's Not the NFL," *Mic*, December 19, 2014, http://mic.com /articles/106886/one-group-has-a-higher-domestic-violence-rate-than-everyone -else-and-it-s-not-the-nfl.

73. Sandra Laville, "Police Abuse: Vulnerable Women and Girls were Targeted by Sexual Predators," *The Guardian*, June 29, 2012, http://www.theguardian.com /uk/2012/jun/29/police-abuse-vulnerable-women-girls.

74. Sue Yacka, "National Report on Hate Violence Against Lesbian, Gay, Bisexual, Transgender, Queer and HIV-Affected Communities Released Today," NCAVP, June 4, 2013, http://www.avp.org/storage/documents/2012_mr_ncavp _hvreport.pdf.

75. Amrit Dhillon, "ATM-style Machine lets Indian Women Report Abuse without Fear," *The Star*, August 25, 2014, http://www.thestar.com/news/world /2014/08/25/atmstyle_machine_lets_indian_women_report_abuse_without _fear.html; see also Barbara Speed, "The ATM at which Indian women can Report Sexual Assault," *CityMetric*, January 6, 2015, http://www.citymetric.com /horizons/atm-which-indian-women-can-report-sexual-assault-613.

76. Kearl, "Three Organizations that Care about Women's Safety in Public Spaces," *Stop Street Harassment*, June 16, 2010, http://www.stopstreetharassment .org/2010/06/three-organizations-that-care-about-womens-safety-in-public/; see also "Anti-Violence Campaign Targets 'Abusive' Attitudes," *BBC*, June 1, 2010, http://www.bbc.com/news/10198459.

77. Kearl, "Asking for it? As if," *Stop Street Harassment*, June 30, 2010, http://www.stopstreetharassment.org/2010/06/asking-for-it-as-if/.

78. Not Ever, "The Campaign," Not Ever, n.d., http://www.notever.co.uk/the -campaign/.

79. Seth Barron, "CM Ferreras Holds Hearing against Street Harassment," Julissa Ferreras, October 28, 2010, http://myemail.constantcontact.com /Julissa-Ferreras-Press-Announcement.html?soid=1102274890321&aid=TC 05i_F0vBY.

80. The New York City Council, "Oversight: Street Harassment of Women and Girls in New York City," The New York City Council, October 28, 2010, 5.

81. Bill de Blasio, "One New York, Rising Together," Bill de Blasio for Mayor, December 2013, http://dnwssx4l7gl7s.cloudfront.net/deblasio/default/page/-/One _New_York_Rising_Together.pdf.

CHAPTER 7: EGYPT AND INDIA CASE STUDIES

1. HarassMap, "HarassMap Reports," HarassMap, n.d., http://harassmap .org/en/resource-center/harassmap-reports/.

2. Holly Kearl, "Lara Logan and Egypt's Next Revolution," *Ms. Blog*, February 16, 2011, http://msmagazine.com/blog/2011/02/16/lara-logan-and-egypts -next-revolution/.

3. Rasha Mohammad Hassan, *Clouds in Egypt's Sky. Sexual Harassment: from Verbal Harassment to Rape. A Sociological Study*. Egyptian Centre for Women's Rights, 2008, http://egypt.unfpa.org/Images/Publication/2010_03 /6eeeb05a-3040-42d2-9e1c-2bd2e1ac8cac.pdf.

4. Reem Leila, "Unsafe Streets," *Al-Ahram*, October 15, 2008, http://weekly .ahram.org.eg/2008/917/eg6.htm.

5. IDRC, "Rebecca Chiao—HarassMap: Social Mapping Sexual Harassment and Violence in Egypt," YouTube, February 11, 2013, https://www.youtube.com /watch?v=hLq7fCUQANM.

6. 60 Minutes, "Laura Logan Breaks Silence on Cairo Assault," *60 Minutes*, May 1, 2011, http://www.cbsnews.com/news/lara-logan-breaks-silence-on-cairo -assault.

7. Ibid.

8. Nadine Marroushi, "Women Police Rape, Who can People Turn to?" *Middle East Eye*, December 27, 2014, http://www.middleeasteye.net/columns /when-police-rape-who-can-people-turn-1347802948.

9. Sarah el Deeb, "Alarming Assaults on Women in Egypt's Tahrir," *Huffington Post*, June 6, 2012, http://www.huffingtonpost.com/huff-wires/20120606 /egypt-sexual-assault/.

10. Patrick Kingsley, "80 Sexual Assaults in One Day—The Other Story of Tahrir Square," *The Guardian*, July 5, 2013, http://www.theguardian.com/world /2013/jul/05/egypt-women-rape-sexual-assault-tahrir-square.

11. Al Jazeera Staff, "Egypt Still has a Sexual Assault Problem," *Al Jazeera America*, July 17, 2014, http://america.aljazeera.com/articles/2014/7/17/egypt -still-has-asexualassaultproblem.html; see also Nadine Marroushi, "When Police Rape, Who can People Turn to?" *Middle East Eye*, December 27, 2014, http:// www.middleeasteye.net/columns/when-police-rape-who-can-people-turn -1347802948.

12. CNN Wire Staff, "Egypt's Million Woman March Fizzles into Shouting Matches," *CNN*, March 8, 2011, http://edition.cnn.com/2011/WORLD/meast /03/08/egypt.women/?hpt=T2; see also Ahmed Awadalla, "Faggots for Whores? Or What happened to Women's March in Tahrir," Rebel with a Cause, March 8, 2011, http://rwac-egypt.blogspot.com/2011/03/faggots-for-whores-or-what -happened-to.html.

13. Kearl, "Harassers Attack Anti-Sexual Assault Protest at Tahrir Square in Egypt," *Stop Street Harassment*, June 9, 2012, http://www.stopstreetharassment .org/2012/06/june8protest/.

14. Kearl, "Egyptian Women Refuse to be Silent by Assaults," *Ms. blog*, June 10, 2012, http://msmagazine.com/blog/2012/06/10/egyptian-women-refuse -to-be-silenced-by-assaults/.

15. Kingsley, "Tahrir Square Sexual Assaults Reported during Anniversary Clashes," *The Guardian*, January 27, 2013, http://www.theguardian.com/world /2013/jan/27/tahrir-square-sexual-assaults-reported.

16. HRW, "Egypt: Military 'Virginity Test' Investigation a Sham," Human Rights Watch, November 9, 2011, http://www.hrw.org/news/2011/11/09/egypt -military-virginity-test-investigation-sham.

17. Jenny Hauser, "Female Egyptian Protesters Highlight Sexual Harassment," Storyful, November 25, 2011, http://storyful.com/stories/1000014443.

18. Kirkpatrick, "Mass March by Cairo Women in Protest Over Abuse by Soldiers," New York Times, December 20, 2011, http://www.nytimes.com/2011 /12/21/world/middleeast/violence-enters-5th-day-as-egyptian-general-blames -protesters.html?.

19. Rosie Swash, "How Egyptians are Fighting Harassment in the Streets," *The Guardian*, November 5, 2012, http://www.theguardian.com/lifeandstyle /2012/nov/05/egyptians-fighting-harassment-streets.

20. Serena Hollmeyer Taylor et al., " 'When She Stands Among Men': Sexual Harassment of Women at Political Protests in Cairo, January 2011–August 2013," *Al Nakhlah*, June 10, 2014, http://alnakhlah.org/2014/06/10/when-she -stands-among-men-sexual-harassment-of-women-at-political-protests-in-cairo -january-2011-august-2013/#_ftn37.

21. Daily News Egypt, "Anti-harassment Group to Form Eid Operation Rooms," *Daily News Egypt*, July 26, 2014, http://www.dailynewsegypt.com /2014/07/26/anti-harassment-group-form-eid-operation-rooms/.

22. Al Jazeera Staff, "Egypt still has a Sexual Assault Problem," *Al Jazeera America*, July 17, 2014, http://america.aljazeera.com/articles/2014/7/17/egypt -still-has-asexualassaultproblem.html; see also Marroushi, "When police rape."

23. Kingsley, "Doubt Remains in Egypt Despite Sisi's Action Against Sexual Harassment," *The Guardian*, June 13, 2014, http://www.theguardian.com /world/2014/jun/13/doubts-remain-in-egypt-despite-sisis-action-against-sexual -harassment.

24. Ibid.

25. Yasmin El-Rifae, "Egypt's Sexual Harassment Law: An Insufficient Measure to End Sexual Violence," *Middle East Institute*, July 17, 2014, http://www .mei.edu/content/at/egypts-sexual-harassment-law-insufficient-measure-end -sexual-violence.

26. Ibid.

27. U.N. Women, "UN Egypt Calls for Firm Stand on Violence Against Women," UN Women, June 11, 2014, http://www.unwomen.org/en/news/stories /2014/6/new-anti-sexual-harassment-law-in-egypt.

28. Menan Khater, "Sexual Harassment Still Pervasive in Egypt, Despite New Law," *Daily News Egypt*, November 24, 2014, http://www.dailynewsegypt.com /2014/11/24/sexual-harassment-still-pervasive-egypt-despite-new-law/.

29. Chiao and Abdelmonem, e-mail message to the author.

30. Abdelmonem, e-mail message to the author, December 28, 2014.

31. Egypt Independent, "Initiative: 4 Sexual Harassment Cases by Policemen in 2 Months," *Egypt Independent*, December 29, 2014, http://www.egypt

independent.com/news/initiative-4-sexual-harassment-cases-policemen-2
-months.

32. Ayah Aman, "Egyptian Women Take to Social Media to Expose Harassers," *Egypt Pulse*, January 16, 2015, http://www.al-monitor.com/pulse/originals
/2015/01/egypt-women-sexual-harrassment-social-media.html#.

33. Samer Fawzer Aziz, Facebook message to the author, January 19, 2015.

34. Chiao and Abdelmonem, e-mail message to the author.

35. IBN Live, I want to Live, Delhi Braveheart told her Mother and Brother,"
IBN Live, December 29, 2012, http://ibnlive.in.com/news/i-want-to-live-delhi
-braveheart-told-her-mother-and-brother/312896-3-244.html.

36. Dean Nelson, "Delhi Gang-rape Victim Dies of Organ Failure," *Telegraph*, December 28, 202, http://www.telegraph.co.uk/news/worldnews/asia/india
/9770345/Delhi-gang-rape-victim-dies-of-organ-failure.html.

37. Arup Roychoudhury and Annie Banerji, "India's Gang-rape Protesters
Defy Moves to Quell Outrage," *Reuters*, December 23, 2012, http://www.reuters
.com/article/2012/12/23/us-india-protests-idUSBRE8BM02X20121223.

38. Soutik Biswas, "How India Treats its Women," *BBC*, December 29, 2012,
http://www.bbc.com/news/world-asia-india-20863860.

39. U.N. Women, "UN Women Supported Survey in Delhi Shows 95 per cent
of Women and Girls Feel Unsafe in Public Spaces," UN Women, February 20,
2013, http://www.unwomen.org/en/news/stories/2013/2/un-women-supported
-survey-in-delhi.

40. The Hindu, "Eve-teasing, Teenager Commits Suicide," *The Hindu*, December 8, 2012, http://www.thehindu.com/todays-paper/tp-national/tp-newdelhi
/eveteased-teenager-commits-suicide/article4176838.ece.

41. The Times of India, "Eve-teasing Prompts Girls to End Life," *The Times
of India*, December 16, 2012, http://timesofindia.indiatimes.com/city/ranchi/Eve
-teasing-prompts-girl-to-end-life/articleshow/17631246.cms?refer.

42. Sky News, "Gang-Rape in India: Teen Victim Kills Herself," *Sky News*,
December 28, 2012, http://news.sky.com/story/1030759/gang-rape-in-india-teen
-victim-kills-herself.

43. Bharat Yagnik, "Man Thrashed for Protesting Eve teasing," *The Times of
India*, December 28, 2012, http://timesofindia.indiatimes.com/city/ahmedabad
/Man-thrashed-for-protesting-eve-teasing/articleshow/17797390.cms.

44. Parth Shastri, "Man Stabbed to Death in Ahmedabad Eve-teasing," *The
Times of India*, November 28, 2012, http://timesofindia.indiatimes.com/city
/ahmedabad/Man-stabbed-to-death-in-Ahmedabad-over-eve-teasing/articleshow
/17403034.cms?referral=PM.

45. Gautam S. Mengle, "Dombivali Youth's Murder Brings Eve-teasing Menace into Sharp Focus Again," *The Indian Express*, December 11, 2012, http://
archive.indianexpress.com/news/dombivali-youth-s-murder-brings-eveteasing
-menace-into-sharp-focus-again/1043383/0.

46. Jason Overdorf, "India: Protests Resume after Delhi Gang Rape Victim
Dies," *Global Post*, December 29, 2012, http://www.globalpost.com/dispatch/
news/regions/asia-pacific/india/121229/india-protests-resume-delhi
-gang-rape-victim-dies

47. Harmeet Shah Singh, "Indian Prime Minister Calls for Calm After Violence Erupts during Anti-rape Rallies," *CNN*, January 4, 2013, http://www.cnn.com/2012/12/23/world/asia/india-rape-protests/index.html?hpt=wo_c1.

48. Kearl, "India Tragedy Seen as a Transitional Moment," *Women's Media Center*, January 10, 2013, http://www.womensmediacenter.com/feature/entry/india-tragedy-seen-as-transitional-moment.

49. Radhika Takru, e-mail message to the author, January 8, 2013.

50. DNA India, "Charge Sheet in Delhi Gang-rape Case Likely Today," *DNA India*, January 3, 2013, http://www.dnaindia.com/india/report-charge-sheet-in-delhi-gang-rape-case-likely-today-1784917.

51. The Times of India, "Delhi Gang Rape: CJI Altamas Kabir Calls for Speedy Trial of Case," *The Times of India*, http://timesofindia.indiatimes.com/india/Delhi-gang-rape-CJI-Altamas-Kabir-calls-for-speedy-trial-of-case/articleshow/17859854.cms?referral=PM.

52. Holly Kearl, "India Tragedy Seen as a Transitional Moment," *Women's Media Center*, January 10, 2013, http://www.womensmediacenter.com/feature/entry/india-tragedy-seen-as-transitional-moment.

53. Ibid.

54. Jagori, "Projects," Jagori, accessed February 14, 2015, http://www.jagori.org/projects.

55. Blank Noise, accessed February 14, 2015, http://blog.blanknoise.org/.

56. Sarah Goodyear, "'I Pledge to Walk Alone': Activists Demand Safer Cities for Women in India," *CityLab*, January 22, 2013, www.citylab.com/politics/2013/01/activists-demand-safer-cities-women-india/4446/.

57. Soutik Biswas, "India Gang Rape: Thousands of Women March in Delhi," *BBC*, January 2, 2013, http://www.bbc.com/news/world-asia-india-20886253.

58. The Deccan Herald, "They Cross-dress for a Cause," *The Deccan Herald*, January 12, 2013, http://www.deccanherald.com/content/304804/men-skirts-pledge-support-women.html.

59. Blank Noise, "Safe City Pledge," Facebook, January 2013, https://www.facebook.com/events/511318265558394/.

60. Kearl, "On March 8, #RingTheBell," *Stop Street Harassment*, March 1, 2013, http://www.stopstreetharassment.org/2013/03/march-8-ringthebell/.

61. Joanna Sugden, "Delhi Men Say Sorry," *The Wall Street Journal*, March 16, 2013, http://blogs.wsj.com/indiarealtime/2013/03/16/delhi-men-say-sorry/.

62. Nancy Schwartzman, "Harnessing Mobile Tech to Prevent Sexual Assault," *Huffington Post,* June 2, 2013, http://www.huffingtonpost.com/nancy-schwartzman/circle-of-6-app_b_2999887.html.

63. The Times of India, "Supreme Court Issues Directions to Curb Sexual Harassment of Women in Public Transport," *The Times of India*, December 2, 2012, http://timesofindia.indiatimes.com/india/Supreme-Court-issues-directions-to-curb-sexual-harassment-of-women-in-public-transport/articleshow/17445499.cms.

64. BBC News, "Delhi Gang-rape Victim Dies in Hospital in Singapore," *BBC*, December 28, 2012, http://timesofindia.indiatimes.com/india/Supreme-Court

-issues-directions-to-curb-sexual-harassment-of-women-in-public-transport
/articleshow/17445499.cms.

65. Kearl, "Street Lights and Short Grass: Local Strategies Help Improve Global Women's Security," *Ms*, Summer 2013, 23.

66. Nita Bhalla, "Indians Ask What has Changed since Delhi Gang Rape as Uber Driver Accused," Reuters, December 8, 2014, http://www.reuters.com/article/2014/12/08/us-india-rape-safety-idUSKBN0JM1UO20141208.

67. Mona Iskander, "One Year Since the Brutal New Delhi Gang Rape, has change come to India?" *PBS News Hour*, December 15, 2013, http://www.pbs.org/newshour/rundown/one-year-since-the-brutal-delhi-gang-rape-has-change-come-to-india/.

68. Bhalla, "Indians Ask What has Changed."

69. Rama Lakshmi, "In New Delhi, A Help Line for Women is Flooded with Calls," *Washington Post*, June 21, 2013, http://www.washingtonpost.com/world/asia_pacific/in-new-delhi-a-help-line-for-women-is-flooded-with-calls/2013/06/21/819becfc-d751-11e2-b418-9dfa095e125d_story.html.

70. Ibid.

71. Pamela Philipose, "That Call for Help: How Effective are Helplines?" Jagori, November 24, 2014, http://www.jagori.org/call-help-how-effective-are-helplines.

72. Niharika Mandhana and Heatlher Timmons, "India Passes Sweeping Bill on Crimes Against Women," *New York Times*, March 21, 2013, http://india.blogs.nytimes.com/2013/03/21/india-passes-sweeping-bill-on-crimes-against-women/.

73. Bhalla, "Indians Ask What has Changed."

74. U.N. Women, "India Visit Starts with a Meeting with Community Members on Safety," UN Women, November 8, 2014, http://www.unwomen.org/en/news/stories/2014/11/ed-visits-delhi-safe-cities-programme.

75. U.N. Women, "Better Lighting, Wider Pavements: Steps Towards Preventing Sexual Violence in New Delhi," UN Women, May 6, 2013, http://www.unwomen.org/en/news/stories/2013/5/better-lighting-wider-pavements-steps-towards-preventing-sexual-violence-in-new-delhi.

76. Priyali Sur, "Are Women Traveling into a Safer 2015?" *The World Bank*, January 15, 2015, http://blogs.worldbank.org/voices/are-women-traveling-safer-2015.

CHAPTER 8: WHAT COMES NEXT?

1. "Gay and Bisexual Men Street Harassment Focus Group," conducted by the author, September 9, 2013.

2. Kathryn Travers, phone interview with the author, December 9, 2014.

3. Marty Langelan, phone interview with the author, December 7, 2014.

4. Langelan e-mail communication with the author, February 8, 2015.

5. Lea Goelnitz, "Germany: Stopping Sexist Advertisements," *Stop Street Harassment*, January 27, 2015, http://www.stopstreetharassment.org/2015/01 http://www.spigen.com/collections/iphone-5s-5/stopping-sexist-ads/.

6. Agustin Fuentes, "The Real Reason Sexual Violence is so Widespread," *Psychology Today*, July 24, 2014, https://www.psychologytoday.com/blog/bust ing-myths-about-human-nature/201407/the-real-reason-sexual-violence-is-so -widespread.

7. Vanita Sundaram, "Schools Aren't Teaching Enough About Sexism. It's the Best Way to End Dating Violence," *Washington Post*, January 7, 2015, http://www.washingtonpost.com/posteverything/wp/2015/01/07/schools-arent -arent-teaching-enough-about-sexism-its-the-best-way-to-end-dating-violence/.

8. Sharita Forrest, "Boys Who Bully Peers More Likely to Engage in Sexual Harassment," *Medical Press,* October 30, 2014, http://medicalxpress.com/news /2014-10-boys-bully-peers-engage-sexual.html.

9. Holly Kearl, "Unsafe and Harassed in Public Spaces: A National Street Harassment Report," *Stop Street Harassment*, June 3, 2014, http://www.stop streetharassment.org/our-work/nationalstudy/, 32.

10. Dr. Amy Sarch, e-mail message to the author, September 17, 2014. Used by permission.

11. Nikki der Gaag, "Because I am a Girl: The State of the World's Girls 2010– Digital and Urban Frontiers: Girls in a Changing Landscape," PLAN Interna- tional, 2010, http://resourcecentre.savethechildren.se/sites/default/files/documents /4905.pdf, p. 110.

12. Jessie Mawson, "UNICEF Supports Efforts to End Sexual Harassment of Girls and Women in Bangladesh," UNICEF, July 21, 2010, http://www.unicef .org/infobycountry/bangladesh_55216.html.

13. Gillian Gaynair, "The Ambassador," International Center for Research on Women, June 9, 2010, http://www.icrw.org/media/news/ambassador.

14. "Project Summary in English," Touche Pas à Ma Pote, n.d., e-mailed to Holly Kearl by Pauline Pourtois on December 16, 2014.

15. METRAC, "Game Changer: Evaluating 'What It Is,' a Game Challenging Sexual Violence Against Youth," METRAC, October 2012, http://www.metrac .org/resources/game-changer-evaluating-what-it-is-a-game-challenging -sexual-violence-against-youth/

16. Catherine Porter, "Ontario Schools will Offer Gender Studies, Thanks to Five Young Women," *The Star,* April 26, 2013, http://www.thestar.com/news /gta/2013/04/26/ontario_schools_will_offer_gender_studies_thanks_to_five _young_women_porter.html.

17. Kearl, "Unsafe and Harassed in Public Spaces," 33.

Bibliography

"4 in 10 Young Women in London Sexually Harassed Over Last Year." *End Violence Against Women Coalition*, May 25, 2012. Accessed January 18, 2015. http://www.endviolenceagainstwomen.org.uk/news/20/evaw-coalition -in-the-media.

A Cappella. "Shanghai Subway Tells Scantily Clad Women to Expect Sexual Harassment." *Tea Leaf Nation*, June 25, 2012. Accessed December 15, 2014. http://www.tealeafnation.com/2012/06/shanghai-subway-tells-scantily-clad -women-to-expect-sexual-harassment/.

ABColombia, Sisma Mujer, and U.S. Office on Colombia. *Colombia: Women, Conflict-Related Sexual Violence and the Peace Process*, London: ABColombia: 2013.

"About." *Twitter*, n.d. Accessed November 29, 2014. https://about.twitter.com /company.

"About the Book." *At the Dark End of the Street*, n.d. Accessed January 5, 2015, http://atthedarkendofthestreet.com/.

"ActionAid South Africa Flashmob." *ActionAid*, June 19, 2014. Accessed on December 28, 2014. http://www.actionaidusa.org/south-africa/videos/action aid-south-africa-flashmob.

Agence France-Presse. "After Pink Train Coaches, Malaysia Launches Women-Only Buses." *Inquirer Global Nation*, December 2, 2010. Accessed January 4, 2015. http://globalnation.inquirer.net/cebudailynews/news/view/2010 1202-306599/After-pink-train-coaches-Malaysia-launches-women-only -buses.

Agence France Presse. "Rape Another Risk for Somali Drought Refugees." *Capital News*, August 17, 2011. http://www.capitalfm.co.ke/news/2011/08 /rape-another-risk-for-somali-drought-refugees/.

AH. "Street Harassment is a Trigger for Rape Survivors." *Stop Street Harassment*, July 6, 2010. Accessed December 10, 2014. http://www.stopstreethar assment.org/2010/07/why-street-harassment-is-a-big-deal/.

Akbar, Noorjahan. "A Letter to My Harasser." *World Pulse*, November 24, 2012. Accessed November 28, 2015. https://worldpulse.com/node/61735.

Al Jazeera Staff. "Egypt Still has a Sexual Assault Problem." *Al Jazeera America*, July 17, 2014. Accessed January 18, 2015. http://america.aljazeera.com/arti cles/2014/7/17/egypt-still-has-asexualassaultproblem.html.

Aman, Ayah. "Egyptian Women Take to Social Media to Expose Harassers." *Egypt Pulse*, January 16, 2015. Accessed January 18, 2015. http://www.al-mo nitor.com/pulse/originals/2015/01/egypt-women-sexual-harrassment-social -media.html#.

Anonymous. "Constant Harassment at California Bus Stop." *Stop Street Harassment*, June 20, 2011. Accessed February 20, 2015. http://www.stopstreethar assment.org/2011/06/constant-harassment-at-california-bus-stop/.

Anonymous. "First Harassed at Age 7 on the Streets." *Stop Street Harassment*, June 11, 2014. Accessed December 10, 2014. http://www.stopstreetharassment .org/2014/06/harassedage7/.

Anonymous. "Harassed 17 times in 7 Minutes." *Stop Street Harassment*, February 10, 2014. Accessed December 10, 2014. http://www.stopstreetharassment .org/2014/02/7minutes/.

Ansari, Shabana. "80% of Women in Mumbai Face Sexual Harassment." *DNA India*, March 3, 2012. Accessed January 14, 2015. http://www.dnaindia.com /mumbai/report-80-women-in-mumbai-face-sexual-harassment-1657755.

Anti-Harassment. "Shit Men Say to Men Who Say Shit to Women on the Streets." YouTube, March 19, 2012. Accessed February 2, 2015. https://www.youtube .com/watch?v=5P4eVjwVd_U.

"Anti-Harassment Group to Form Eid Operation Rooms." *Daily News Egypt*, July 26, 2014. Accessed January 18, 2015, http://www.dailynewsegypt.com /2014/07/26/anti-harassment-group-form-eid-operation-rooms/.

"Anti-Violence Campaign Targets 'Abusive' Attitudes." *BBC*, June 1, 2010. Accessed February 16, 2015. http://www.bbc.com/news/10198459.

AQ Online. "Guatemala Debuts 'Women Only' Buses." *Americas Quarterly*, June 16, 2011. Accessed December 29, 2014. http://www.americasquarterly .org/node/2589.

Armutçu, Emel. "Turkish Mayor Advises Women to 'Stay Home' to Avoid Harassment." *Hurriyet Daily News*, May 25, 2011. Accessed December 13, 2014. http://www.hurriyetdailynews.com/default.aspx?pageid=438&n=sit-in -your-homes-unless-you-want-to-be-sexually-harassed-2011-05-25.

"Around the World," *HarassMap*, n.d. Accessed November 28, 2014. http:// harassmap.org/en/what-we-do/around-the-world/.

Asafoetida. "Then I See His Penis Out!" YouTube, September 4, 2010. Accessed November 28, 2014. https://www.youtube.com/watch?v=iIlObKYwUyI.

Ashford, Tara. "Australia: Was #IllRideWithYou Worth It?" *Stop Street Harassment*, January 18, 2015. Accessed January 18, 2015. http://www.stopstreet harassment.org/2015/01/illridewithyouworthit/.

Awadalla, Ahmed. "Faggots for Whores? Or What happened to Women's March in Tahrir." Rebel with a Cause, March 8, 2011. Accessed January 18, 2015. http://rwac-egypt.blogspot.com/2011/03/faggots-for-whores-or-what-happened-to.html.

Ax, Joseph, and Marina Lopes "New York City ends legal defense of stop-and-frisk police tactic." Reuters, January 30, 2014. Accessed January 5, 2015. http://www.reuters.com/article/2014/01/30/us-usa-newyork-stopandfrisk-id USBREA0T1JY20140130.

Bagby, Dyana. "Trans women brutally attacked on Atlanta's MARTA." GA Voice, May 26, 2014. Accessed January 9, 2015. http://thegavoice.com/trans-women-attacked-atlantas-marta/.

"Bangladeshis Raise Voice Against Sexual Harassment." Hindustan Times, June 19, 2010. Accessed January 14, 2015. http://www.hindustantimes.com/world-news/bangladeshis-raise-voice-against-sexual-harassment/article1-560011.aspx.

Barron, Seth. "CM Ferreras Holds Hearing against Street Harassment." Julissa Ferreras, October 28, 2010. Accessed December 28, 2014. http://myemail.constantcontact.com/Julissa-Ferreras-Press-Announcement.html?soid=1102 274890321&aid=TC05i_F0vBY.

Bates, Laura. Everyday Sexism. London: Simon & Schuster UK Ltd, 2014.

Bates, Laura. "Everyday Sexism Speech to the UN: 'Sexism and Sexual Harassment is not a 'Women's Issue'—It is a Matter of Human Rights." New Statesman, March 13, 2014. Accessed December 28, 2014. http://www.newstatesman.com/2014/03/everyday-sexism-speech-un-sexism-and-sexual-harassment-not-womens-issue.

Bennett, Roxanna. "Yes, All Women." Gender Focus, May 26, 2014. Accessed January 3, 2015. http://www.gender-focus.com/2014/05/26/yes-all-women/#sthash.TG5ZIHJW.dpuf.

"Better Lighting, Wider Pavements: Steps Towards Preventing Sexual Violence in New Delhi." UN Women, May 6, 2013. Accessed January 13, 2015. http://www.unwomen.org/en/news/stories/2013/5/better-lighting-wider-pavements-steps-towards-preventing-sexual-violence-in-new-delhi.

Bhalla, Nita. "Indians Ask What has Changed since Delhi Gang Rape as Uber Driver Accused." Reuters, December 8, 2014. Accessed December 10, 2014. http://www.reuters.com/article/2014/12/08/us-india-rape-safety-idUSKBN 0JM1UO20141208.

Bianco, Marcie. "One Group has a Higher Domestic Violence Rate Than Everyone Else—And It's Not the NFL." Mic, December 19, 2014. Accessed December 29, 2014. http://mic.com/articles/106886/one-group-has-a-higher-domestic-violence-rate-than-everyone-else-and-it-s-not-the-nfl.

Bint Afeich, Noura. "Saudi Women Turn to Social Media to Combat Harassment." Al-Monitor, March 26, 2012. Accessed December 28, 2015. http://www.al-monitor.com/pulse/culture/2014/02/sexual-harassment-rise-saudi-arabia.html#.

Biswas, Soutik. "How India Treats its Women." BBC, December 29, 2012. Accessed January 18, 2015. http://www.bbc.com/news/world-asia-india-20863860.

Biswas, Soutik. "India Gang Rape: Thousands of Women March in Delhi." *BBC*, January 2, 2013. Accessed January 19, 2015. http://www.bbc.com/news/world -asia-india-20886253.

Blank Noise. "Safe City Pledge." *Facebook*, January 2013. Accessed January 19, 2015. https://www.facebook.com/events/511318265558394/.

de Blasio, Bill. "One New York, Rising Together." Bill de Blasio for Mayor, December 2013. Accessed January 3, 2015. http://dnwssx4l7gl7s.cloudfront.net/de blasio/default/page/-/One_New_York_Rising_Together.pdf.

"Blog." Blank Noise, n.d., Accessed February 14, 2015. http://blog.blanknoise .org/.

Boboltz, Sara. "#AliveWhileBlack Highlights the Ugly Discrimination Black America Knows Too Well." *Huffington Post*, December 4, 2014. Accessed January 8, 2015. http://www.huffingtonpost.com/2014/12/04/alivewhileblack -hashtag-twitter_n_6271820.html.

Bogado, Aura. "De-centering Whiteness is Essential to Thinking About Street Harassment." *Colorlines*, October 30, 2014. Accessed November 28, 2014. http://colorlines.com/archives/2014/10/decentering_whiteness_is_essential _to_thinking_about_street_harassment.html.

"Bolivia Approves a Landmark Law against Harassment of Women Political Leaders." UN Women, June 11, 2012. Accessed January 5, 2015, http://www .unwomen.org/en/news/stories/2012/6/bolivia-approves-a-landmark-law-ag ainst-harassment-of-women-political-leaders.

"Bolivian Women Battle Against Culture of Harassment." *BBC,* March 11, 2014. Accessed December 8, 2014. http://www.bbc.com/news/world-latin-america -26446066.

Bowers, Katie, and Nefertiti Martin. " 'Bring Your Brother Day' Workshop on Street Harassment." *Stop Street Harassment*, March 30, 2012. Accessed December 10, 2014. http://www.stopstreetharassment.org/2012/03/bring-your -brother.

Boyle, Robyn. "Two Complaints A Day in Brussels for Street Harassment." *The Bulletin*, October 14, 2014. Accessed December 4, 2014. http://www.xpats .com/two-complaints-day-brussels-street-harassment.

Brame, Robert, Shawn D. Bushway, Ray Paternoster, and Michael G. Turner. "Demographic Patterns of Culmative Arrest Prevalence by Ages 18 and 23." *Crime & Delinquency*, January 6, 2014. Accessed January 9, 2015. http://cad .sagepub.com/content/early/2013/12/18/0011128713514801.full.pdf+html.

Brooks Gardner, Carol. *Passing By: Gender and Public Harassment.* Berkeley, CA: University of California Press, 1995.

"bSafe Personal Safety Alarm." Google Play, August 14, 2013. Accessed November 28, 2014. https://play.google.com/store/apps/details?id=com.bipper.app .bsafe&hl=en.

Burns, Crosby, and Philip Ross. "Gay and Transgender Discrimination Outside the Workplace: Why We Need Protections in Housing, Health Care, and Public Accommodations." *American Progress*, July 19, 2011. Accessed January 16, 2015. https://www.americanprogress.org/issues/lgbt/report/2011/07/19 /9927/gay-and-transgender-discrimination-outside-the-workplace/.

"Bum Groping is Not Sexual Harassment in Austria." *Austrian Independent*, November 22, 2012. Accessed December 4, 2014. http://austrianindependent .com/news/General_News/2012-11-22/12686/Bum_groping_is_not_sexual _harrasment_in_Austria.

Butcher, Mike. "Clever bsafe Panic Alarm App Launches in U.S. with Free Offer to New Yorkers." *TechCrunch*, June 26, 2013. Accessed November 13, 2014. http://techcrunch.com/2012/06/26/clever-bsafe-panic-alarm-app-launches-in -us-with-free-offer-to-new-yorkers/.

Cabral, Nuala, and Mari Morales-Williams. "Black Women Activists Talk Back: How We Can End Street Harassment Through Transformative Justice." Black Youth Project, October 31, 2014. Accessed January 8, 2015. http://www .blackyouthproject.com/2014/10/black-women-activists-talk-back-how-we -can-end-street-harassment-through-transformative-justice/.

Calas, Sophie. "Hey Police Officer, What Does Being 'Pretty' Have To Do With Assault?" *Stop Street Harassment*, January 19, 2012. Accessed December 10, 2014. http://www.stopstreetharassment.org/2012/01/revolutionbar/.

"The Campaign." Not Ever, n.d. Accessed February 16, 2015. http://www.note ver.co.uk/the-campaign/.

Carmon, Irn. "How to Shout Down a Perv: Tips and Tricks from the Subway Badass." *Jezebel*, December 17, 2010. Accessed December 3, 2014. http://jeze bel.com/5714562/tips-on-how-to-handle-pervs-from-subway-badass-nicola -briggs.

Carter, Samuel, and Emily May. "Hollaback! State of the Streets Report, 2011." *Hollaback!* December 2011. Accesed December 9, 2014. http://issuu.com/holla back/docs/finalstate_of_the_streets_12.19?e=4099169/3126329.

Caspari, Von Lisa. "Der #aufschrei und seine Folgen." *Zeit Online*, January 23, 2014. Accessed December 18, 2014. http://www.zeit.de/politik/deutschland /2014-01/sexismus-debatte-folgen.

Chang, David. "Man Knocked Unconscious After Defending Women From Catcallers: Police." *NBC Bay Area*, August 13, 2014. Accessed February 7, 2015. http://www.nbcbayarea.com/news/national-international/Man-Punched -Knocked-Unconscious-During-Rittenhouse-Square-Attack-270588441 .html.

Chang, Sarah. "Street Harassment in Boston." *Stop Street Harassment*, July 2, 2014. Accessed December 10, 2014. http://www.stopstreetharassment.org /2014/07/street-harassment-in-boston/.

"Charge Sheet in Delhi Gang-Rape Case Likely Today." *DNA India*, January 3, 2013. Accessed January 19, 2015. http://www.dnaindia.com/india/report -charge-sheet-in-delhi-gang-rape-case-likely-today-1784917.

"Check it out—A Sign Made Entirely of Fail." Feminist Philosophers, June 15, 2012. Accessed November 28, 2014. https://feministphilosophers.wordpress .com/2012/06/15/check-it-out/.

Chemaly, Soraya, Jaclyn Friedman, and Laura Bates. "An Open Letter to Face-book." *Huffington Post*, May 21, 2013. Accessed December 3, 2014. http:// www.huffingtonpost.com/soraya-chemaly/an-open-letter-to-faceboo_1_b_330 7394.html.

Chemaly, Soraya, Jaclyn Friedman, and Laura Bates. "May 28, 2013." WAM!, May 28, 2013. Accessed December 10, 2014. http://www.womenactionmedia.org/fbagreement/.

Chemaly, Soraya, Jaclyn Friedman, and Laura Bates. "Take Action to End Gender-Based Hate Speech on Facebook." *Women, Action & The Media*, n.d. Accessed November 28, 2014 http://www.womenactionmedia.org/facebookaction.

Chirciu, Simona-Maria. "Romania: Organizing a Street Harassment March." *Stop Street Harassment*, January 14, 2015. Accessed January 14, 2015. http://www.stopstreetharassment.org/2015/01/romaniashmarch/.

CNN Wire Staff. "Egypt's Million Woman March Fizzles into Shouting Matches." *CNN*, March 8, 2011. Accessed January 18, 2015. http://edition.cnn.com/2011/WORLD/meast/03/08/egypt.women/?hpt=T2.

Cocozza, Paula. "Oppressed Majority: The Film About a World Run By Women That Went Viral." *The Guardian*, February 11, 2014. Accessed November 28, 2014. http://www.theguardian.com/lifeandstyle/womens-blog/2014/feb/11/oppressed-majority-film-women-eleonore-pourriat.

Colomé, Sarah. "USA: Flash Mob Against Harassment on CTA." *Stop Street Harassment*, November 7, 2014. Accessed December 10, 2014. http://www.stopstreetharassment.org/2014/11/flashmobcta/.

Colomé, Sarah. "USA: Our Oppressions are Intertwined." *Stop Street Harassment*, October 20, 2014. Accessed December 10, 2014. http://www.stopstreetharassment.org/2014/10/intertwinedoppressions/.

Cosgrave, Ellie. "I Danced Against Sexual Assault on the Tube to Reclaim It for Women." *The Guardian*, July 23, 2013. Accessed January 4, 2015. http://www.theguardian.com/commentisfree/2013/jul/23/danced-sexual-assault-tube-women.

Crabtree, Steve, and Faith Nsubuga. "Women Feel Less Safe than Men in Many Developed Countries." Gallup, July 6, 2012. Accessed January 15, 2015. http://www.gallup.com/poll/155402/women-feel-less-safe-men-developed-countries.aspx.

"Creating Safe Public Spaces," UN Women, n.d. Accessed on December 28, 2014. http://www.unwomen.org/en/what-we-do/ending-violence-against-women/creating-safe-public-spaces.

el-Dabh, Basil. "99.3% of Egyptian Women Experienced Sexual Harassment: Report." *Daily News Egypt*, April 28, 2013. Accessed November 28, 2014. http://www.dailynewsegypt.com/2013/04/28/99-3-of-egyptian-women-experienced-sexual-harassment-report/.

el-Deeb, Sarah. "Alarming Assaults on Women in Egypt's Tahrir." *Huffington Post*, June 6, 2012. Accessed January 28, 2015. http://www.huffingtonpost.com/huff-wires/20120606/egypt-sexual-assault/.

Dagres, Holly. "Workshop Idea: Fight Harassment 101." *Stop Street Harassment*, July 10, 2013. Accessed December 10, 2014. http://www.stopstreetharassment.org/2013/07/fh101/.

Dang-Vu, Huong, and Thomas Le Jeannie. "Femmes agressées au domicile ou à l'extérieur: une analyse des risques." National Institute of Statistics and

Economic Studies, 2013. Accessed January 20, 2015. http://www.insee.fr/fr
/ffc/docs_ffc/ES448G.pdf.

Davidson, Terry. "Cops: School Uniforms May Attract Pervs." *Canoe News*,
October 8, 2011. Accessed December 14, 2014. http://cnews.canoe.ca/CNEWS
/Canada/2011/10/07/18799506.html.

"Delhi and Beyond: Concrete Action for Safer Cities" Google Map, Huairiou
Commission, n.d., Accessed February 3, 2015. https://www.google.com/maps
/d/viewer?oe=UTF8&ie=UTF8&msa=0&mid=zHkzk8nfZBkI.kYRnz3La
VFmY.

"Delhi Gang Rape: CJI Altamas Kabir Calls for Speedy Trial of Case." *The Times
of India*, January 2, 2013. Accessed Feburary 3, 2015. http://timesofindia
.indiatimes.com/india/Delhi-gang-rape-CJI-Altamas-Kabir-calls-for-speedy
-trial-of-case/articleshow/17859854.cms?referral=PM.

"Delhi Gang-Rape Victim Dies in Hospital in Singapore." *BBC*, December 28,
2012. Accessed January 19, 2015. http://timesofindia.indiatimes.com/india
/Supreme-Court-issues-directions-to-curb-sexual-harassment-of-women-in
-public-transport/articleshow/17445499.cms.

"Delhi Joins UN Initiative to Make Urban Areas Safer for Women." *NTV*,
November 22, 2010. Accessed November 29, 2014. http://www.ndtv.com
/article/cities/delhi-joins-un-initiative-to-make-urban-areas-safer-for-women
-67905.

Dewey, Caitlin. "Almost as Many People Use Facebook as Live in the Entire
Country of China." *Washington Post*, October 29, 2014. Accessed December
3, 2014. http://www.washingtonpost.com/news/the-intersect/wp/2014/10/29
/almost-as-many-people-use-facebook-as-live-in-the-entire-country-of-china/.

Dettmer, Jamie. "Libya Women Report Increased Harassment." *Voice of America*,
November 1, 2013. Accessed February 15, 2015. http://www.voanews.com
/content/libya-women-report-increased-harassment/1781596.html.

Dhillon, Amrit. "ATM-Style Machine Lets Indian Women Report Abuse Without Fear." *The Star*, August 25, 2014. Accessed December 4, 2014. http://www
.thestar.com/news/world/2014/08/25/atmstyle_machine_lets_indian_women
_report_abuse_without_fear.html.

Drucker, Susan J., and Gary Grumpert. "Shopping Women, and Public Space."
In *Voices in the Street: Explorations in Gender, Media, and Public Space*,
edited by Susan J. Drucker and Gary Gumpert, 119–136. Cresskill, NJ:
Hampton Press, Inc, 1996.

Drucker, Susan J., and Gary Grumpert. "Voices in the Street: Explorations in
Gender, Media, and Public Space." In *Voices in the Street: Explorations
in Gender, Media, and Public Space*, edited by Susan J. Drucker and Gary
Gumpert, 1–14. Cresskill, NJ: Hampton Press, Inc, 1996.

Dugan, Andrew. "In U.S., 37% Do Not Feel Safe Walking at Night Near Home."
Gallup Poll, November 24, 2014. Accessed November 29, 2014. http://www
.gallup.com/poll/179558/not-feel-safe-walking-night-near-home.aspx.

Duggan, Maeve. "Online Harassment." *Pew Research*, October 22, 2014.
Accessed December 28, 2014. http://www.pewinternet.org/2014/10/22/online
-harassment/.

Economic and Social Council. Commission on the Status of Women: Report on the fifty-seventh session. United Nations, April 2, 2013. Accessed December 16, 2014. http://www.un.org/ga/search/view_doc.asp?symbol=E/2013/27.

"Egypt: Military 'Virginity Test' investigation a sham." *Human Rights Watch*, November 9, 2011. Accessed January 18, 2015. http://www.hrw.org/news/2011/11/09/egypt-military-virginity-test-investigation-sham.

Elphick, Nicole. "Belgium to Ban Sexist Comments." *Daily Life Australia*, March 17, 2014. Accessed January 3, 2015. http://www.dailylife.com.au/news-and-views/news-features/belgium-to-ban-sexist-comments-20140317-34w68.html.

"Eve-Teasing Prompts Girls to End Life." *The Times of India*, December 16, 2012. Accessed January 18, 2015. http://timesofindia.indiatimes.com/city/ranchi/Eve-teasing-prompts-girl-to-end-life/articleshow/17631246.cms?refer.

"Eve-Teasing, Teenager Commits Suicide." *The Hindu*, December 8, 2012. Accessed January 18, 2015. http://www.thehindu.com/todays-paper/tp-national/tp-newdelhi/eveteased-teenager-commits-suicide/article4176838.ece.

Fairchild, Kimberly, and Laurie A. Rudman, "Everyday stranger harassment and women's self-objectification," *Social Justice Research*, 21, no. 3 (2008): 338–357.

Fasila, Dofa. "Women Should Not Wear Miniskirts on Angkot: Jakarta Governor." *The Jakarta Globe*, September 16, 2011. Accessed December 13, 2014. http://thejakartaglobe.beritasatu.com/archive/women-should-not-wear-mini skirts-on-angkot-jakarta-governor/.

Fayer, Joan. "Changes in Gender Use of Public Space in Puerto Rico." In *Voices in the Street: Explorations in Gender, Media, and Public Space*, edited by Susan J. Drucker and Gary Gumpert, 211–224. Cresskill, NJ: Hampton Press, Inc, 1996.

Feeney, Michael J. "Teen Rapper Astronomical Kid Angry with Guy Ogling His Ma, So He Makes a YouTube hit." *Daily News*, October 14, 2010. Accessed November 28, 2014. http://www.nydailynews.com/new-york/teen-rapper-astro nomical-kid-angry-guys-ogling-ma-youtube-hit-article-1.187010.

Feeney, Nolan. "The Most Powerful #YesAllWomen Tweets." *Time,* May 25, 2014. Accessed November 28, 2014. http://time.com/114043/yesallwomen-hashtag-santa-barbara-shooting/.

Feis, Aaron. "Woman's Throat Slashed After Rejecting Man's Advances," *New York Post*, October 8, 2014. Accessed December 15, 2015. http://nypost.com/2014/10/08/womans-throat-slashed-after-rejecting-mans-advances/.

Feldmar, Jamie. "Following Sexual Assaults, Cyclists Rally to Escort Park Slope Women Home." *Gothamist*, September 20, 2011. Accessed December 28, 2014. http://gothamist.com/2011/09/20/following_sexual_assaults_cyclists.php.

Ferdman, Robert A. "4.4 Billion People Around the World Still Don't Have Internet. Here's Where They Live." *Washington Post*, October 2, 2014. Accessed November 28, 2014. http://www.washingtonpost.com/blogs/wonkblog

/wp/2014/10/02/4-4-billion-people-around-the-world-still-dont-have-internet-heres-where-they-live/.

Fey, Tina. *Bossypants*. New York: Reagan Arthur Books, 2011.

"Filming Insults: Street Harassment Prompts New Brussels Law." *RT*, September 5, 2012. Accessed December 8, 2014. http://rt.com/news/law-fines-insults-brussels-421/.

Fine, Michelle, Nick Freudenberg, Yasser Payne, Tiffany Perkins, Kersha Smith, and Katya Wanzer. "'Anything Can Happen With Police Around: Urban Youth Evaluate Strategies of Surveillance in Public Places." *Journal of Social Issues* 59 (2003):141–158.

Forrest, Sharita. "Boys Who Bully Peers More Likely to Engage in Sexual Harassment." *Medical Press*, October 30, 2014. Accessed November 29, 2014. http://medicalxpress.com/news/2014-10-boys-bully-peers-engage-sexual.html.

Frustrated and Disgusted. "Harassers at Work and in the Parking Lot Prompt Move." *Stop Street Harassment*, August 6, 2010. Accessed February 20, 2015. http://www.stopstreetharassment.org/2010/08/harassers-at-work-in-the-parking-lot-prompt-move/.

Fuentes, Agustin. "The Real Reason Sexual Violence is So Widespread." *Psychology Today*, July 24, 2014. Accessed January 14, 2015. https://www.psychologytoday.com/blog/busting-myths-about-human-nature/201407/the-real-reason-sexual-violence-is-so-widespread.

der Gaag, Nikki. *Because I am a Girl: The State of the World's Girls 2010—Digital and Urban Frontiers: Girls in a Changing Landscape*. PLAN International, 2010. Accessed November 27, 2014. http://resourcecentre.savethechildren.se/sites/default/files/documents/4905.pdf.

Gabrielson, Ryan, Ryann Grochowski Jones, and Eric Sagara. "Deadly Force, in Black and White." *ProPublica*, October 10, 2014. Accessed January 7, 2015. http://www.propublica.org/article/deadly-force-in-black-and-white.

"Game Changer: Evaluating 'What It Is,' A Game Challenging Sexual Violence Against Youth." METRAC, October 2012. Accessed November 12, 2013. http://www.metrac.org/resources/game-changer-evaluating-what-it-is-a-game-challenging-sexual-violence-against-youth/

"Gang-Rape in India: Teen Victim Kills Herself." *Sky News*, December 28, 2012. Accessed January 19, 2015. http://news.sky.com/story/1030759/gang-rape-in-india-teen-victim-kills-herself.

Garcia Calderon Orbe, Gabriela. "3 Videos Turn the Tables on Street Harassment of Women in Latin America." *Global Voices*, December 11, 2014. Accessed December 12, 2014. http://globalvoicesonline.org/2014/12/11/3-videos-turn-the-tables-on-street-harassment-of-women-in-latin-america/.

Garcés, Andrew Willis. "Ruta Pacífica: Colombian Women Against Violence," Upside Down World, February 4, 2009. http://upsidedownworld.org/main/colombia-archives-61/1699-ruta-pacifica-colombian-women-against-violence

"Gay and Bisexual Men Street Harassment Focus Group." Conducted by Holly Kearl, September 9, 2013.

Gaynair, Gillian. "The Ambassador." International Center for Research on Women, June 9, 2010. Accessed on January 28, 2015. http://www.icrw.org /media/news/ambassador.

Gibbs, Samuel. "Instagram Reaches 200 Million Users." *The Guardian*, March 26, 2014. Accessed December 10, 2014. http://www.theguardian.com/tech nology/2014/mar/26/instagram-200-million-users-facebook-mobile-photo -sharing.

Goelnitz, Lea. "Germany: Stopping Sexist Advertisements." *Stop Street Harassment*, January 27, 2015. Accessed January 27, 2015. http://www.stopstreet harassment.org/2015/01/stopping-sexist-ads/.

Goldberg, Michelle. "Feminist Writers are so Besieged by Online Abuse that Some Have Begun to Retire." *Washington Post*, February 20, 2015. Accessed February 20, 2015. http://www.washingtonpost.com/opinions/online-femi nists-increasingly-ask-are-the-psychic-costs-too-much-to-bear/2015/02/19 /3dc4ca6c-b7dd-11e4-a200-c008a01a6692_story.html.

Goodyear, Sarah. " 'I Pledge to Walk Alone': Activists Demand Safer Cities for Women in India." CityLab, January 22, 2013. Accessed January 19, 2015. www.citylab.com/politics/2013/01/activists-demand-safer-cities-women-india /4446/.

Gordy, Cynthia. "Recy Taylor: A Symbol of Jim Crow's Forgotten Horror." *The Root*, February 9, 2011. Accessed January 5, 2015. http://www.theroot.com /articles/culture/2011/02/recy_taylor_a_symbol_of_jim_crows_forgotten _horror.html.

Grove, Tilly. "UK: Street Harassment, the Initiation into Adulthood." *Stop Street Harassment*, September 26, 2013. Accessed December 10, 2014. http://www .stopstreetharassment.org/2013/09/adulthood/.

Guimares, Thiago. "REVEALED: The Demographic Trends for Every Social Network." *Business Insider*, December 12, 2014. Accessed December 28, 2014. http://www.businessinsider.com/2014-social-media-demographics-update -2014-9#ixzz3MYu0wMNL.

"HarassMap Reports." *HarassMap*, n.d. Accessed December 4, 2014. http://haras smap.org/en/resource-center/harassmap-reports/.

Harding, Eleanor. "Student Suffers Horrific Injuries After She is Punched in the Face at Notting Hill Carnival For Telling Men To Stop Groping Her." *The Daily Mail*, August 27, 2014. Accessed January 5, 2015, http://www.daily mail.co.uk/news/article-2735612/Horrific-injuries-woman-punched-face-Not ting-Hill-Carnival-telling-man-stop-groping-her.html.

Harthorne, Michael. "Police: Men Threaten To Shoot Woman Who Ignored Their Advances." *Komo News*, November 17, 2014. Accessed February 3, 2015. http://www.komonews.com/news/crime/Police-Men-threaten-to-shoot-woman -who-ignored-their-advances-282938701.html?mobile=y.

Hauser, Jenny. "Female Egyptian Protesters Highlight Sexual Harassment." Storyful, November 25, 2011. Accessed January 18, 2015. http://storyful.com /stories/1000014443.

Heideman, Elizabeth. "#YesAllWomen, But Not Really: How Feminism Leaves the Disabled Behind." *The Daily Beast*, November 24, 2014. Accessed December 3,

2014. http://www.thedailybeast.com/articles/2014/11/24/yesallwomen-but-not
-really-how-feminism-leaves-the-disabled-behind.html.

Henry, Elsa S. "Street Harassment 102: When You're Blind and a Woman." *Feminist Sonar*, September 7, 2012. Accessed December 5, 2014. http://feminist
sonar.com/2012/09/street-harassment-102-when-youre-blind-and-a-woman/.

Hernandez, Rigoberto. "'Stop Telling Women to Smile': Denouncing 'Jackals' and Catcalling in Mexico." *NPR*, February 10, 2015. Accessed February 11, 2015. http://www.npr.org/blogs/codeswitch/2015/02/10/384994475/stop-tell
ing-women-to-smile-denouncing-jackals-and-catcalling-in-mexico.

Hess, Amanda. "Why Women Aren't Welcome on the Internet." *Pacific Standard Magazine*, January 6, 2014. Accessed February 20, 2015. http://www.psmag
.com/health-and-behavior/women-arent-welcome-internet-72170.

Hill, Amelia, and Juliette Jowit. "Sexist Remarks and Wolf-Whistles Could Become Criminal Offences." *The Guardian*, March 7, 2012. Accessed November 29, 2014. http://www.theguardian.com/society/2012/mar/08/sexist-com
ments-to-become-criminal-offence.

Hirokawa, Kasumi. "Phone Camera Shutters and Women-Only Cars: Japan's Answer to Chikan." *Stop Street Harassment*, July 10, 2014. Accessed December 10, 2014. http://www.stopstreetharassment.org/2014/07/phone-camera
-shutters/.

Hlavka, Heather R. "Normalizing Sexual Violence: Young Women Account for Harassment and Abuse." *Gender & Society* (2014). Accessed December 10, 2014. http://gas.sagepub.com/content/early/2014/02/28/0891243214526468
.full?keytype=ref&siteid=spgas&ijkey=1zjS.dsfVDs32.

Hoby, Hermione. "The Woman in 10 Hours Walking in NYC: 'I Got People Wanting To Slit My Throat.'" *The Guardian*, December 17, 2014. Accessed December 28, 2014. http://www.theguardian.com/lifeandstyle/2014/dec/17/the
-woman-in-10-hours-walking-in-nyc-i-got-people-wanting-to-slit-my-throat.

Hodge, Nathan, and Jenny Gross. "Pakistani Girls' Education Activist Malala Yousafzai Rose to Global Prominence After Taliban Shooting." *The Wall Street Journal*, October 10, 2014. Accessed January 8, 2015, http://www.wsj.com
/articles/pakistani-girls-education-activist-malala-yousafzai-rose-to-global
-prominence-after-taliban-shooting-1412942763.

"Hollaback! iPhone and Droid Apps." *Hollaback*!, n.d. Accessed December 4, 2014. http://www.ihollaback.org/resources/iphone-and-droid-apps/.

Hollaback! Brussels. "Chalk Walk: Women in Brussels Reclaim the Places Where They Were Harassed." *Stop Street Harassment*, March 25, 2012. Accessed December 10, 2014. http://www.stopstreetharassment.org/2012/03/chalkwalk/.

Hollmeyer Taylor, Serena, Amy Tan, Phoebe Sloane, Maggie Tiernan, and Faiqa Mahmood. "'When She Stands Among Men': Sexual Harassment of Women at Political Protests in Cairo, January 2011—August 2013." *Al Nakhlah*, June 10, 2014. Accessed January 18, 2015. http://alnakhlah.org/2014/06/10
/when-she-stands-among-men-sexual-harassment-of-women-at-political-pro
tests-in-cairo-january-2011-august-2013/#_ftn37.

"How and Why We Began." HarassMap, n.d. Accessed November 28, 2014. http://harassmap.org/en/who-we-are/how-and-why-we-began/.

" 'I Want to Live,' Delhi Braveheart told Her Mother and Brother." *IBN Live*, December 29, 2012. Accessed January 18, 2015. http://ibnlive.in.com/news /i-want-to-live-delhi-braveheart-told-her-mother-and-brother/312896-3-244 .html.

Iaccino, Ludovica. "Belgium: Sexual Harassment Punished with Imprisonment Under New Law." *International Business Times*, March 17, 2014. Accessed December 8, 2014. http://www.ibtimes.co.uk/belgium-sexual-harassment-puni shed-imprisonment-under-new-law-1440582.

Ians. "Bangladeshis Raise Voice Against Sexual Harassment." *Hindustan Times*, June 19, 2010. Accessed January 19, 2015. http://www.hindustantimes.com /world-news/bangladeshis-raise-voice-against-sexual-harassment/article1 -560011.aspx.

IDRC. "Rebecca Chiao—HarassMap: Social Mapping Sexual Harassment and Violence in Egypt." YouTube, February 11, 2013. Accessed November 29, 2014. https://www.youtube.com/watch?v=hLq7fCUQANM.

"In Brief: Safe Cities Global Initiative." UN Women, 2014. Accessed January 5, 2015. http://www.unwomen.org/~/media/headquarters/attachments/sections /library/publications/2014/un%20women%20safe%20cities%20brief-us -web.pdf.

"India visit Starts with a Meeting with Community Members on Safety." UN Women, November 8, 2014. Accessed January 5, 2015. http://www.unwomen .org/en/news/stories/2014/11/ed-visits-delhi-safe-cities-programme.

"Indonesian Women Don Miniskirts in Rape Protest." *The Jakarta Globe*, September 18, 2011. Accessed December 14, 2014. http://thejakartaglobe .beritasatu.com/archive/indonesian-women-don-miniskirts-in-rape-protest /466109/.

International Telecommunication Union. "Measuring the Information Soci- ety." ITU, 2013. Accessed December 10, 2014. http://www.itu.int/en/ITU -D/Statistics/Documents/publications/mis2013/MIS2013_without_Annex _4.pdf.

"Initiative: 4 Sexual Harassment Cases by Policemen in 2 Months." *Egypt Inde- pendent*, December 29, 2014. Accessed January 18, 2015. http://www.egypt independent.com/news/initiative-4-sexual-harassment-cases-policemen-2 -months.

Irshad, Ghazala. "Attention Men: If You Attack a Woman In Tahrir Square, You Might Get Your Ass Kicked, Finally." *Gawker*, December 6, 2012. Accessed December 15, 2014. http://gawker.com/5966368/attention-men-if-you-attack -a-woman-in-tahrir-square-you-might-get-your-ass-kicked-finally.

Irwin, Demetria. "#YouOkSis: Online Movement Launches to Combat Street Harassment." *The Grio*, August 2, 2014. Accessed December 3, 2014. http:// thegrio.com/2014/08/02/youoksis-online-movement-launches-to-combat -street-harassment/.

Iskander, Mona. "One Year Since the Brutal New Delhi Gang Rape, has Change Come to India?" *PBS News Hour*, December 15, 2013. Accessed January 19, 2015. http://www.pbs.org/newshour/rundown/one-year-since-the-brutal-delhi -gang-rape-has-change-come-to-india/.

Islam, Zyman. "Not Safe Even Among People." *The Daily Star*, January 29, 2014. Accessed 15 January 2015. http://www.thedailystar.net/not-safe-even -among-people-8895.

"ITU Releases 2014 ICT Figures." ITU, May 5, 2014. Accessed February 1, 2015. http://www.itu.int/net/pressoffice/press_releases/2014/23.aspx.

JaguarGrin. "Police in Toronto Say Grow Thicker Skin about Street Harassment." *Stop Street Harassment*, February 22, 2012. Accessed December 10, 2014. http://www.stopstreetharassment.org/2012/02/thickerskin/.

Jeenbaeva, Aikanysh, and the BFCSQ team. "Kyrgyzstan: Street Harassment of Transgender People in Bishkek." *Stop Street Harassment*, October 20, 2013. Accessed December 10, 2014. http://www.stopstreetharassment.org/2013/10 /kyrgyzstantransgender/.

"Joining Forces with UN-Habitat to Promote Women's Voice, Access and Safety in Sustainable Urban Development." UN Women, June 11, 2013. Accessed on December 28, 2014. http://www.unwomen.org/en/news/stories/2013/6/joining -forces-with-un-habitat.

Jones, Mirabelle. "Catcalling Cards." I am Not an Object, September 14, 2012. Accessed November 29, 2014. http://iamnotanobject.tumblr.com/post/3154 4486531/catcalling-cards.

"Judge Resigns Over Subway Sexual Harassment." *The Korea Herald*, April 23, 2011. Accessed December 3, 2014. http://www.koreaherald.com/view.php?ud =20110423000008.

Kaberia, Judie. "Somali Women Raped Enroute to Kenya." *CapitalNews*, August 8, 2011. Accessed February 15, 2015. http://www.capitalfm.co.ke/news /2011/08/hungry-somali-women-raped-enroute-to-kenya/.

Kamat, Pallavi. "India: Festivals and Street Harassment." *Stop Street Harassment*, September 9, 2013. Accessed December 10, 2014. http://www.stopstreethara ssment.org/2013/09/india-festivals/.

Kamat, Pallavi. "India: Public Transport, Private Harassment." *Stop Street Harassment*, August 15, 2013. Accessed December 10, 2014. http://www.stop streetharassment.org/2013/08/mumbaitransport/.

Karmarkar, Ujwala Shenoy. "No More Roadside Romeos: Is Stalking a Tragedy in the Making?" *Women's Web*, September 3, 2014. Accessed January 5, 2015, http://www.womensweb.in/2014/09/no-more-roadside-romeos-is-stalking-a -tragedy-in-the-making/.

Kearl, Holly. "2014: The Year of the Tipping Point (Part 2)." *Stop Street Harassment*, December 29, 2014. Accessed December 29, 2014. http://www.stop streetharassment.org/2014/12/2014-part-2/.

Kearl, Holly. "700 Anti-Violence Posters Pasted Throughout Kabul, Afghanistan." *Stop Street Harassment*, December 26, 2011. Accessed December 10, 2014. http://www.stopstreetharassment.org/2011/12/posterskabul/.

Kearl, Holly. "Asking for it? As if." *Stop Street Harassment*, June 30, 2010. Accessed December 10, 2014. http://www.stopstreetharassment.org/2010/06 /asking-for-it-as-if/.

Kearl, Holly. "Buses and Metros Carry Messages Against Harassment." *Women's Media Center*, April 12, 2013. Accessed February 3, 2015. http://www.womens

mediacenter.com/feature/entry/buses-and-metros-carry-messages-against
-harassment.

Kearl, Holly. "Call Them Out, Literally." *Stop Street Harassment*, January 30, 2012. Accessed December 10, 2014. http://www.stopstreetharassment .org/2012/01/callthem/.

Kearl, Holly. "Car Harassers Can Go To Jail in Missouri!" *Stop Street Harassment*, September 22, 2010. Accessed February 3, 2015. http://www.stopstreet harassment.org/2010/09/car-harassers-can-go-to-jail-in-missouri/.

Kearl, Holly. *Cross-Regional Report: Mapping Access to and Use of Mobile Phones to Prevent, Document, and Respond to Sexual Violence Against Women and Girls in Urban Public Spaces*. New York: UN Women, June 2015.

Kearl, Holly. "Egypt: Protests Against Harassment This Week." *Stop Street Harassment*, July 6, 2012. Accessed December 10, 2014. http://www.stop streetharassment.org/2012/07/egypt2protests/.

Kearl, Holly. "Egyptian Women Refuse to be Silent by Assaults." *Ms*. Blog, June 10, 2012. Accessed January 18, 2015. http://msmagazine.com/blog/2012 /06/10/egyptian-women-refuse-to-be-silenced-by-assaults/.

Kearl, Holly. "Harassers Attack Anti-Sexual Assault Protest at Tahrir Square in Egypt." *Stop Street Harassment*, June 9, 2012. Accessed January 19, 2015. http://www.stopstreetharassment.org/2012/06/june8protest/.

Kearl, Holly. "India: New Reporting Site and #SafeCityPledge Events." *Stop Street Harassment*, January 1, 2013. Accessed December 10, 2014. http://www .stopstreetharassment.org/2013/01/indiajan1/.

Kearl, Holly. "India Tragedy Seen as a Transitional Moment." *Women's Media Center*, January 10, 2013. Accessed January 2, 2015. http://www.womens mediacenter.com/feature/entry/india-tragedy-seen-as-transitional-moment.

Kearl, Holly. *International Anti-Street Harassment Week 2013 Report, Stop Street Harassment*: 2013.

Kearl, Holly. *International Anti-Street Harassment Week 2014 Report, Stop Street Harassment*: 2014.

Kearl, Holly. "Interview with Organizer of Afghanistan Anti-Street Harassment March." *Stop Street Harassment*, July 16, 2011. Accessed December 10, 2014. http://www.stopstreetharassment.org/2011/07/interviewnoorjahan akbar/.

Kearl, Holly. "June 20: Lebanese Day of Blogging against Sexual Harassment." *Stop Street Harassment*, June 17, 2011. Accessed December 10, 2014. http:// www.stopstreetharassment.org/2011/06/june-20-lebanese-day-of-blogging -against-sexual-harassment/.

Kearl, Holly. "Kansas City, MO, Passes Anti-Harassment Ordinance." *Stop Street Harassment*, October 3, 2014. Accessed November 28, 2014. http:// www.stopstreetharassment.org/2014/10/shordinance/.

Kearl, Holly. "Lara Logan and Egypt's Next Revolution." Ms. Magazine blog, February 16, 2011. Accessed January 19, 2015. http://msmagazine.com/blog /2011/02/16/lara-logan-and-egypts-next-revolution/.

Kearl, Holly. "Laws Protecting Women from Upskirt Photo Assaults Fall Short." *The Daily Beast*, March 12, 2014. Accessed December 10, 2014. http://www

.thedailybeast.com/witw/articles/2014/03/12/tighten-laws-on-upskirt-photos
.html.

Kearl, Holly. "Male Allies Win Awards!" *Stop Street Harassment*, September 11, 2012. Accessed December 10, 2014. http://www.stopstreetharassment.org /2012/09/male-allies-win-awards/.

Kearl, Holly. "On March 8, #RingTheBell." *Stop Street Harassment*, March 1, 2013. Accessed January 19, 2015. http://www.stopstreetharassment.org/2013 /03/march-8-ringthebell/.

Kearl, Holly. "Our Streets, Our Rights." *Stop Street Harassment*, December 10, 2012. Accessed February 20, 2015. http://www.stopstreetharassment.org /2012/12/our-streets-our-rights/.

Kearl, Holly. Panel Speech at the 3rd International Conference on Women's Safety. Delhi, India, November 23, 2010.

Kearl, Holly. "Part 2: Redefining Rape and Street Harassment: 1880s—1920s," *Stop Street Harassment*, October 3, 2013. Accessed December 10, 2014. http://www.stopstreetharassment.org/2013/10/redefiningrape2/.

Kearl, Holly. "Patrols Against Harassment in Egypt." *Stop Street Harassment*, August 22, 2012. Accessed December 10, 2014. http://www.stopstreethara ssment.org/2012/08/patrols-against-harassment-in-egypt/.

Kearl, Holly. "Safety Audits and Surveying." *Stop Street Harassment*, n.d. Accessed December 10, 2014. http://www.stopstreetharassment.org/toolkits /audits/#audit.

Kearl, Holly. "#ShoutingBack Stories Flood Twitter." *Stop Street Harassment*, January 8, 2013. Accessed December 10, 2014. http://www.stopstreetharass ment.org/2013/01/shoutingback/.

Kearl, Holly. "Sri Lanka Campaign Reached 30,000 Commuters in One Week." *Stop Street Harassment*, August 9, 2012. Accessed December 10, 2014. http:// www.stopstreetharassment.org/2012/08/30000/.

Kearl, Holly. "Stories About Being #Grabbed Trended on Twitter." *Stop Street Harassment*, May 18, 2014. Accessed December 10, 2014. http://www.stop streetharassment.org/2014/05/grabbed/.

Kearl, Holly. "Street Harassment Fuels a Viral Documentary." *Ms.* Blog, August 7, 2012. Accessed November 28, 2014. http://msmagazine.com/blog/2012/08 /07/street-harassment-fuels-a-viral-documentary/.

Kearl, Holly. "Street Lights and Short Grass: Local strategies help improve global women's security. *Ms*, Summer 2013.

Kearl, Holly. "Take Down Pro-Harassment Sign!" Change.org, June 2012. Accessed December 10, 2014. https://www.change.org/p/take-down-pro-harass ment-sign.

Kearl, Holly. "Three Organizations That Care About Women's Safety in Public Spaces." *Stop Street Harassment*, June 16, 2010. Accessed February 15, 2015. http://www.stopstreetharassment.org/2010/06/three-organizations-that-care -about-womens-safety-in-public/.

Kearl, Holly. "Tweet #INeverAskforIt." *Stop Street Harassment*, February 17, 2010. Accessed December 10, 2014. http://www.stopstreetharassment.org /2010/02/tweet-ineveraskforit/.

Kearl, Holly. "Unsafe and Harassed in Public Spaces: A National Street Harassment Report." Accessed December 10, 2014. *Stop Street Harassment*, June 3, 2014. http://www.stopstreetharassment.org/our-work/nationalstudy/.

Kearl, Holly. "Way to go Togo's." *Stop Street Harassment*, November 21, 2011. Accessed December 10, 2014. http://www.stopstreetharassment.org/2011/11/togos3/.

Kearl, Holly. "WMATA Taking Steps to Curb Sexual Harassment." *Greater Washington*, March 6, 2013. Accessed November 28, 2014. http://greater greaterwashington.org/post/17914/wmata-taking-steps-to-curb-sexual-har assment/.

Kearl, Holly. "Yes to Carrots: It's Not a Compliment." *Stop Street Harassment*, February 25, 2013. Accessed December 10, 2014. http://www.stopstreethar assment.org/2013/02/yestocarrots/.

Kehoe, Karrie. "Exclusive Poll: Does Single-Sex Public Transport Help or Hinder Women?" *Reuters*, October 29, 2014. Accessed January 3, 2015. http://uk .reuters.com/article/2014/10/29/women-poll-carriages-idUKL6N0S42MD 20141029.

Khalil, Nama. "Blue Bra Graffiti (Bahia Shehab)." Design and Violence, September 3, 2014. Accessed January 4, 2015. http://designandviolence.moma.org /blue-bra-graffiti-bahia-shehab/.

Khater, Menan. "Sexual Harassment Still Pervasive in Egypt, Despite New Law." *Daily News Egypt*, November 24, 2014. Accessed January 18, 2015. http:// www.dailynewsegypt.com/2014/11/24/sexual-harassment-still-pervasive-egypt -despite-new-law/.

Kingsley, Patrick. "80 Sexual Assaults in One Day—The Other Story of Tahrir Square." *The Guardian*, July 5, 2013. Accessed January 19, 2015. http://www .theguardian.com/world/2013/jul/05/egypt-women-rape-sexual-assault-tahrir -square.

Kingsley, Patrick. "Doubt Remains in Egypt Despite Sisi's Action Against Sexual Harassment." *The Guardian*, June 13, 2014. Accessed January 18, 2015. http://www.theguardian.com/world/2014/jun/13/doubts-remain-in-egypt -despite-sisis-action-against-sexual-harassment.

Kingsley, Patrick. "Tahrir Square Sexual Assaults Reported During Anniversary Clashes." *The Guardian*, January 27, 2013. Accessed January 18, 2015. http:// www.theguardian.com/world/2013/jan/27/tahrir-square-sexual-assaults -reported.

Kirkpatrick, David. "Mass March by Cairo Women in Protest Over Abuse by Soldiers." *New York Times*, December 20, 2011. Accessed January 8, 2015. http://www.nytimes.com/2011/12/21/world/middleeast/violence-enters-5th -day-as-egyptian-general-blames-protesters.html?.

Kissling, Elizabeth Arveda. "Street Harassment: The Language of Sexual Terrorism." *Discourse Society* (1991). Accessed December 10, 2014. http://das.sage pub.com/content/2/4/451.abstract.

Krieger, Daniel. "Why Women-Only Transit Options Have Caught On." *The Atlantic*, Feb. 8, 2012. Accessed December 4, 2014. http://www.theatlantic

cities.com/commute/2012/02/why-women-only-transit-options-have-caught/1171/.

Kwan, Raymond. "Don't Dress Like a Slut: Toronto Cop." *Excalibur—York University's Community Newspaper*, February 16, 2011. Accessed December 14, 2014. http://www.excal.on.ca/dont-dress-like-a-slut-toronto-cop/.

Lakshmi, Rama. "In New Delhi, A Help Line for Women is Flooded with Calls." *Washington Post*, June 21, 2013. Accessed January 13, 2015. http://www.washingtonpost.com/world/asia_pacific/in-new-delhi-a-help-line-for-women-is-flooded-with-calls/2013/06/21/819becfc-d751-11e2-b418-9dfa095e125d_story.html.

Lambert, Logan. "Harasser Uses Sexually Violent Language In Front of Cop, Cop Laughs." *Stop Street Harassment*, July 18, 2011. Accessed December 10, 2014. http://www.stopstreetharassment.org/2011/07/harasser-uses-sexually-violent-language-in-front-of-cop-cop-laughs/.

"Laura Logan Breaks Silence on Cairo Assault." *60 Minutes*, May 1, 2011. Accessed November 29, 2014. http://www.cbsnews.com/news/lara-logan-breaks-silence-on-cairo-assault.

Laville, Sandra. "Police abuse: Vulnerable Women and Girls were Targeted by Sexual Predators." *The Guardian*, June 29, 2012. Accessed December 28, 2014. http://www.theguardian.com/uk/2012/jun/29/police-abuse-vulnerable-women-girls.

Leila, Reem. "Unsafe Streets." *Al-Ahram*, October 15, 2008. Accessed November 28, 2014. http://weekly.ahram.org.eg/2008/917/eg6.htm.

Lewis, Kim. "Somali Women Face Rape, Sexual Assault as They Flee Famine." *Voice of America*, August 1, 2011. Accessed February 15, 2015. http://www.voanews.com/content/somali-women-face-rape-sexual-assault-as-they-flee-famine----126598458/160072.html.

Lewis-McCoy, L'Heureux Dumi. "Parallels of Street Harassment & Police Harassment." *Stop Street Harassment*, May 5, 2011. Accessed November 29, 2015. http://www.stopstreetharassment.org/2011/05/parellels-of-street-harassment-police-harassment/.

"LGBT Persons' Experiences of Discrimination and Hate Crime in the EU and Croatia." European Union Agency for Fundamental Rights, 2013. Accessed January 14, 2015. http://fra.europa.eu/sites/default/files/eu-lgbt-survey-factsheet_en.pdf.

Linthicum, Kate. "Bicyclist Harassment Outlawed by Los Angeles City Council." *LA Times*, July 21, 2011. Accessed November 28, 2014. http://articles.latimes.com/2011/jul/21/local/la-me-bicycle-law-20110721.

Lior, Ilan. "Vast Majority of Tel Aviv Women Report Sexual Harassment, Survey Finds." *Haaretz,* November 23, 2011. Accessed January 5, 2015. http://www.haaretz.com/print-edition/news/vast-majority-of-tel-aviv-women-report-sexual-harassment-survey-finds-1.397163.

Logan, Laura S. "The Case of the 'Killer Lesbians.'" *The Public Intellectual*, July 18, 2011. Accessed December 4, 2014. http://thepublicintellectual.org/2011/07/18/the-case-of-the-killer-lesbians/.

Ludwig, Mike. "'Walking While Woman' and the Fight to Stop Violent Policing of Gender Identity." *Truthout*, May 7, 2014. Accessed January 8, 2015. http://www.truth-out.org/news/item/23551-walking-while-woman-and-the-fight-to-stop-violent-policing-of-gender-identity.

MaddieandTaeVEVO. "Maddie & Teo—Girl in a Country Song." YouTube, July 24, 2014. Accessed December 12, 2014. https://www.youtube.com/watch?v=_MOavH-Eivw.

"The Making of International Anti-Street Harassment Week Signs." A Long Walk Home, March 19, 2012. Accessed December 27, 2014. https://www.youtube.com/watch?v=aRkIQoUo2kw.

Males, Mike. "Who are Police Killing?" Center on Juvenile and Criminal Justice. August 26, 2014. Accessed January 8, 2015. http://www.cjcj.org/news/8113.

Mandhana, Niharika, and Heatlher Timmons. "India Passes Sweeping Bill on Crimes Against Women." *The New York Times*, March 21, 2013. Accessed January 13, 2015. http://india.blogs.nytimes.com/2013/03/21/india-passes-sweeping-bill-on-crimes-against-women/.

Marroushi, Nadine. "When Police Rape, Who Can People Turn To?" *Middle East Eye*, December 27, 2014. Accessed January 18, 2015. http://www.middleeasteye.net/columns/when-police-rape-who-can-people-turn-1347802948.

Martinson, Jane. "Police Act to Halt Sex Harassment on London Buses and Trains." *The Guardian*, July 21, 2013. Accessed November 29, 2014. http://www.theguardian.com/uk-news/2013/jul/22/sexual-harassment-london-transport.

Mastrine, Julie. "Penn State Students Conduct Anti-Street Harassment Demonstration." *Stop Street Harassment*, October 22, 2012. Accessed December 3, 2014. http://www.stopstreetharassment.org/2012/10/pennstate/.

Mawson, Jessie. "UNICEF Supports Efforts to End Sexual Harassment of Girls and Women in Bangladesh." UNICEF, July 21, 2010. Accessed November 28, 2014. http://www.unicef.org/infobycountry/bangladesh_55216.html.

May, Emily. "Statement About Recent Street Harassment PSA." *Hollaback*! October 30, 2014. Accessed November 28, 2014. http://www.ihollaback.org/blog/2014/10/30/statement-about-recent-street-harassment-psa/.

May, Emily, and Allison Sesso. "Hollaback! State of the Streets Report, 2014." *Hollaback*! December 2014. Accessed December 9, 2014. http://issuu.com/hollaback/docs/sots14v4.

Mbondgulo Wondieh, Zoneziwoh. "Cameroon: Safe Cities Walk." *Stop Street Harassment*, October 30, 2013. Accessed December 10, 2014. http://www.stopstreetharassment.org/2013/10/cameroon-safe-cities-walk/.

Mbondgulo Wondieh, Zoneziwoh. "Cameroon Workshop to Raise Awareness and Build Allies with Adolescents." *Stop Street Harassment*, December 14, 2013. Accessed January 13, 2015. http://www.stopstreetharassment.org/2013/12/cameroon16daysworkshop/.

McCullagh, Kathryn. "Tweeting about sexism may improve a woman's well-being." *British Psychological Society*, EurekaAlert!, January 30, 2015. Accessed February 3, 2015. http://www.eurekalert.org/pub_releases/2015-01/bps-tas013015.php.

McKinney, Kelsey. "Maddie & Tae Top the Charts with Feminist Country Music." *VOX*, December 11, 2014. Accessed November 28, 2014. http://www.vox .com/2014/8/7/5966739/country-music-feminist.

McNeil, Patrick. "Harassing Men on the Street." Feministe, October 15, 2012. Accessed November 28, 2015. http://www.feministe.us/blog/archives/2012 /10/15/harassing-men-on-the-street/.

McNeil, Patrick. "Street Harassment at the Intersections: The Experiences of Gay and Bisexual Men." The George Washington University Dissertation, 2014. Accessed 20 December 2014. http://gradworks.umi.com/15/50/1550487.html.

Mengle, Gautam S. "Dombivali Youth's Murder Brings Eve-Teasing Menace into Sharp Focus Again." *The Indian Express*, December 11, 2012. Accessed January 13, 2015. http://archive.indianexpress.com/news/dombivali-youth-s -murder-brings-eveteasing-menace-into-sharp-focus-again/1043383/0.

METRAC. "Not Your Baby." iTunes, n.d. Accessed February 3, 2015. https:// itunes.apple.com/us/app/not-your-baby/id545191859?mt=8.

"MetroEgy." YouTube, n.d., Accessed January 3, 2015. https://www.youtube .com/user/MetroEgy?feature=watch;

Mia, Salim. "Bangladesh 'Eve teasing' Takes a Terrible Toll." *BBC*, June 11, 2010. Accessed November 28, 2014. http://www.bbc.co.uk/news/10220920.

Middlecamp, Lindsey. "Talk Back to Your Harassers with these Cards!" *Stop Street Harassment*, June 10, 2014. Accessed December 10, 2014. http://www .stopstreetharassment.org/2014/06/cardsagainstharassment/.

Miles-McLean, Haley, Miriam Liss, Mindy J. Erchull, Caitlin M. Robertson, Charlotte Hagerman, Michelle A. Gnoleba, and Leanna J. Papp. "'Stop Looking at Me!' Interpersonal Sexual Objectification as a Source of Insidious Trauma." *Psychology of Women Quarterly* (2014). Accessed December 10, 2014. http:// pwq.sagepub.com/content/early/2014/11/03/0361684314561018?papetoc.

Millhiser, Ian. "Judge to Woman Sexually Assaulted by Cop: 'When You Blame Others, You Give Up Your Power to Change." *Think Progress*, September 7, 2012. Accessed December 15, 2014. http://thinkprogress.org/justice/2012/09 /07/809861/judge-to-woman-sexually-assaulted-by-cop-when-you-blame -others-you-give-up-your-power-to-change/?mobile=nc.

"Minister to Take Part in Miniskirt March." *News24*, February 16, 2012. Accessed November 29, 2014. http://www.news24.com/SouthAfrica/Politics /Minister-to-take-part-in-miniskirt-march-20120216.

"Miss Alice Reighly, President of the Anti-Flirt Club." Library of Congress, Call 12295, v.1, February 27, 1923. Accessed, February 15, 2015. http://www.loc .gov/pictures/item/2002695741/.

"Mission and Description." Huairou Commission, n.d. Accessed November 29, 2014. http://huairou.org/mission-and-description.

Mohammad Hassan, Rasha. *Clouds in Egypt's Sky. Sexual Harassment: from Verbal Harassment to Rape. A Sociological Study*. Egyptian Centre for Women's Rights, 2008. Accessed December 10, 2014. http://egypt.unfpa.org /Images/Publication/2010_03/6eeeb05a-3040-42d2-9e1c-2bd2e1ac8cac.pdf.

Mohapatra, Samhati. "Yellow-and-Green Gender Revolution on 3 Wheels." *New Indian Express*, October 25, 2014. Accessed January 23, 2015. http://www

.newindianexpress.com/magazine/Yellow-and-Green-Gender-Revolution-on
-3-Wheels/2014/10/25/article2491608.ece.

Moloney, Anastasia. "Colombia Steps Up Campaign to Combat Sexual Harassment on Buses." Thomas Reuters Foundation, November 4, 2014. Accessed
November 29, 2014. http://www.trust.org/item/20141105160728-yro0i/.

Msimang, Sisonke. "The Backlash Against African Women." *The New York
Times*, January 10, 2015. Accessed January 15, 2015, http://www.nytimes
.com/2015/01/11/opinion/sunday/the-backlash-against-african-women
.html.

"National Report on Hate Violence Against Lesbian, Gay, Bisexual, Transgender,
Queer, and HIV-Affected Communities Released Today." National Coalition
of Anti-Violence Programs, June 4, 2013. Accessed January 8, 2015. http://
www.avp.org/storage/documents/2012_mr_ncavp_hvreport.pdf.

NDTV. "Outrage in Assam After Mob Publicly Strips, Molests Girl in Guwahati,"
YouTube, July 13, 2012. Accessed December 15, 2014. https://www.youtube
.com/watch?v=vGW2HL92VEw&feature=related.

NDTV Correspondent. "MMS scandal: Molested and Harassed, Sisters Driven
to Suicide." *NDTV*, May 28, 2010. Accessed December 4, 2014. http://www
.ndtv.com/article/cities/mms-scandal-molested-and-harassed-sisters-driven-to
-suicide-28192.

Nelson, Dean. "Delhi Gang-Rape Victim Dies of Organ Failure." *Telegraph*,
December 28, 2012. Accessed January 18, 2015. http://www.telegraph.co.uk
/news/worldnews/asia/india/9770345/Delhi-gang-rape-victim-dies-of-organ
-failure.html.

Nelson, Laura J. "Survey: Sexual Harassment Makes 20% of Metro Riders Feel
Unsafe." *LA Times*, May 7, 2014. Accessed December 4, 2014. http://www
.latimes.com/local/lanow/la-me-ln-passengers-feel-unsafe-20140507-story
.html.

Nichols, James. "Monica Jones, Transgender Woman, Convicted of 'Manifesting
Prostitution." *Huffington Post*, April 16, 2014. Accessed February 16, 2015.
http://www.huffingtonpost.com/2014/04/16/monica-jones-transgender_n
_5159638.html.

"Nigeria Anti-Gay Law: Fears Over New Legislation." *BBC*, January 14, 2012.
Accessed December 14, 2014. http://www.bbc.com/news/world-africa-2572
8845.

" 'No Groping' on Bogota's Buses." Love Matters, April 22, 2011. Accessed
January 23, 2015. http://lovematters.in/en/news/no-groping-bogotas-buses.

Nolen, Stephanie. "Finding Solace in Delhi's Women-Only Subway Car." *The
Globe & Mail*, February 23, 2012. Accessed December 4, 2014. http://www
.theglobeandmail.com/news/world/worldview/finding-solace-in-delhis-women
-only-subway-car/article548716/.

Nyawira Mwangi, Linnet. "Kenya: He Mistook My Kindness for Weakness."
Stop Street Harassment, January 15, 2015. Accessed January 15, 2015. http://
www.stopstreetharassment.org/2015/01/kindness-for-weakness/.

O'Connor, Clare. "New App Launched in Time for Super Bowl Lets You
Call Out Brands for Sexist Ads." Forbes.com, January 27 2014. Accessed

December 28, 2014. http://www.forbes.com/sites/clareoconnor/2014/01/27
/new-app-launched-in-time-for-super-bowl-lets-you-call-out-brands-for
-sexist-ads/.

Olivia Parsons, Clare. "Reputation and Public Appearance: The De-Eroticization
of the Urban Street." In *Voices in the Street: Explorations in Gender, Media,
and Public Space*, edited by Susan J. Drucker and Gary Gumpert, 59–70.
Cresskill, NJ: Hampton Press, Inc, 1996.

"Our New Strategy for Ending Poverty." ActionAid, n.d. Accessed on December
28, 2014. http://www.actionaid.org/who-we-are/our-new-strategy-ending
-poverty.

Overdorf, Jason. "India: Protests Resume After Delhi Gang Rape Victim Dies."
Global Post, December 29, 2012. Accessed January 12, 2015. http://www.
globalpost.com/dispatch/news/regions/asia-pacific/india/121229/india-protests
-resume-delhi-gang-rape-victim-dies

"Oversight: Street Harassment of Women and Girls in New York City." The
New York City Council, October 28, 2010.

Oxygen/Markle Pulse Poll. "Harassment of Women on the Street is Rampant;
87% of American Women Report Being Harassed on the Street By a Male
Stranger." The Free Library, June 22, 2000. Accessed January 30, 2015. http://
www.thefreelibrary.com/Oxygen%2FMarkle+Pulse+Poll+Finds%3A+Harass
ment+of+Women+on+the+Street+Is . . . -a062870396.

P.M. "No, Officers, Harassment, Following and Assault Does Not Equal 'Flirting.' " *Stop Street Harassment Blog*, April 9, 2011. Accessed December 10,
2014. http://www.stopstreetharassment.org/2011/04/no-officers-harassment
-following-and-assault-does-not-equal-flirting/.

Pachal, Pete. "How the #YesAllWomen Hashtag Began." *Mashable*, May 26,
2014. Accessed November 28, 2014. http://mashable.com/2014/05/26/yes
allwomen-hashtag/.

"Pakistan's Educational Challenges." *CNN*, October 10, 2014. Accessed January
8, 2015. http://www.cnn.com/2013/10/09/world/asia/infographic-pakistan
-education/.

Pérez-Rodríguez, Adriana. "Colombia: Harassment and Armed Conflict." *Stop
Street Harassment*, February 13, 2013. Accessed December 10, 2014. http://
www.stopstreetharassment.org/2013/02/colombiaarmedconflict/.

Philipose, Pamela. "That Call for Help: How Effective are Helplines?" Jagori,
November 24, 2014. Accessed December 29, 2015. http://jagori.org/call-help
-how-effective-are-helplines.

Plank, Elizabeth. "#NotBuyingIt App Could Put an End to Sexist Advertisements."
Mic, March 21, 2013, Accessed January 3, 2015. http://mic.com/articles/30592
/notbuyingit-app-could-put-an-end-to-sexist-advertisements.

"Poll reveals 1/4 Women Do Not Feel Safe on London Public Transport." End
Violence Against Women, March 30, 2012. Accessed November 29, 2014.
http://www.endviolenceagainstwomen.org.uk/news/14/poll-reveals-14
-women-dont-feel-safe-on-london-public-transport.

Poole, Melanie. "When We Talk about Police Shootings, We Need to Talk about
Gender." Feministing, December 17, 2014. Accessed January 7, 2015. http://

feministing.com/2014/12/17/when-we-talk-about-police-shootings-we-need-to
-talk-about-gender/.

Popkin, Susan and Robin Smith. "Girls in the 'Hood—What Violence Means for
Girls." Urban Institute, September 14, 2011. Accessed February 12, 2015.
http://blog.metrotrends.org/2011/09/what-violence-means-for-girls/.

Porter, Catherine. "Ontario schools will offer gender studies, thanks to five young
women." *The Star,* April 26, 2013. Accessed November 28, 2014. http://
www.thestar.com/news/gta/2013/04/26/ontario_schools_will_offer_gender
_studies_thanks_to_five_young_women_porter.html.

Pratt, Seanna. "Lesbian Couples and Street Harassment." *GERM Magazine,*
September 3, 2014. Accessed January 22, 2015. http://www.germmagazine
.com/lesbian-couples-and-street-harassment/.

"Preocupantes cifras de acoso a mujeres en Transmilenio." *Noticias RCN,* May
9, 2014. Accessed November 29, 2014. http://www.noticiasrcn.com/nacional
-bogota/preocupantes-cifras-acoso-mujeres-transmilenio.

"Project Guardian." British Transit Police, n.d. Accessed November 30, 2014.
http://www.btp.police.uk/advice_and_information/how_we_tackle_crime
/project_guardian.aspx.

"Projects." Jagori, n.d., Accessed February 14, 2015. http://www.jagori.org
/projects.

"Racial Profiling," ACLU, n.d. Accessed January 8, 2015. https://www.aclu.org
/racial-justice/racial-profiling.

Ramakrishnan, Kavita B. "Inconsistent Legal Treatment of Unwanted Sexual
Advances: A Study of the Homosexual Advance Defense, Street Harassment,
and Sexual Harassment in the Workplace." *Berkeley Journal of Gender,
Law & Justice* 26 (2011): 291–355.

"Rape on the rise in aftermath of Haiti quake." *The Grio,* March 16, 2010.
Accessed February 15, 2015. http://thegrio.com/2010/03/16/rape-on-the-rise
-in-aftermath-of-haiti-quake/.

Rebel.grrrl. Instagram. Accessed February 17, 2015. http://instagram.com/rebel
.grrrl.

Reddy, Sumathi. "A Thin Line on Skirts." *Wall Street Journal,* September 30,
2011. Accessed January 3, 2015. http://www.wsj.com/articles/SB10001424052
970204226204576601174240952328.

"Report of The Sentencing Project to the United Nations Human Rights Committee Regarding Racial Disparities in the United States Criminal Justice
System." The Sentencing Project, August 2013. Accessed January 5, 2015.
http://sentencingproject.org/doc/publications/rd_ICCPR%20Race%20
and%20Justice%20Shadow%20Report.pdf.

Richter, Ash M. "The Wall Street Ogle-In of 1970." *All Day,* November 2014.
Accessed February 15, 2015. http://allday.com/post/1619-the-wall-street-ogle
-in-of-1970.

"Riding a Bus in Kathmandu: Gender and Transport in Nepal." The World Bank,
March 17, 2014. Accessed December 3, 2014. http://www.worldbank.org/en
/news/feature/2014/03/17/riding-a-bus-in-kathmandu-gender-and-transport
-in-nepal.

el-Rifae, Yasmin. "Egypt's Sexual Harassment Law: An Insufficient Measure to End Sexual Violence." *Middle East Institute*, July 17, 2014. Accessed January 18, 2015. http://www.mei.edu/content/at/egypts-sexual-harassment-law-insuf ficient-measure-end-sexual-violence.

Robbie. "I Think I Gave Them a Tiny Scare." *Stop Street Harassment*, September 2, 2014. Accessed December 10, 2014. http://www.stopstreetharassment.org /2014/09/tinyscare/.

Rodriguez, Salvador. "60% of World's Population Still Won't Have Internet by the End of 2014." *LA Times*, May 7, 2014. Accessed November 20, 2015. http://www.latimes.com/business/technology/la-fi-tn-60-world-population-3 -billion-internet-2014-20140507-story.html.

Rose, Rebecca. "Man Stabbed for Asking Someone to Stop Catcalling His Girl-friend." *Jezebel*, November 20, 2014. Accessed February 7, 2015. http://jezebel .com/and-this-is-why-more-men-men-who-are-pissed-off-at-str-1661480851 ?utm_campaign=socialflow_jezebel_facebook&utm_source=jezebel_face book&utm_medium=socialflow.

Rosenthal, Lindsay. "Eliminate Violence Against Women and Girls? There's An App for That." *Science Progress*, March 8, 2013. Accessed November 20, 2015. http://scienceprogress.org/2013/03/eliminate-violence-against-women -and-girls-worldwide-there%E2%80%99s-an-app-for-that/.

Rosin, Hanna. "The Problem with that Catcalling Video." *Slate*, October 29, 2014. Accessed November 28, 2014. http://www.slate.com/blogs/xx_factor /2014/10/29/catcalling_video_hollaback_s_look_at_street_harassment_in_nyc _edited_out.html.

Roychoudhury, Arup, and Annie Banerji. "India's Gang-Rape Protesters Defy Moves to Quell Outrage." *Reuters*, December 23, 2012. Accessed January 18, 2015. http://www.reuters.com/article/2012/12/23/us-india-protests-idUSBRE 8BM02X20121223.

Saavedra, Chloe. "Woman Reports Street Harassment, NYPD Officer Laughs." *Stop Street Harassment*, October 6, 2013. Accessed December 10, 2014. http:// www.stopstreetharassment.org/2013/10/nypdlaughs/.

"Safe Cities for Women." ActionAid, n.d. Accessed on December 28, 2014. http:// www.actionaid.org/safe-cities-for-women.

Safe Cities for Women: From Reality to Rights. ActionAid, May 2014. Accessed February 3, 2015. http://global.safecitiesforwomen.org/wp-content/uploads /sites/5/2014/02/safe-cities.pdf.

"Safe Cities Programme: Women's Right to the City." ActionAid, September 2014 newsletter, PDF emailed to the author by Christy Abraham on December 30, 2014.

Safetipin. "Our Vision," n.d., http://ww.safetipin.com/our-vision; see also Ayesha Vemuri, "Meet Safetipin: A Mobile Application That Tells Exactly How Safe Any Locality is For You," Youth Kiawaaz, 20 November 2013. Accessed December 10, 2014. http://www.youthkiawaaz.com/2013/11/meet-safetipin -mobile-application-tells-exactly-safe-locality/.

"Safety." METRAC, n.d. Accessed November 28, 2014. http://www.metrac.org /what-we-do/safety/.

Sanchez, Nathalie. "Cultural Machismo in Latino Communities." *Stop Street Harassment*, March 30, 2011. Accessed December 10, 2014. http://www.stop streetharassment.org/2011/03/cultural-machismo-in-latino-communities/.

"Saudi Arabia Sexual Harassment Video Sparks Social Media Outrage." *Al Arabiya*, October 24, 2013. Accessed November 28, 2014. http://english .alarabiya.net/en/News/middle-east/2013/10/24/Saudi-Arabia-sexual-harass ment-video-sparks-social-media-outrage-.html.

"Saudi Mulls Hefty Punishment for Sexual Harassment." *BBC,* October 14, 2014. Accessed November 29, 2014. http://www.bbc.com/news/blogs-news -from-elsewhere-29619205.

Schulz, Dorothy, and Susan Gilbert. "Women and Transit Security: A New Look at an Old Issue." Proceedings of the Women's Travel Issues Second National Conference, October 25–27, 1996. Baltimore, MD, page 551.

Schwartzman, Nancy. "Harnessing Mobile Tech to Prevent Sexual Assault." *Huffington Post*, April 2, 2013. Accessed November 20, 2015. http://www .huffingtonpost.com/nancy-schwartzman/circle-of-6-app_b_2999887.html.

"See Something, Text Something: Metro Transit Police Launch Text Tips Service." Washington Metropolitan Area Transit Authority, October 3 2013. Accessed November 13, 2014. http://www.wmata.com/about_metro/news/PressRelease Detail.cfm?ReleaseID=5584.

Segall, Sandra. "Three in Four Chilean Women Regularly Harassed in Public, Study Finds." *Santiago Times*, May 5, 2014. Accessed December 14, 2014. http://santiagotimes.cl/three-four-chilean-women-regularly-harassed-public -study-finds/.

Segrave, Kerry. *Beware the Masher: Sexual Harassment in American Public Places, 1880–1930.* Jefferson, NC: McFarland & Company, 2014.

"Serial Killer on Motorcycle may be to Blame for 12 Slayings: Police." *Global News*, August 5, 2014. Accessed January 5, 2015, http://globalnews.ca/news /1492999/serial-killer-on-motorcycle-may-.

Setiawati, Indah. "Men, Women Have Separate Busway Queue Lines." *The Jakarta Post*, June 10, 2010. Accessed January 3, 2015. http://www.thejakarta post.com/news/2010/06/10/men-women-have-separate-busway-queue-lines .html.

"Sexual Harassment Myths," HarassMap, n.d. Accessed November 28, 2014. http://harassmap.org/en/resource-center/harassment-myths/.

Shah Singh, Harmeet. "Indian Prime Minister Calls for Calm After Violence Erupts During Anti-Rape Rallies." *CNN*, January 4, 2013. Accessed December 28, 2015. http://www.cnn.com/2012/12/23/world/asia/india-rape-protests /index.html?hpt=wo_c1.

Sharma, Kuber. "I Flashed a Mob and I Liked It." *Stop Street Harassment*, June 2, 2011. Accessed December 10, 2014. http://www.stopstreetharassment.org /2011/06/i-flashed-a-mob-and-i-liked-it/.

Shastri, Parth. "Man Stabbed to Death in Ahmedabad Eve-Teasing." *The Times of India*, November 28, 2012. Accessed December 29, 2015. http:// timesofindia.indiatimes.com/city/ahmedabad/Man-stabbed-to-death-in -Ahmedabad-over-eve-teasing/articleshow/17403034.cms?referral=PM.

Shaw, Anny. "Artists Fight Violence Against Women in Egypt." *The Art Newspaper*, August 20, 2014. Accessed December 4, 2014. http://old.theartnewspaper.com/articles/Artists-fight-violence-against-women-in-Egypt/33419

Shaw, Margaret, Caroline Andrew, Carolyn Whitzman, Fran Klodawsky, Kalpana Viswanath, and Crystal Legacy. "Introduction: Challenges, opportunities and tools." In *Building Inclusive Cities: Women's safety and their right to the city*, edited by Margaret Shaw, Caroline Andrew, Carolyn Whitzman, Fran Klodawsky, Kalpana Viswanath, and Crystal Legacy, 1–16. New York: Routledge, 2013.

Sheils, Conor. "Egyptian Cops Using Grindr to Hunt Gays." *Cairoscene*, August 31, 2014. Accessed December 15, 2015. http://www.cairoscene.com/ViewArticle.aspx?AId=13967-Egyptian-Cops-Using-Grindr-To-Hunt-Gays.

Shoot, Brittany. "Resilience in Slums a Lesson for Cynical Western Feminists." *Ms. Blog*, November 24, 2010. Accessed December 4, 2014. http://msmagazine.com/blog/2010/11/24/resilience-in-slums-a-lesson-for-cynical-western-feminists/.

Smale, Alison. "A Student's Death Exposes German Struggle for a Multicultural Ideal." *The New York Times*, December 2, 2014. Accessed February 7, 2015. http://www.nytimes.com/2014/12/03/world/europe/tugce-albayrak-death-rattles-germany.html?_r=1.

Smith, Joanne. "Young Women of Color Break the Silence. Now What?" *Women's eNews*, December 4, 2014. Accessed January 8, 2015. http://womensenews.org/story/equalitywomen%E2%80%99s-rights/141203/young-women-color-break-the-silence-now-what#.VIDWGaTF-VZ.

Sobol, Rosemary Regina, Meredith Rodriguez and Steve Schmadeke. "Father dies shielding daughter, 15: 'I'm going to make him proud.'" *Chicago Tribune*, March 21, 2014. Accessed February 7, 2015. http://articles.chicagotribune.com/2014-03-21/news/chi-father-died-protecting-teenage-daughter-her-mother-says-20140320_1_daughter-disability-benefits-chest.

Solomon, Akiba. "On that Street Harassment Video and Race." *Colorlines*, October 30, 2014. Accessed December 4, 2014. http://colorlines.com/archives/2014/10/on_that_street_harassment_video_and_race.html.

Son, Thai. "Vietnam Capital Plans All-Female Buses Following Reports of Sexual Harassment." *Thanh Nien News,* December 25, 2014. Accessed December 5, 2014. http://www.thanhniennews.com/society/vietnam-capital-plans-allfemale-buses-following-reports-of-sexual-harassment-36725.html.

Speed, Barbara. "The ATM at Which Indian Women can Report Sexual Assault." CityMetric, January 6, 2015. Accessed January 19, 2015. http://www.citymetric.com/horizons/atm-which-indian-women-can-report-sexual-assault-613.

Staff. "Egyptian Rights Group Rejects 'Women-Only' Taxi." *Egypt Independent*, July 27, 2011. Accessed December 5, 2014. http://www.egyptindependent.com/news/egyptian-rights-group-rejects-women-only-taxis.

Stamoulis, Kathryn. " 'Hey Baby' Hurts." *Psychology Today*, August 19, 2011. Accessed February 20, 2015. http://www.psychologytoday.com/blog/the-new-teen-age/201108/hey-baby-hurts.

Stanković, Marija. "Serbia: Street Harassment Survey has an Impact." *Stop Street Harassment*, December 29, 2014. Accessed December 29, 2014. http://www.stopstreetharassment.org/2014/12/serbiaspsmfinalreport/.

"Statistics." YouTube, n.d. Accessed December 4, 2014. https://www.youtube.com/yt/press/statistics.html.

Stock, Wendy. "Togo's Restaurant Trivializes Street Harassment." *Stop Street Harassment*, November 4, 2011. Accessed December 10, 2014. http://www.stopstreetharassment.org/2011/11/togos/.

"Stop-and-Frisk Data." NYCLU, n.d. Accessed January 15, 2015. http://www.nyclu.org/content/stop-and-frisk-data.

Stop Street Harassment. "The Astronomical Kid Testifies at NYC Council Hearing on Street Harassment." YouTube, October 29, 2010. Accessed December 4, 2014. https://www.youtube.com/watch?v=awwzjnxicQo.

Stop Street Harassment. "Sawsan Gad—Street Harassment Talk." YouTube, March 20, 2012. Accessed December 2, 2014. https://www.youtube.com/watch?v=dwwa0qqsDfw.

Strangio, Chase. "Arrested for Walking While Trans: An Interview with Monica Jones." ACLU, April 2, 2014. Accessed February 16, 2015. https://www.aclu.org/blog/lgbt-rights-criminal-law-reform-hiv-aids-reproductive-freedom-womens-rights/arrested-walking.

"Street harassment." Google Trends, n.d., Accessed December 13, 2014. http://www.google.com/trends/explore#q=%22Street%20harassment%22.

Sugden, Joanna. "Delhi Men Say Sorry." *The Wall Street Journal*, March 16, 2013. Accessed January 19, 2015. http://blogs.wsj.com/indiarealtime/2013/03/16/delhi-men-say-sorry/.

Sundaram, Vanita. "Schools Aren't Teaching Enough about Sexism. It's the Best Way to End Dating Violence," *Washington Post*, January 7, 2015. Accessed January 12, 2015. http://www.washingtonpost.com/posteverything/wp/2015/01/07/schools-arent-arent-teaching-enough-about-sexism-its-the-best-way-to-end-dating-violence/.

"Supreme Court Issues Directions to Curb Sexual Harassment of Women in Public Transport." *The Times of India*, December 2, 2012. Accessed January 19, 2015. http://timesofindia.indiatimes.com/india/Supreme-Court-issues-directions-to-curb-sexual-harassment-of-women-in-public-transport/articleshow/17445499.cms.

Sur, Priyali. "Are Women Traveling into a Safer 2015?" The World Bank, January 15, 2015. Accessed January 19, 2015. http://blogs.worldbank.org/voices/are-women-traveling-safer-2015.

Suzee in the City. "Women in Graffiti: A Tribute to the Women of Egypt." Suzeeinthecity, January 7, 2013. Accessed November 29, 2014. http://suzeeinthecity.wordpress.com/2013/01/07/women-in-graffiti-a-tribute-to-the-women-of-egypt/.

Swash, Rosie. "How Egyptians are Fighting Harassment in the Streets." *The Guardian*, November 5, 2012. Accessed January 18, 2015. http://www.theguardian.com/lifeandstyle/2012/nov/05/egyptians-fighting-harassment-streets.

"Swaziland bans 'rape-provoking' mini-skirts, low-rise jeans." *Indian Express*, December 31, 2012. Accessed December 14, 2014. http://archive.indianexpress .com/news/%22swaziland-bans-rapeprovoking-miniskirts-lowrise-jeans%22 /1049615/.

"Taking Harassment Off The Streets." *Tribune 242*, April 1, 2014. Accessed November 28, 2014. http://www.tribune242.com/news/2014/apr/01/taking -harassment-off-the-streets/?news.

Tarrant, Shira. "Shit Men Say to Men about Street Harassment." *Ms*. Blog, April 4, 2012. Accessed December 3, 2014. http://msmagazine.com/blog/2012/04 /04/sht-men-say-to-men-about-street-harassment/.

"Teenager Killed in Egypt While Defending Women from Sexual Harassment." *Egyptian Streets*, October 6, 2014. Accessed February 7, 2015. http://egyptian streets.com/2014/10/06/teenager-killed-in-egypt-while-defending-women-from -sexual-harassment/.

Телеканал ОНТ, "EURO-2012: Holland Fans and Ukranian Reporter, Funny Video, Kharkiv." YouTube, June 15, 2012. Accessed December 14, 2014. https://www.youtube.com/watch?v=XmQlb_N-K64.

Thein, Cherry. "Whistle Campaign a Hit on City Buses." *Myanmar Times*, February 27, 2012. Accessed January 14, 2015. http://www.mmtimes.com/index .php/national-news/yangon/1161-whistle-campaign-a-hit-on-city-buses.html.

"They Cross-Dress for a Cause." *The Deccan Herald*, January 12, 2013. Accessed January 20, 2015. http://www.deccanherald.com/content/304804/men-skirts -pledge-support-women.html.

"Third International Conference on Women's Safety—Building Inclusive Cities." Women in Cities International, 2010. Accessed on December 28, 2014. http:// www.femmesetvilles.org/index.php/en/conferences/third-international-confe rence-on-women-s.

"Third International Conference on Women's Safety: Building Inclusive Cities— Conference Programme." Women in Cities International and Jagori, November 22, 2010 (print copy).

Thomas Reuters Foundation. "Most Dangerous Transport Systems for Women." Trust.org, October 31, 2014. Accessed December 4, 2014. http://www.trust .org/spotlight/most-dangerous-transport-systems-for-women/.

Toukan, Nadine. "Jordan: Women's Basic Rights for Dignity and Social Cohesion." *Global Voices Online*, June 27, 2012. Accessed January 2, 2015. http:// globalvoicesonline.org/2012/06/27/jordan-womens-basic-rights-for-dignity -and-social-cohesion/.

Trotter, Alan. "@RantingOwl has a great train harassment story to tell." *Storify*, February 6, 2015. Accessed February 7, 2015. https://storify.com/alantrotter /commuter-harrassment.

"UN Egypt Calls for Firm Stand on Violence Against Women." UN Women, June 11, 2014. Accessed January 18, 2015. http://www.unwomen.org/en/news /stories/2014/6/new-anti-sexual-harassment-law-in-egypt.

UN Women Multi Country Office of India, Bhutan, Maldives, and Sri Lanka, ICRW Asia Regional Office, "Safe Cities Free From Violence Against Women and Girls: Baseline Findings from the 'Safe City Delhi Programme," December 2012. Accessed January 15, 2015. https://www.icrw.org/files/publications/Baseline%20Research%20of%20Safe%20Cities%20programme%20(1)[smallpdf.com].pdf.

"UN Women Supported Survey in Delhi Shows 95 Percent of Women and Girls Feel Unsafe in Public Spaces." UN Women, February 20, 2013. Accessed January 18, 2015. http://www.unwomen.org/en/news/stories/2013/2/un-women-supported-survey-in-delhi.

Valladares, Danilo. "Guatemala: Women-Only Buses Against Sexual Harassment." *Inter Press Service*, June 2011. Accessed January 3, 2015. http://www.ipsnews.net/2011/06/guatemala-women-only-buses-against-sexual-harassment/.

Vallejo Rivera, Elizabeth, and Maria Paula Rivarola Monzon. "La violencia invisible: acoso sexual callejero en Lima Metropolitana y Callao." El Instituto de Opinion Publica de la PUCP, December 2013. Accessed December 28, 2015. http://textos.pucp.edu.pe/texto/Cuadernos-de-Investigacion-N-4---La-violencia-invisible-acoso-sexual-callejero-en-Lima-Metropolitan.

Verbruggen, Yola. "Yangon's Women Start to Fight Sexual Harassment." *The Bangkok Post*, October 19, 2014. Accessed January 4, 2015. http://www.bangkokpost.com/print/438372/.

"Violence Against Women." ActionAid, n.d. Accessed on December 28, 2014. http://www.actionaid.org/what-we-do/womens-rights/violence-against-women.

Viswanath, Kalpana. "Gender Inclusive Cities Programme—Implementing Change for Women's Safety," in *Building Inclusive Cities: Women's safety and their right to the city,* edited by Margaret Shaw, Caroline Andrew, Carolyn Whitzman, Fran Klodawsky, KalpanaViswanath, and Crystal Legacy, 75–89. New York: Routledge, 2013.

Volokh, Eugene. "Belgium Bans a Wide Range of Sexist Speech." *The Washington Post*, March21, 2014. Accessed December 8, 2014. http://www.washington-post.com/news/volokh-conspiracy/wp/2014/03/21/belgium-bans-a-wide-range-of-sexist-speech/.

Wallace, Arturo. "Colombian Anti-Groping Squad goes to Work." *BBC*, August 25, 2010. Accessed November 29, 2014. http://www.bbc.com/news/world-latin-america-28925622.

Watson, Laurel B., Jacob M. Marszalek, Franco Dispenza, Christopher M. Davids. "Understanding the Relationships Among White and African American Women's Sexual Objectification Experiences, Physical Safety Anxiety, and Psychological Distress." *Sex Roles* (2015). Accessed January 15, 2015. http://link.springer.com/article/10.1007/s11199-014-0444-y/fulltext.html.

"What is At Stake in the Colombian Peace Process?" *BBC*, January 15, 2015. Accessed February 15, 2015. http://www.bbc.com/news/world-latin-america-19875363.

"What Men Are Really Saying When Catcalling Women," YouTube, August 7, 2014. Accessed December 10, 2014. https://www.youtube.com/watch?v=lUJ24mblCLY.

"Who Wants to Know!? The Government responds to 'Femme de la rue.'" Holla-back Brussels, August 8, 2012. Accessed December 9, 2014. http://brussels .ihollaback.org/2012/08/08/government-responds-Hollaback-replies/.

World Economic Forum. *The Global Gender Gap Report: 2014.* 2014. Accessed December 10, 2014. http://www3.weforum.org/docs/GGGR14/GGGR_Com pleteReport_2014.pdf.

"World's Population Increasingly Urban with More Than Half Living in Urban Areas." United Nations, July 10, 2014. Accessed February 13, 2015. http:// www.un.org/en/development/desa/news/population/world-urbanization-pros pects-2014.html.

WUSA 9 Staff. "Is Sexual Harassment a Problem on Metro?" *WUSA 9,* February 21, 2012. Accessed November 28, 2014. http://www.wusa9.com/story /local/2012/02/21/3933809/.

Yacka, Sue. "National Report on Hate Violence Against Lesbian, Gay, Bisexual, Transgender, Queer and HIV-Affected Communities Released Today." NCAVP, June 4, 2013. Accessed January 4, 2015. http://www.avp.org/storage/docu ments/2012_mr_ncavp_hvreport.pdf.

Yagnik, Bharat. "Man Thrashed for Protesting Eve Teasing." *The Times of India,* December 28, 2012. Accessed January 18, 2015. http://timesofindia.indiatimes .com/city/ahmedabad/Man-thrashed-for-protesting-eve-teasing/articleshow /17797390.cms.

Young, Danielle. "Shot Down: Mother of Three Killed Because She Said No to a Man's Advances." Michigan Chronicle, October 8, 2014. Accessed November 27, 2014. http://michronicleonline.com/2014/10/08/shot-down-mother-of -three-killed-because-she-said-no-to-a-mans-advances/.

Zambrano, Raul, and Ruhiya Kristine Seward. *Mobile Technologies and Empowerment: Enhancing Human Development through Participation and Innovation.* United Nations Development Programme. 2012. Accessed December 10, 2014. http://www.undpegov.org/sites/undpegov.org/files/undp_mobile_techno logy_primer.pdf.

Zweynert, Astrid. "More than 4 Billion People Forecasts to Remain Uncon-nected Online—UN Report." Thomas Reuters Foundation, October 8, 2013. Accessed November 28, 2014. http://www.trust.org/item/20131008152926 -w1xfd/?source=hpeditorial&siteVersion=mobile.

Index

About the Author

HOLLY KEARL is the founder of the nonprofit organization Stop Street Harassment, a consultant for entities like the Aspen Institute, the U.S. State Department, and the U.N. Women's Global Safe Cities Initiative, a facilitator with the OpEd Project and an adjunct professor at George Mason University.

Kearl authored the book *Stop Street Harassment: Making Public Places Safe and Welcoming for Women* (Praeger, 2010) and the national study *Unsafe and Harassed in Public Spaces: A National Street Harassment Report* (2014) and co-authored the national study *Crossing the Line: Sexual Harassment in Schools* (2011). She has given more than 250 media interviews about these topics, written more than 60 articles for news outlets such as CNN, *The New York Times*, the *Washington Post*, and the *Guardian*, and given more than 130 talks.

Kearl received a master's degree in Public Policy and Women's Studies from George Washington University and bachelor's degrees in history and women's studies from Santa Clara University.